Thy Kingdom Come

THY KINGDOM COME

J. Dwight Pentecost

VICTOR BOOKS.

A DIVISION OF SCRIPTURE PRESS PUBLICATIONS INC.
USA CANADA ENGLAND

Unless otherwise indicated, all Scripture quotations are from the *Holy Bible, New International Version,* © 1973, 1978, 1984, International Bible Society. Used by permission of Zondervan Bible Publishers. Other quotations are from the *King James Version* (KJV).

Library of Congress Cataloging-in-Publication Data

Pentecost, J. Dwight.
  Thy kingdom come / J. Dwight Pentecost.
    p.   cm.
  Includes bibliographical references.
  ISBN 0-89693-549-3
  1. Kingdom of God—Biblical teaching. 2. Bible—History of Biblical events.
3. History (Theology)—Biblical teaching. 4. Covenants (Theology) I. Title.
BT94.P386 1990
231.7′2—dc20
                                                                89-49604
                                                                    CIP

1 2 3 4 5 6 7 8 9 10   Printing/Year 94 93 92 91 90

Contents

To
"the Blessed and only Potentate,
the King of kings,
and
Lord of lords"
who by His promise,
"I will come again,"
brought HOPE

and to
my grandchildren
Kara Jane
and
John Lawrence
who, by their coming,
brought JOY
this book is dedicated

Preface

Early in my study of the Scriptures I was deeply disturbed by the accusations of those who saw all biblical history as the outworking of an implied covenant of redemption against those who held, as I did, to a distinction between God's program for Israel and His program for the church in the present age. These theologians claimed that they alone had a system that unified the Scriptures into a consistent whole; any other, they insisted, destroyed the unity of the Bible.

Almost unconsciously, as I studied, I found myself looking for that theme in Scripture which would unite the entire body of revelation. It seemed too simplistic simply to say that God's purpose in history was to glorify Himself, although that certainly is true.

In the course of my teaching students who were preparing themselves for a ministry of the Word of God, I was privileged to instruct them in a course on the biblical covenants. I later added a course on the kingdom of God. After teaching these as separate courses I began to realize that the two were inseparable, for God's kingdom program was the outworking of His eternal and unconditional covenants. It became possible to trace the development of that kingdom through Scripture from Genesis to Revelation, and that theme provided a unifying structure that bound all the Bible together into a unit, and by which all the history recorded there could be understood and related.

It was through the encouragement of my students that I gave myself to this lengthy task. The results of these years of study are presented to others with the desire that they too may come to understand the outworking of God's plan to establish a kingdom here on the earth over which His Son rules as King of kings and Lord of lords.

I am grateful to the students who expanded my thinking througn their responses and reactions to the material presented. They have helped to clarify my understanding of the subject. I am deeply grateful to Mr. Ken Durham who has devoted much time to editing and refining the original manuscript for presentation in this form.

May the Lord be pleased to use this work to give us understanding in what Christ had in mind when He taught His disciples to pray, "THY KINGDOM COME."

J. Dwight Pentecost
Dallas, Texas

Introduction:
The Kingdom of the God of Heaven

The great theme of God's kingdom program can be found throughout the Bible, from Genesis to Revelation. It is a theme that unifies
all of Scripture. Through it the Bible records the progressive unfolding of a program in which God reveals His sovereign authority. And
through it God demonstrates His right to rule through various forms
of a kingdom He establishes here on earth, beginning in Genesis
and consummating in the reign of Jesus Christ as King of kings and
Lord of lords in the Book of Revelation.

In spite of all that the Scripture has to say on this subject, however, we are faced with a number of different interpretations and
explanations concerning the nature or purpose of the kingdom of
God.

What is the kingdom of God?

Some understand the kingdom of God to be synonymous with the
eternal state, or heaven, where the saints of God go following physical death. Those who hold this view of the kingdom say it has no
relationship whatsoever to the earth.

Others understand the kingdom as a nonmaterial or "spiritual"
kingdom in which God rules over the hearts of men, so that while
God's kingdom is related to the present, it is unrelated to the earth.
It is entirely spiritual, not material.

Still others view the kingdom as purely earthly, without any
spiritual realities attached to it. It is a future political and social

11

structure achieved by the efforts of humanity, a goal reached through social and economic evolution. Some with this same general concept believe the kingdom of God will be a nationalistic movement on the part of Israel that will reconstitute that nation as an independent political state.

Another more common interpretation sees the kingdom as synonymous with the visible organized church. In other words, the church becomes the kingdom of God, a dominion which is both spiritual and political.

And finally, there are those who view the kingdom as an earthly manifestation of the universal sovereignty of God. The kingdom is a realm in which God rules in the affairs of men, so that the kingdom is conceived as being both spiritual and material.

Admittedly, it seems impossible to navigate this maze of interpretations. Were it not for the clarity of the Bible when allowed to explain itself, we would get hopelessly bogged down in theories and speculation. But truths related to the kingdom of God are not determined by the writings of men. Only through an inductive study of the Word of God may we understand this great subject. That means we must carefully study words according to their meaning to the original writers and readers; we must understand each passage according to its contexts (literary, historical, and cultural); and we must allow Scripture to interpret Scripture rather than assigning our own arbitrary interpretations.

The meaning of the word

A logical starting point is understanding the word itself. Within the word *kingdom (basilea)*, there are three interrelated ideas which must be considered in establishing a biblical concept of the term.

The right to rule
The first of these concepts or ideas is the right to rule—the authority vested in a king, or the sovereignty or dominion granted to someone reigning over a kingdom.

This idea is clearly seen in Christ's parable in Luke 19:11-27. Because His listeners "thought that the kingdom of God should immediately appear" (v. 11), the Lord told of a nobleman who "went into a far country to receive for himself a kingdom and to return" (v. 12). This parable is actually based on the historical event

12

of a journey to Rome that Archelaus, son of Herod, made in order to be confirmed by the Roman emperor Augustus as a ruler in Palestine. Thus it shows that to "receive the kingdom" meant that someone was invested with the authority to rule.

This same idea is seen in Revelation 17:12, where we read that "the ten horns you saw are ten kings, who have not yet received a kingdom, but who for one hour will receive authority as kings along with the beast." Notice that the terms *kingdom* and *authority* (power) are used interchangeably. The ten are given the right to exercise sovereign rule and share the same authority or power the beast exercises in his kingdom.

Therefore the word *kingdom* includes the concept of a person's right to rule.

The realm of rule

The second concept is that of a *realm* in which ruling authority is exercised. This involves the subjects of the one in authority rather than the authority himself. The Lord's statement that "the kingdom of God will be taken away from you and given to a people who will produce its fruit" (Matt. 21:43) shows that He has subjects in view. The same idea is seen in the announcement, "The kingdom of God is near. Repent and believe the good news!" (Mark 1:15) Because only people can repent, the kingdom must include a realm in which kingdom authority is exercised over people.

Again, in Acts 1:6 the Eleven asked, "Lord, are You at this time going to restore the kingdom to Israel?" The word *restore* implies reestablishing what had previously existed. Since Israel's kingdom in the Old Testament involved a specific realm of rule, that concept must be seen here as well. This undoubtedly was Paul's viewpoint when he wrote, "In the presence of God and of Christ Jesus, who will judge the living and the dead, and in view of His appearing and His kingdom . . . " (2 Tim. 4:1). Since death and resurrection involve people, the meaning of the word *kingdom* in this passage must be "realm."

The same concept is seen in the writing of John who recorded that heavenly voices proclaimed, "The kingdom of the world has become the kingdom of our Lord and of His Christ, and He will reign for ever and ever" (Rev. 11:15). Since the kingdom of this world obviously is a reference to a specific realm, that idea must be included in the *kingdom* "of our Lord and of His Christ."

13

The reality of rule

The third concept inherent in the idea of *kingdom* is that of the actual *exercise of royal authority*. Even if a sovereign has the right to rule and a realm in which to rule, there cannot be an actual kingdom apart from the active exercise of that authority.

The relationship between possessing authority and exercising authority is found in various contexts in Scripture. In Matthew 16:19 Christ said to Peter, "I will give you the keys of the kingdom of heaven; whatever you bind on earth will be bound in heaven, and whatever you loose on earth will be loosed in heaven." It is clear in this statement that the authority Christ bestowed was to be exercised.

Similarly, Belshazzar's proclamation, "Whoever reads this writing and tells me what it means . . . will be made the third highest ruler in the kingdom" (Dan. 5:7, 16), showed that he thoroughly expected the one who received authority to exercise it. Darius' appointment of 120 princes "to rule throughout the kingdom" (6:1) also shows that the ideas of *realm* and the exercise of *authority* are intertwined, for "Daniel so distinguished himself among the administrators and the satraps by his exceptional qualities that the king planned to set him over the whole kingdom" (v. 3).

Most significantly, in relation to Christ's earthly ministry we see that Pilate—having interrogated Christ—declared that he found no charge on which He could be condemned. Why? Though Pilate recognized that Christ claimed to be king (John 19:14-15), he declared Him without fault (vv. 4, 6) because he saw that Jesus was not actually exercising the authority He claimed for Himself.

Essential to the meaning of the word *kingdom* is the actual exercise of authority in a realm over which one has the sovereign right to rule. If the exercise of authority is not in view, the concept of kingdom is not present.

Clearing up contradictions

How do we put all this together in reaching a workable understanding of the word *kingdom?* Obviously we must include the three basic concepts of *authority, realm,* and *exercised rule.* Many have erred in their basic concepts of the kingdom by omitting one or more of these ideas—often to support a preconceived theological concept of God's kingdom. This is a mistake we want to avoid.

We do, however, want to extend our understanding of the biblical word *kingdom* in general to the *kingdom of God* in particular. What has made this troublesome for many is that throughout the Bible there seem to be numerous contradictions concerning the kingdom over which God rules. On one hand, the kingdom is described in terms that are strictly eternal—but on the other hand it is described as temporal, with a definite historical beginning, progress, and termination. In the same way, in some passages it is depicted as universal, while in others it is clearly local. Further, the kingdom of God on many occasions is seen to be the direct administration of the sovereignty of God, while in other instances it is characterized as an indirect administration through appointed administrators.

Two aspects of the kingdom

To clear up this seeming confusion, we must recognize that the kingdom over which God rules is not self-contradictory; instead, it has two separate aspects that can be described a number of ways. One might say there is an *eternal* aspect as well as a *temporal* aspect; it has a *universal* nature as well as a *local* nature; or there is an *immediate* sense of the kingdom in which God rules directly, and a *mediated* sense of the kingdom in which God rules indirectly through appointed representatives.

To "set the stage" for better understanding the kingdom of God from the outset, we need to look at four essential truths that characterize its *eternal* aspect. The nature of the kingdom is derived from the person of God and is a reflection of what is found in Him.

It is timeless

First, since God is eternal, a timeless element characterizes His kingdom. Numerous Scriptures demonstrate that God has always possessed absolute sovereignty over all His creation and that He rules as king eternally. For example:

The Lord is King forever and ever (Ps. 10:16).

But You, O God, are my king from of old (Ps. 74:12).

But the Lord is the true God; He is the living God, the eternal King (Jer. 10:10).

15

Your kingdom is an everlasting kingdom, and Your dominion endures through all generations (Ps. 145:13).

You, O Lord, reign forever; Your throne endures from generation to generation (Lam. 5:19).

Simply and biblically stated, God's kingdom is as eternal as He Himself is eternal.

It is universal
Second, since God is omnipresent, the Bible clearly makes reference to the unlimited scope of God's sovereignty over His kingdom, as in the following passages:

Yours, O Lord, is the greatness and the power and the glory and the majesty and the splendor, for everything in heaven and earth is Yours. Yours, O Lord, is the kingdom; You are exalted as head over all (1 Chron. 29:11-12).

The Lord has established His throne in heaven, and His kingdom rules over all (Ps. 103:19).

Where can I go from your Spirit? Where can I flee from your presence? If I go up to the heavens, You are there; if I make my bed in the depths, You are there. If I rise on the wings of the dawn, if I settle on the far side of the sea, even there Your hand will guide me, Your right hand will hold me fast (Ps. 139:7-10).

The Most High is sovereign over the kingdoms of men and gives them to anyone He wishes (Dan. 4:17, 25, 32).

Though they dig down to the depths of the grave, from there My hand will take them. Though they climb up to the heavens, from there I will bring them down (Amos 9:2).

It is clear from Scripture that God's sovereignty is exercised over heaven and earth—even hell itself. There is simply no realm outside of God's authority; God's kingdom is as universal as God is omnipresent.

It is administered through appointed representatives
The Bible also makes it evident that while God exercises absolute authority over all things, His sovereignty may be exercised or ad-

ministrated through individuals. While God is the primary cause, these agents or administrators can be secondary causes. Consider these passages:

> But God sent me [Joseph] ahead of you to preserve for you a remnant on earth and to save your lives by a great deliverance. So then, it was not you who sent me here, but God. . . . You intended to harm me, but God intended it for good to accomplish what is now being done, the saving of many lives (Gen. 45:7-8; 50:20).

> The king's heart is in the hand of the Lord (Prov. 21:1).

> Woe to the Assyrian, the rod of My anger, in whose hand is the club of My wrath! I send him against a godless nation, I dispatch him against a people who anger Me, to seize loot and snatch plunder (Isa. 10:5-6).

> This is what the Lord says to His anointed, to Cyrus, whose right hand I take hold of to subdue nations before him . . . I will go before you . . . so that you may know that I am the Lord, the God of Israel, who calls you by name. . . . I call you by name and bestow on you a title of honor, though you do not acknowledge Me (Isa. 45:1-4).

This truth is further illustrated in Jeremiah 25:8-12; 27:4-8; 51:11-24, 27. That is, God deals sovereignly through men, some of whom recognize it, some of whom reject it, and some of whom are ignorant of it. Yet in every such situation God's will is executed. This not only is true in the realm of humanity, but in nature as well. The psalmist observed, "Lightning and hail, snow and clouds, stormy winds do His bidding" (Ps. 148:8). Thus, nothing ever transpires apart from God's sovereign will. God's kingdom is as varied in its implementation as God is omniscient.

It is miraculous
There are occasions when God's sovereignty is manifested through the direct intervention of God in the affairs of men. These demonstrations of His sovereignty are what we call miracles. The connection between biblical miracles and God's sovereignty is seen in many passages, including:

But I will harden Pharaoh's heart, and though I multiply My miraculous signs and wonders in Egypt, He will not listen to you. Then I will lay My hand on Egypt and with mighty acts of judgment I will bring out My divisions, My people the Israelites. And the Egyptians will know that I am the Lord when I stretch out My hand against Egypt and bring the Israelites out of it (Ex. 7:3-5).

The Lord does whatever pleases Him, in the heavens and on the earth, in the seas and all their depths. He makes clouds rise from the ends of the earth; He sends lightning with the rain, and brings out the wind from His storehouses. He struck down the firstborn of Egypt, the firstborn of men and animals. He sent His signs and wonders into your midst, O Egypt, against Pharaoh and all his servants. He struck down many nations and killed mighty kings (Ps. 135:6-10).

In reality, the question of miracles at its simplest is a question of whether an infinite, sovereign God has the power as well as the right to demonstrate that power within the sphere over which He rules. God's kingdom is as diverse as God is omnipotent. Thus Scripture reveals that God's kingdom is eternal, universal, may be administered through individuals as secondary causes, and may be evidenced through miraculous intervention in the affairs of men. Since God is in control of the world of nature as well as the world of men, He is able, through His control, to direct the course of history to accomplish His purposes. Rejection of or rebellion against God's authority does not diminish or eliminate His rule.

Summary

What have we observed? First, we have seen that in order to understand the biblical concept of *kingdom*, we must recognize that it involves several ideas, including the *right* to rule, a *realm* in which ruling authority is exercised, and the *reality* of that authority actually being exercised.

Second, in laying the foundation for clearing up misconceptions concerning God's kingdom, we have understood that the Bible presents truth concerning two aspects of the kingdom of God: the *eternal* aspect as well as the *temporal* aspect.

And finally, the kingdom is characterized by four essential truths:
(1) It is *timeless,*
(2) It is *universal,*
(3) It is *providential,*
(4) It is *miraculous.*
In eternity past, before the creation of angels or the creation of the earth and the population of it with man, a kingdom existed in the sphere of "the heavenlies" because of the relationship existing among the members of the Trinity. God the Father was sovereign. God the Son, although equal in person, was subordinate to the Father. God the Holy Spirit was the active executor of the will of the Father (Gen. 1:2-3). Thus in eternity past there was a kingdom, involving the right to rule, as well as the sphere in which the right operated and the rule was exercised. Indeed, all the elements essential to a kingdom were present.

Next we will begin tracing the Bible's development of God's kingdom, beginning with prehistory, or the angelic realm.

1

The Kingdom of God in Prehistory

From the beginning, the sphere in which God ruled His kingdom was the heavens. The subjects of His rule were the created angelic beings. Those who dwelt in God's kingdom were called upon to "Praise the Lord, you His angels, you mighty ones who do His bidding, who obey His word. Praise the Lord, all His heavenly hosts, you His servants who do His will. Praise the Lord, all His works everywhere in His dominion" (Ps. 103:20-22; see Job 38:7).

By virtue of their creation, angels were to fulfill several important roles.

The kingdom administration of angels

First, angels were created *to be the subjects of and administrators in God's kingdom.* As such they were characterized by wisdom (2 Sam. 14:20; Ezek. 28:12); strength (Ps. 103:20); and beauty (Ezek. 28:12). It is apparent from Scripture that the angelic realm was divided into different ranks of angels, each with individual position and function, as seen in Ephesians 3:10 where Paul makes reference to the principalities and powers in heavenly places.

Second, the angels were created *to minister.* In Psalm 104:4 they are referred to as God's "messengers" (NIV) or "ministers" (KJV). Again in Hebrews 1:14 they are said to be "ministering spirits sent to serve those who will inherit salvation." As ministers they are administrators of God's kingdom, executors of His will in keeping with His sovereign authority.

21

Third, the angels were also created *to worship.* In Isaiah 6:1-3 there is a unique reference to *seraphim* which means "burning ones," perhaps referring to the reflected glory of God seen in them. These seraphim surround and overshadow the throne of God, crying to one another, "Holy, holy, holy, is the Lord Almighty" (v. 3).

Ezekiel makes reference to four living creatures (Ezek. 1:5) which later are identified as cherubim (Ezek. 10). These same creatures appear in Revelation before the throne of God, where "day and night they never stop saying: 'Holy, holy, holy is the Lord God Almighty, who was, and is, and is to come'" (4:8).

While the cherubim are distinguished from the seraphim, together they are worshipers before the throne of God. The cherubim are associated with the "wheels" of Ezekiel 1, which signify movement and motion, or worship of the One sitting on the throne. Ezekiel also pictures the cherubim's role as protectors or stewards of the glory of God.

Thus we see that in the development of His kingdom, God instituted a kingdom in the realm of the heavenlies. This kingdom was made up of angelic beings divided into different ranks with different privileges and responsibilities. By design, all angelic beings were servants and worshipers of God. Because all were subject to the sovereign authority of the One who ruled as king, there was perfect harmony within the kingdom.

Angelic opposition to the kingdom

The first opposition and rebellion against the sovereign authority of God is recorded in two significant passages, Ezekiel 28:1-19 and Isaiah 14:12-15. These important passages each must be considered in order to understand the unfolding program of the kingdom of God.

Ezekiel 28:1-19
In Ezekiel 28:1-10, the prophet addressed a message to an earthly monarch who was ruling in the city of Tyre. This ruler claimed for himself the right that belonged to God to rule over Israel, setting himself against God's covenant people. Motivated by pride and conceit, the king of Tyre thought that he could subjugate the covenant people. And because he had assumed prerogatives that belonged to God alone, the prophet announced God's judgment on this king.

But in Ezekiel 28:12 the prophet looked beyond the limits of earthly authority and addressed a lamentation to someone who was using this earthly king to accomplish his purpose. Specifically, the message of verses 12-19 was addressed to Satan, who was working out his purposes through the earthly king of Tyre.

We see from verse 14 that the one referred to in verse 12 as the king of Tyre was in fact an angelic being—one of the cherubim. He was a created being (vv. 13, 15) who had been appointed by God to minister in "Eden, the garden of God" (v. 13), a reference to the very presence of God Himself. His position is made even more clear in verse 14: "You were anointed as a guardian cherub, for so I ordained you. You were on the holy mount of God; you walked among the fiery stones." Thus we see that this angelic being ministered in the presence of God's throne, and he personally witnessed the glory that belonged to Him as sovereign.

Moreover, this one was the wisest of God's created angelic beings (v. 12) and was characterized by exceptional beauty (v. 13). It wasn't even necessary for him to take up a musical instrument in order to bring glory to God who had created him—his beauty itself accomplished that. Further, this one was "blameless in [his] ways from the day [he was] created till wickedness was found in [him]" (v. 15).

He was created perfect, not sinful, but didn't remain that way. Because of his beauty, his wisdom, and his glory (or his glorified position before the throne of God), he became filled with pride. Although he was responsible for none of these traits, he acted as though he was the author of them all. And his pride led to his rebellion against God, who immediately exercised His sovereignty over the rebel by pronouncing judgment on him (vv. 17-19).

Thus in Ezekiel we see that Satan was the wisest and most beautiful of God's created angelic beings. He was appointed to the privilege of ministry in the presence of God's throne and glory. But motivated by pride because of his wisdom, beauty, and position, Satan sinned by rebelling against the God who had created him. Consequently he came under the judgment of God, showing the sovereign authority of the One who has the right to rule.

Isaiah 14:12-14
Just as Ezekiel 28 describes the fall of Satan, Isaiah 14:12-14 describes the actual sin that led to that fall. The same personality Ezekiel addressed as the king of Tyre, Isaiah addressed as Lucifer,

"son of the dawn" (v. 12), referring to the glory and the beauty associated with this angelic being.

In his message, Isaiah recorded five specific instances in which the will of Lucifer was set against the will of God. These *five "I wills"* are manifestations of Lucifer's rebellion.

First he said, *"I will ascend to heaven"* (v. 13). While Lucifer already was privileged to minister in the heavenlies, here "heaven" refers to the dwelling place of the all-sovereign God. Lucifer wanted to take over as his own the dwelling place that rightfully belonged to God. He wanted to occupy heaven not as a servant, but as sovereign!

Second he said, *"I will raise my throne above the stars of God"* (v. 13). Here "the stars of God" refers to the host of created angelic beings. As creator of the angelic realm, God alone possessed the right to rule and to be sovereign over a kingdom in which the angels were His subjects. Lucifer, however, resolved to take over the authority that belonged to God alone. He wanted to assume rulership over all of God's kingdom.

Third he said, *"I will sit enthroned on the mount of assembly, on the utmost heights of the sacred mountain"* (v. 13). The "assembly" refers again to the created angelic realm, where Lucifer planned to elevate himself as the one in authority. The "sacred mountain" in Scripture is often associated with the seat of God's authority—thus Lucifer is affirming his desire to usurp the authority of God.

Fourth he asserted, *"I will ascend above the tops of the clouds"* (v. 14). Frequently in Scripture "the clouds" refer to the dwelling place of God, which here shows that Lucifer wanted to exalt himself above God as well as the created angelic beings. In other words, he wanted to bring God under subjection to himself.

Fifth and finally, Lucifer's desire was expressed in the words, *"I will make myself like the most high"* (v. 14). God is sovereign and God is responsible to no one outside of Himself. What Lucifer expressed was his desire to be independent of any authority except himself. But because God alone is sovereign and possesses eternal, uncreated life, Lucifer could not hope to attain the sovereignty or the life that belongs solely to God.

It is the part of the creature to be subject to the creator, just as it is the responsibility of those who are in the kingdom of the God of heaven to acknowledge His authority to rule.

But Lucifer rejected God's authority and rebelled against His sovereign authority. He repudiated God's right to rule. He rejected his responsibility as a subject of the kingdom to remain in subjection to the King, and instead offered himself to the angelic realm as an alternative king who—according to his own affirmation—had a superior right to rule.

The two kingdoms

This rebellion constituted a challenge to God's sovereignty, and it continues today in active rebellion against the kingdom of the God of heaven. Through this rebellion the one who bore the glorious name of Lucifer, son of the morning, is now referred to as "that ancient serpent called the devil or Satan" (Rev. 12:9).

The extent of Satan's kingdom

But there's more. When Satan rebelled, he instituted his own counterfeit of God's kingdom, a program entirely opposed to God's authority and His right to rule. To do this, Satan enticed the angels of God to follow him in his rebellion, with the result that innumerable multitudes of angels followed him in revolt. Evidence of this angelic rebellion can be seen in Revelation 12:9 where reference is made to "his (Satan's) angels." Further, Revelation 12:4 may indicate Satan's influence was so extensive that he drew a third of the created angelic hosts after him!

The authority of Satan's kingdom

In the false kingdom created by his rebellion, Satan is "the god of this age" (2 Cor. 4:4) and has assumed sovereign authority. Elsewhere we are told he is "the ruler of the kingdom of the air" (Eph. 2:2), and that "the whole world is under the control of the evil one" (1 John 5:19). Clearly the Bible teaches Satan is the authority behind the counter-kingdom program he instituted against God.

The characteristics of Satan's kingdom

Because Satan's kingdom was instituted by lawlessness and rebellion, its chief characteristics are *lawlessness and rebellion* against the authority of God. All who are in Satan's kingdom oppose God, elevating themselves above Him who alone has the right to rule and be worshiped (2 Thes. 2:4).

Satan's kingdom also is characterized by *darkness rather than light* (Col. 1:13). Since Satan is a liar and the father of lies, his kingdom is further characterized by *deceit and deception* (Rev. 13:14). Satan does not operate in the realm of truth; rather, his kingdom is characterized by denial of truth and by error.

Moreover, Satan's kingdom is not characterized by righteousness but by *sin* (Rom. 6:16-17), not by godliness but by *ungodliness* (Ps. 1:3-6; Rom. 5:6), not by holiness but by *unholiness* (1 Tim. 1:9). Satan's kingdom is characterized not by obedience but by *disobedience* (Eph. 2:2), and not by life but by *death* (Eph. 2:5).

The realm of Satan's kingdom

The Bible also makes it clear that the realm of Satan's kingdom is the heavenlies. In Ephesians 6:12 Paul reminds believers they are struggling "against the spiritual forces of evil in the heavenly realms." This is the same expression used in Ephesians 1:3 for the realm in which "God has blessed us . . . with every spiritual blessing in Christ."

For this reason Satan's kingdom must operate in the same realm in which the kingdom of the God operates. All of the angels who followed Satan in his original rebellion constitute the subjects of this kingdom. And apparently they have been organized by the head of the kingdom of darkness to follow the organization of God's kingdom in the angelic realm. This is confirmed by Paul's reference to the "the rulers . . . the authorities . . . the powers of this dark world and . . . the spiritual forces of evil in the heavenly realms" (Eph. 6:12). Satan is not omnipresent—as God is—and must carry out the work of his kingdom through the fallen angels, or demons, who are the subjects of that kingdom.

Summary

Therefore we see that the Bible reveals two kingdoms existing in the realm of the heavenlies. The first is the kingdom of the God of heaven, with the unfallen angels as its subjects, while the second is the kingdom of Satan, with the fallen angels as its subjects. The two are in absolute opposition to each other. At no point will there be any agreement between the two—they are diametrically opposed to one another.

While God's kingdom is as timeless as God Himself, Satan's kingdom had its beginning with Satan's rebellion. Thus the two kingdoms are not to be misconstrued as coexistent from eternity past While good existed eternally because God is good, evil was introduced by Lucifer's rebellion against the kingdom of God.

Although God passed judgment on that false ruler and his false kingdom (Luke 10:18), and its ultimate subjugation to Himself is certain (Phil. 2:10), that subjugation has not yet been accomplished. Therefore two kingdoms coexist in the heavenly realm: the kingdom of God and the kingdom of Satan.

2

The Kingdom of God Established on Earth

Who has the right to rule?

The lawless rebellion of Satan against God raised a question of gigantic importance. Who is God? Who has the right to rule? The authority which had been recognized throughout God's eternal kingdom and exercised in the angelic realm had been challenged. God might have answered that question by imposing a deserved judgment on Satan and those who followed him in his rebellion. That would have conclusively demonstrated to all the subjects of God's kingdom that He alone is God, that He has the right to rule and the right to receive worship from those in His kingdom.

But God sovereignly chose another method by which this question would be settled: He created the heavens and the earth. This creation was designed to provide a new sphere in which God's kingdom might be administered and through which the question of right-to-rule would ultimately be concluded.

The creation of heaven and earth

Scripture begins with the affirmation that God created the heavens and the earth. Such is the universal testimony of the Scriptures (Deut. 4:32; Ps. 89:11-12; Isa. 42:5, 45:7, 12; John 1:3; Col. 1:16; Heb. 1:2, 11:3). The only witness to the fact of creation as well as the means of creation is found in the testimony of the Creator Himself—there were no other witnesses to creation. Either God's testimony as to the fact and purpose of creation is to be believed, or God is a liar. In our study we will make no attempt to *prove* the fact that God created, but rather we *assume* this fact on the basis of the testimony of the Creator who is God and who cannot lie (see Heb 11:1-3).

Genesis 1:1 tells us God created. The name for God here is *Elohim*, which is used some 2,570 times in the Bible. This name stresses the sovereign omnipotence that belongs to the One who bears it. Therefore creation is a manifestation of the sovereign power and authority of the Creator. "The heavens and the earth" in verse 1 is a reference to the expanse of the universe. In verse 2, however, our attention is turned from the general to the specific and attention is focused on a small part of the universe—the earth—for it was on the earth rather than in the universe as a whole that God's purposes were to be fulfilled.

In Colossians 1:16 Paul affirmed that "all things were created by Him and for Him." He asserted not only that God was Creator, but also the significant fact that there was purpose in Creation. "All things were created . . . for him," that is, to fulfill His purposes, to serve His ends. Creation was more than a demonstration of sovereign omnipotence, although Isaiah 45:12 substantiates that truth. Rather, the earth was specifically brought into existence as a manifestation of the sovereign will of God who would work out His purposes in this sphere·

Four deficiencies

The earth as a part of the original creation of the universe (referred to in Gen. 1:1) lay for an indeterminate time in a state characterized by four deficiencies (1:2).

First, it was said to be "without form" (the Hebrew word *tohu*). The earth was an unformed state It had not been put into a usable shape. Second, it was characterized as being "void" (the Hebrew word *bohu*). It was empty and unproductive Third, it was characterized by "darkness." The unformed and empty earth was wrapped in darkness. Fourth, it was referred to as "the deep." This word signifies a surging activity that could refer to the surface only or to the entire earth itself.

The earth in that state could not fulfill the purposes God had in mind when He created the heavens and the earth Isaiah declared,

29

"For this is what the Lord says—He who created the heavens, He is God; He who fashioned and made the earth, He founded it; He did not create it to be empty, but formed it to be inhabited—He says: 'I am the Lord, and there is no other'" (Isa. 45:18). Isaiah affirmed what Paul would affirm in Colossians 1:16, that God had not prepared the earth to remain in an empty, useless, darkened, surging state. It was to become a sphere occupied by those who would become subjects of the kingdom of the God of heaven.

Removing the deficiencies

What we find, then, in Genesis 1:3-31 are the successive· steps through which God removed the deficiencies that characterized the earth, in order to provide a place to populate with those who would become subjects of His kingdom. This work of forming the earth was the work of the triune God. God the Father was active (Gen. 1:3). God the Son was active (John 1:3). And God the Holy Spirit was active, for Genesis 1:2 states that the Spirit of God "was hovering over the waters." The word *hovering* signifies a protective watch over the earth even in its then unformed, empty, darkened, and seething state.

Without belaboring the point, it is concluded that this work took place in six consecutive twenty-four-hour days. While in Scripture a "day" (the Hebrew *yom*) may refer to a long period or an epoch—as in "the day of the Lord," which is an extended period of time—the normal usage of the word *day* in Scripture refers to a twenty-four-hour period. This is especially true when the word is modified by a number or numeric adjective, or when there is reference to morning and/or evening, as in Genesis 1:5: "And there was evening, and there was morning—the first day."

According to verses 3-5, on the first day God removed deficiency number three—darkness. Because the light of the sun did not appear until the fourth day, the light God caused to shine was not the light of the sun. Instead, this light must have been the shining of that essential glory that belongs to God Himself. The God of glory who had formed this earth to serve His purposes dispelled the darkness that had enveloped it. It was God's presence in this earthly sphere that brought light and caused a separation between light and darkness.

The second day God removed deficiency number one by forming

that which was previously unformed into distinct matter in order to make it productive. The word *firmament* literally means "that which is hammered out," and refers to a gaseous ocean surrounding the earth, or to air space that separated the heavens above from the earth beneath. The water-laden clouds above the earth were separated from the seething mass below by the firmament between. Thus God formed what had been useless into a useful place.

On day three God separated out of the water that which would constitute the dry land, thus removing deficiency number four. This also made it possible for God to remove deficiency number two. The earth, empty and unproductive in its original state, now blossomed with herbs and fruit trees.

On the fourth day, light was assigned to the luminaries in the heavens to provide light for the earth. The purpose of this, according to verse 14, was first to "separate the day from the night," or to mark time. Second, they were to be "as signs," evidently meaning indications of forthcoming weather (Matt. 16:2-3). Next, they were to be for "seasons." Varying relationships between the earth and the sun would provide the four seasons of the year. And finally, these luminaries were to be for "days and years." This seems to refer to special times that would be set aside for worship or for rest. The sun and moon would give light to the earth until those in the kingdom would no longer need their light because they would walk in the light of God's glory (Rev. 21:23).

On the fifth day God again moved to remove deficiency number two when he said, "Let the water teem with living creatures, and let birds fly above the earth across the expanse of the sky" (Gen. 1:20). At the end of the fifth day, only the earth itself was left without living creatures. So on the sixth day God finalized His plan to provide a new sphere in which His kingdom program might develop. God first populated the earth with three classes of animals (vv. 24-25), and then He climaxed His work of creation with the formation of a unique creature (vv. 26-27).

Then God said, "Let Us make man in Our image, in Our likeness, and let them rule over the fish of the sea and the birds of the air, over the livestock, over all the earth, and over all the creatures that move along the ground." So God created man in His own image, in the image of God He created him; male and female He created them.

31

Two aspects of man

In this climactic statement concerning the creative program of God, two things are asserted about man. First, concerning his nature, three times it is said that man was made in God's image, and once that he was made in God's likeness. The second affirmation has to do with God's purpose for man in Creation. God said, "Let them rule." This purpose is stated again in verse 28 where God said "Rule. . . ."

The image of God

Because God is a spirit, the image of God in man is not physical. Nor is it moral, for man was not created as a holy being. Holiness is absolute and unchangeable. Therefore, had man been created holy he could not have sinned. Instead, man was created with an untried innocence, which could be tested.

God is a person with all the essential components of personality—intellect, emotion, and will. With the mind God could know, with the heart He could love, and with the will He could choose. Man, distinct from the animals, was endowed with the essential components of personality so that he could exercise those qualities Godward: with the mind to know God, with the heart to love God, and with the will to obey God. Thus as a person man was in the image or likeness of God.

The assignment to rule

The concept of dominion is inherent in the image or likeness given to man. God is sovereign, and man was to exercise delegated authority and thus reflect the authority that belongs to the Creator. In exercising dominion, man would subjugate all creation to the Creator. He would establish a kingdom in this sphere, one in which the God of heaven ruled and demonstrated His right to rule. This purpose for man is reaffirmed in Psalm 8:5-8 and again in Hebrews 2:6-8, and even though this purpose has not yet been realized, it ultimately will be—through the reign of the Son of Man at His second advent.

After God had created man, God prepared a special environment in which he was to be placed. "Now the Lord God had planted a garden in the east, in Eden; and there He put the man He had formed" (Gen. 2:8). Thus God had prepared a kingdom over which He would rule, and had established a theocracy here on earth.

Theocracy on earth

Theocracy simply means "God ruling." God's rule in His eternal kingdom was direct exercise of sovereign authority. God's rule in the angelic realm again was a direct rule. After the creation of the new sphere in which God's kingdom would be developed, however, God delegated authority to man to rule as His representative. The right to rule belonged to God—but the One who had the right to rule could delegate His responsibility in the administration of that kingdom or in the exercise of that authority. Such administration through a delegated representative constitutes a theocracy.

Man's authority in this theocracy was not only over the physical earth, but also over every living thing God had created and placed on the earth. In Genesis 1:26, God said that man was to have dominion over the fish, the birds, the cattle, and every creeping thing, as well as over the physical earth itself. This was reiterated in Genesis 1:29. It becomes clear, then, that the earth became the sphere of God's kingdom. Man was the administrator in that kingdom, and all created living things were subjects of that kingdom.

With the establishment of the kingdom of the God of heaven here in this earthly sphere, His purpose for creation had been accomplished. "God saw all that He had made, and it was very good" (Gen. 1:31). "By the seventh day God had finished the work He had been doing; so on the seventh day He rested from all his work" (2:2).

God's purpose for man

There was no need for further creative work. God's purpose for Creation had been accomplished with the establishment of a miniature theocracy in Eden in which He ruled as sovereign through man as His delegated representative. This was God's unchanging purpose for man and for the earth, as clearly seen in Psalm 8.

There the psalmist asked, "When I consider Your heavens, the work of Your fingers, the moon and the stars, which You have set in place, what is man that You are mindful of him, the son of man that You care for him?" (Ps. 8:3-4) In contrast to the vast expanse of the universe, man seems to be a very insignificant part of Creation— thus the psalmist was asking what God's purpose was for man, as man. The angels had inhabited the expanse of the universe, yet it was not angels who were crowned with glory and honor. Rather, it was man who was so glorified and dignified. What is it that has given man this glory and this honor? The answer is found in verse 6: "You made him ruler over the works of Your hands." Man as man was appointed as God's theocratic administrator, and his authority extends "over the works of [God's] hands; [He] put everything under his feet: all flocks and herds, and the beasts of the field, the birds of the air, and the fish of the sea, all that swim the paths of the seas" (vv. 6-8). It was the delegated authority given to man to exercise rulership in God's kingdom that brought him to a position of glory and honor.

The writer of Hebrews made the same affirmation by quoting Psalm 8:4-6. He made the observation that man was the ruler over all that was in this realm: "In putting everything under him, God left nothing that is not subject to him" (Heb. 2:8). The authority of man over the earth was as extensive as the authority of God over the earth, for man as man was God's duly appointed theocratic administrator.

But this same writer knew he must also make the observation, "Yet at present we do not see everything subject to him." The earth and everything in it is not in subjection to man, nor by implication, in subjection to God Himself. This means God's purpose for Creation has not yet been realized, and that the kingdom of the God of heaven has not yet been established on this earth as God intended it should be. However, even though that kingdom has not yet been realized, God's purpose for the earth *must* come to its designated fulfillment. Otherwise Satan will have gained a permanent victory by dispossessing God of His authority, of His right to rule, and of His right to be worshiped.

Adam began to exercise the authority entrusted to him by God, for he not only occupied the garden but worked it and took care of it (Gen. 2:15). Further, he exercised dominion over animal creation by giving names to all cattle, to all fowl of the air, to every beast of the field (v. 20). The naming of Eve again was an exercise of the dominion entrusted to Adam. In stating the original law of marriage Adam said, "For this reason a man will leave his father and mother and be united to his wife, and they will become one flesh" (v. 24), recognizing that headship responsibility and dominion were given to man as man, and that headship was to be exercised in the home established by marriage.

The fall of man

Thus we see that man was not only constituted as head of this miniature theocracy, but Adam—as administrator in the theocracy—exercised the dominion entrusted to him by God.

But God did not surrender His right to rule in this theocracy, as seen in Genesis 2:16-17: "And the Lord God commanded the man, 'You are free to eat from any tree in the garden; but you must not eat from the tree of the knowledge of good and evil, for when you eat of it you will surely die.'"

No such prohibitions were placed on the subjects of the kingdom in the angelic realm. It was the responsibility of the creature to be in subjection to the Creator. Satan did not originally rebel against a specific commandment of God, but rather against the obligation that rested on him because he was a created being. But in the miniature theocracy in the Garden of Eden a specific prohibition was placed on man. This prohibition was not instituted because the fruit of the tree of knowledge of good and evil was poisonous, for all that God had created was good. Moreover, God had said "I give you every seed-bearing plant on the face of the whole earth and every tree . . . they will be yours for food" (1:29).

The prohibition against eating of the tree of knowledge of good and evil was given to test man's recognition of and subjection to the authority of God. Man was not to assume that, because he had been given delegated authority to rule as God's administrator in the theocracy, he was independent of God or not responsible to God's law. Those who are in the kingdom must obey the rule of the King. Obedience to that rule becomes a test as to whether one is in the kingdom.

Lucifer in his original rebellion had refused to submit to the authority of God and had declared himself independent of God. Now man in this new form of the kingdom was tested to see whether he would submit to the authority of God out of recognition of God's right to rule, or whether he, like Satan, would reject God's right to rule and declare himself to be independent of God's law.

The prohibition, then, was not to rob man of that which would have been a pleasure to him, but rather to test his *recognition of* and *submission to* the authority of the One who is sovereign in the kingdom of God. Just how long Adam and Eve remained in a state of obedience and continued as citizens of the kingdom of the God of heaven on earth we do not know, but the time came when their obedience was tested by Satan, as recorded in Genesis 3.

Satan, the wisest of God's created angelic beings, appropriated the body of the wisest of God's earthly creatures and used it as the instrument through which he approached Eve. The first question that Satan addressed to Eve—"Did God really say, 'You must not eat from any tree in the garden'?"—shows that Satan had full knowledge of the restrictions God had placed on the subjects of His kingdom. Eve's response—"We may eat fruit from the trees in the garden" (v. 2)—shows that Eve recognized the liberty that God had given her and Adam; but her statement, "But God did say, 'You must not eat fruit from the tree that is in the middle of the garden,'" shows that she also recognized the limitation God had placed upon their liberty

The words she added— and you must not touch it"—does not so much reveal an attempt by Eve to add to the restrictions that God had placed on them as it indicates a realization of how stringent God's requirement actually was. Eve recognized the penalty for disobedience to the command of God, for she stated, "Or you will die" (v. 3). Thus the prohibition God had laid on His subjects as well as the penalty for transgression of that law were very clear to Adam and Eve. Satan, whom Christ refers to as a liar and the father of lies, used a lie to categorically deny the penalty for transgression of the law of God. He said, "You will not surely die" (v. 4).

Satan went on to plant seeds of doubt concerning the love of God for the subjects of His kingdom. He inferred in verse 5 that God had placed the prohibition on them out of jealousy, to withhold from them something beneficial. Satan also implied that transgressing the law of God would make them equal to God. This is a subtle repetition of Lucifer's sin in which he desired to be like the Most High. It suggested to Adam and Eve that if they would only transgress the command of God, they would become like God.

The flesh, the eyes, the pride of life

In 1 John 2:16 we are told that when Satan assaults a soul, he does it by appealing to the lust of the flesh, the lust of the eyes, or the pride of life. These are the only channels through which Satan can enter a citadel. Here in the first temptation we discover that Satan used all three of these channels in tempting Eve.

We read that, "The woman saw that the fruit of the tree was good for food" (Gen. 3:6). That was an appeal to the lust of the flesh. Next, it was "pleasing to the eye." That was the lust of the eyes. And third, it was "also desirable for gaining wisdom," clearly an appeal to pride. Overcome by the temptation, "She took some and ate it. She also gave some to her husband, who was with her, and he ate it." This was willful, deliberate disobedience of the kingdom subjects to the law the kingdom ruler had laid down. Like Lucifer in the beginning, they wanted to be like God, and they believed the lie of Satan that by disobedience they could become like Him.

It is interesting to observe that when this sin is referred to throughout Scripture, it is not referred to as the sin of Eve—but rather as the sin of Adam! The phrase in verse 6, "with her," seems to suggest that Adam was at Eve's side when she was tempted by Satan. As God's theocratic administrator, and as the appointed head of the family, it was Adam's responsibility to safeguard Eve and to assure that she remained in submission to the command of God. But Adam failed in his God-given responsibility and permitted Eve to eat of the forbidden fruit.

While it was Eve's responsibility to obey, it was Adam's responsibility as theocratic administrator to see to it that subjects of the kingdom obeyed the law of the kingdom. Adam did not exercise this responsibility; therefore he was held responsible for the sin of Eve. Added to this was the fact that Adam did not resist the solicitation of Eve. By submitting to her he gave up his headship.

Two kingdoms

As a result of Adam and Eve's transgression, they experienced spiritual death, which is separation from God. They passed out of the life that belongs to subjects of the kingdom of God, entered into the realm of death, and became subjects of the kingdom of Satan. Up to this point the kingdom of Satan had existed only in the heavenly realm where angels were subject to his authority. Now, however, the kingdom of Satan was established here on the earth, and Adam and Eve became subjects of that kingdom. From that point forward all those born in Adam's line would be born into the kingdom of darkness, into the kingdom of Satan. They would be characterized by the lawless rebellion that characterized Satan and all those in Satan's kingdom. As a result of this sin, two kingdoms would develop side by side in this earthly realm. A recurring theme in the Scriptures, then, shows God developing His kingdom of heaven on earth, and Satan propagating his kingdom of lawlessness and darkness in the same realm.

When God, as was His custom, came into the garden to enjoy fellowship with those who had been subjects of His kingdom, He found Adam and Eve hiding themselves from His presence (Gen. 3:8-9), because they were under conviction of sin. God then exercised the prerogatives of His sovereignty and pronounced judgment on those involved in this transgression.

First, there was the judgment on the serpent, the instrument Satan had used, now condemned to crawl upon the ground (v. 14). Next, judgment was passed on the woman. When she would fulfill God's command to "be fruitful and increase in number; fill the earth" (1:28), she would be reminded of her sin by the pain associated with childbirth. The statement, "Your desire will be for your husband, and he will rule over you" (3:16), reemphasizes the continuing headship of the husband over the wife which was instituted at Creation. In giving the fruit of the tree to Adam, Eve usurped authority over Adam; but God made it clear that Eve's disobedience did not alter God's original design to place the husband as the responsible head in the family.

Next, judgment was placed on the ground when God said, "It will produce thorns and thistles for you" (v. 18). This curse was the means by which Adam was judged. Man was to survive by eating of the fruits of the ground, and because the ground had been cursed, "By the sweat of your brow you will eat your food" (v. 19).

The need for redemption

Thus we see that as a result of the sin of Adam and Eve the earth needs redemption; the creatures on the earth need redemption; and fallen, sinful mankind needs redemption. And God graciously promised a redeemer who would provide that redemption.

In Genesis 3:15 God said, "I will put enmity between you [Satan] and the woman, between your offspring [Satan] and hers; he [the seed of the woman] will crush your [Satan's] head and you [Satan] shall strike his [the seed of the woman's] heel." It is important to note that the head wound is fatal, while a wound to the heel is not. In other words, God promised One who will crush Satan, bring an end to his activity, and eliminate that kingdom which he has introduced here on the earth. In crushing Satan, the One who crushes will endure brief suffering. This is the first hint of a coming Saviour who would provide redemption for all that have been corrupted by Satan's infiltration.

God further manifested His grace when He "made garments of skin for Adam and his wife and clothed them" (v. 21). Through the sacrifice of an innocent animal God provided a way by which Adam and Eve could be brought out of the kingdom of darkness into God's kingdom and have fellowship with Him. The blood of the animal God killed provided a covering for Adam's sin, and the skin of the animal provided a covering for Adam's nakedness. Again, we are provided with a foreshadowing of the way in which God would ultimately deal with sin.

Finally, lest man should live forever in his fallen sinful state, God expelled Adam from the Garden of Eden. The garden was the sphere in which the kingdom of the God of heaven was manifested here on the earth. Exclusion from the garden suggests that Adam, because of his sin, was excluded from the kingdom of God and was left to dwell in the domain of Satan, the kingdom of darkness. God demonstrated His authority by positioning an angel at the gate of the garden (v. 24) to keep Adam from the tree of life until a way had been provided for man to partake of it again (Rev. 2:7, 22:2). Even so, there was anticipation that through a God-provided redemption God's program would ultimately be established on this earth.

Summary

Thus we see that God prepared a new sphere in which He would develop a kingdom, and He populated it with creatures made like Himself so that they might know Him, love Him, and submit themselves to Him because He is worthy.

Satan, however, entered into that sphere and enticed those who were in subjection to God into submission to himself. He usurped God's right to rule, suggesting that he, Satan, possesses the right to rule, and that he—not God—is worthy to be obeyed.

God demonstrated His authority by passing judgment on the earth, its creatures, on Satan, and on mankind—and He promised a coming One through whom this judgment would be executed and by whom subjection would be restored.

3

The Administration of the Kingdom through the Law of Conscience

The law of conscience

Just as the rebellion of Satan did not terminate the kingdom of God, the rebellion of Adam did not terminate God's plan to demonstrate and validate His right to rule in this earthly sphere. But Adam's fall did necessitate a change in the administration of the kingdom.

God's answer to lawlessness was to impose law. While the prohibition placed on Adam and Eve in the garden could be considered law, the first formal law God imposed was the law of conscience. Paul, in fact, wrote that "when Gentiles, who do not have the law [that is, the Law of Moses], do by nature things required by the law [of Moses], they are a law for themselves, even though they do not have the law, since they show that the requirements of the law are written on their hearts, their consciences also bearing witness, and their thoughts now accusing, now even defending them" (Rom. 2:14-15).

Paul defined conscience as the law of God—written universally into the heart of man—revealing what is right and what is wrong, what God approves and what God disapproves. Consequently, men are held responsible for obedience to this law.

In this initial section of Romans the apostle was showing that God is just when He condemns sinners. Men have a revelation of God through creation (1:19-20), which placed responsibility on man. Because they rejected that revelation, men are held accountable (vv. 21-23). The pagan Gentile world justly comes under judgment because they have the law of God written in their hearts and are held responsible for the observance of and submission to that law. Men are not left in ignorance as to what is right or wrong, for the law of God, or conscience, makes that very clear.

Life under conscience

Beginning in Genesis 4, then, God administered His kingdom on the earth through this law of conscience. The first thing conscience teaches a man is that he is responsible to worship the Creator, thus the two sons of Adam and Eve brought the evidences of their worship to the Lord. Abel brought of the flocks of which he was a keeper, and Cain the fruits of the ground of which he was a tiller.

According to later revelation either form of worship was acceptable to God. The Mosaic Law provided for worship through sacrifice of animals as well as through offerings of grain. The distinction in the offerings was not what was offered; the difference was the attitude in which the offering was made. Hebrews 11:4 reads, "By faith Abel offered God a better sacrifice than Cain did. By faith he was commended as a righteous man, when God spoke well of his offerings." Our attention is directed to the faith that caused Abel to offer his sacrifice, with the inference that Cain offered a sacrifice apart from faith in the One to whom the sacrifice was offered. Thus the sacrifice of Abel was acceptable to God while the sacrifice of Cain was unacceptable.

This incident clearly reveals that faith is the way of access to God and the means of entrance into the kingdom of God. It reveals that one who does not come by faith cannot come to God and is not a member of God's kingdom. In spite of his unbelief, Cain was offered a way of access to God through sacrifice when God said, "If you do not do what is right, sin [literally, a sin offering] is crouching [waiting] at your door" (Gen. 4:7). Thus God revealed to one outside of the kingdom that he could come into the kingdom through blood sacrifice.

Knowledge of the law itself does not mean that the requirements of the law will be fulfilled. Murder was forbidden by the law of conscience, but despite knowing this Cain murdered his brother. Cain rejected the way of righteousness, the way of access to God, and the way of entrance into His kingdom, and by His works he demonstrated that he was a part of the lawless kingdom of Satan.

Cain fled from the presence of the Lord (v. 16) and established a city (v. 17) which became a home for those who rejected the demands of the law of conscience and chose instead to live in rebellion. Later this city became the center of Satan's kingdom of darkness.

In Genesis 4:25 we see that God gave Adam and Eve a son to take the place of Abel. When the first child Cain was born, Eve said, literally translated, "I've gotten a man, even Jehovah" (4:1). Eve seems to have viewed Cain as a successor to Adam as an administrator in God's earthly kingdom. But Cain's unbelief made him ineligible to be an administrator in God's kingdom, and Abel was murdered by Cain. So another administrator needed to be raised up.

When the third child was born to replace Abel he was named Seth which means "appointed one." Again Eve seems to have had in mind a successor as an administrator in the kingdom; and in fact Seth was indeed appointed to a position of administrative authority. He was the one who established the line of whom it was said, "At that time men began to call upon the name of the Lord" (v. 26). Another translation would be, "Men began to call themselves by the name of the Lord." In other words, the descendants of Seth were identifying themselves with the Lord by faith, as subjects of the kingdom of God.

The two administrations under conscience

Thus in the two sons of Adam and Eve we see the development of two kingdoms here on the earth: the kingdom of Satan, centered in the city which Cain built; and the kingdom of God through the line that sprang from Seth.

The descendants of Seth were called "sons of the kingdom" or the "sons of God." From the days of Seth to the days of Noah, the distinction between these two lines or these two kingdoms was very evident. But in Genesis 6 we learn that the distinction was lost through intermarriage. We understand "the sons of God" of Genesis 6:2 to be the Sethites or "the sons of the kingdom of God." The "daughters of men," on the other hand, refer to the Cainites or those who are a part of the kingdom of darkness. The description of Nephilim in verse 4 does not refer to physical stature, but rather to men who assumed great authority over other men. They were administrators in the kingdom of darkness who exerted authority over those in their realm. This seems to be supported by the further statement, "They were the heroes of old, men of renown."

The intermarriage of the sons of God with the daughters of men, therefore, was an attempt to merge the two kingdoms. And the removal of the barrier that separated those in the kingdom of God from those in the kingdom of Satan brought forth an announcement of judgment from the sovereign God: "The Lord saw how great man's wickedness on the earth had become, and that every inclination of the thoughts of his heart was only evil all the time. The Lord was grieved that He had made man on the earth, and His heart was filled with pain. So the Lord said, 'I will wipe mankind, whom I have created, from the face of the earth" (vv. 5-7).

A sovereign God has a right to judge, and judgment is a manifestation of His sovereign authority. The earth had been cursed at the time of Adam's sin and now God purposed to bring a judgment on the earth. Animals had been cursed at the time of Adam's fall and now God purposed to bring judgment on the animal creation. Man had been cursed at the time of Adam's sin and now God purposed to bring a judgment on the human race. The earth, animal creation, and the human race were viewed as being under the authority of Satan; they were subjects of Satan's kingdom of darkness. Now God would manifest His right to rule by bringing judgment on all those who were a part of Satan's kingdom.

Righteous Noah

Noah found grace in the eyes of the Lord (Gen. 6:8). God testified of Noah: "I have found you righteous in this generation" (7:1). The righteousness of Noah was by faith: "By faith Noah, when warned about things not yet seen, in holy fear built an ark to save his family. By his faith he condemned the world and became heir of the righteousness that comes by faith" (Heb. 11:7). Noah's "holy fear" was a reverential respect for the God who had revealed Himself to him.

Noah's faith manifested itself in obedience, as we read: "Noah did everything just as God commanded him" (Gen. 6:22). The grace of God toward those who were in Satan's kingdom was extended in the decades which intervened between the announcement of judgment (6:3) and the execution of the judgment (7:6). During that extended interval Noah was "a preacher of righteousness" (2 Peter 2:5), who evidently proclaimed a coming judgment and exhorted people to escape by offering them salvation through faith. Light was given to those who were in darkness and an opportunity extended for them to leave the kingdom of darkness and to come into the kingdom of the God of heaven. But so great was the hardness of their hearts and the blindness of their minds, none among Noah's generation—outside of his family—responded to his preaching of righteousness.

The Creator on the second day of Creation had separated the moisture-laden clouds into a firmament above the earth and on the third day had separated water in the ocean from the dry land. Now in judgment by the hand of the Creator "all the springs of the great deep burst forth, and the floodgates of the heavens were opened. And rain fell on the earth forty days and forty nights" (Gen. 7:11-12). The waters of the ocean surged across the dry land and the moisture contained in the clouds of the firmament was released so that "the waters rose and increased greatly on the earth, and the ark floated on the surface of the water. All the high mountains under the entire heavens were covered" (vv. 18-19).

That passage, read normally, would indicate a universal flood. Moreover, in the verses that follow there is testimony to the universality of the judgment of death that the Flood brought: "Every living thing that moved on the earth perished—birds, livestock, wild animals, all the creatures that swarm over the earth, and all mankind. Everything on dry land that had the breath of life in its nostrils died. Every living thing on the face of the earth was wiped out; men and animals and the creatures that move along the ground and the birds of the air were wiped from the earth" (vv. 21-23). One cannot escape the use of the words *all* and *every* in this passage. Further it is affirmed, "Only Noah was left, and those with him in the ark" (v. 23). This was clearly a universal judgment on the kingdom of Satan on this earth, and only those who were a part of the kingdom of God were spared.

The kingdom reestablished

After the waters had receded and the ark had rested on the mountains of Ararat, God said to Noah, "Come out of the ark, you and your wife and your sons and their wives. Bring out every kind of living creature that is with you—the birds, the animals, and all the creatures that move along the ground—so they can multiply on the earth and be fruitful and increase in number upon it" (Gen. 8:16-17). So Noah did.

Thus God reestablished His kingdom on earth after the pattern of His original creation in Eden. The kingdom program of God received a new beginning, and Noah and his family constituted the subjects of that kingdom. At the time of their departure from the ark there was no false kingdom operating in the earthly sphere. And because it was fitting that those who are in God's kingdom should recognize God's right to rule and offer acceptable worship to Him, Noah "built an altar to the Lord and, taking some of all the clean animals and clean birds, he sacrificed burnt offerings on it. The Lord smelled the pleasing aroma and said in His heart, 'Never again will I curse the ground because of man, even though every inclination of his heart is evil from childhood'" (vv. 20-21).

Summary

And so it was that after the Fall, God placed man under the law of conscience. In submitting themselves to the law men were submitting themselves to God and showing themselves to be in the kingdom of the God of heaven.

The false kingdom of Satan soon manifested itself in the activities of Cain, who became the progenitor of many who were in Satan's kingdom. God demonstrated His right to rule by bringing about a catastrophic judgment on all who were in the kingdom of Satan, and began a new form of theocratic administration through Noah.

4

The Administration of the Kingdom through Human Government

As we saw in the previous chapter, the administration of God's kingdom through conscience meant that each individual was *personally* responsible for his subjection to the law of God. But men were total failures under this form of theocratic administration, so God chose to administer His kingdom by bringing individuals into subjection to His administrators, people who received a God-given injunction to control the lawlessness of men.

In Genesis 9 we see that the same responsibility given to Adam was given to Noah. He was to be fruitful and multiply and replenish the earth (v. 1). Because Noah was made the administrator of God's kingdom on the earth, he was to exercise authority over every living creature on land and sea. This right to rule as a theocratic administrator was to produce dread on the part of all those who were subject to his authority (v. 2).

Curbing lawlessness

The extent of the authority given to Noah as a theocratic administrator is found in Genesis 9:6: "Whoever sheds the blood of man, by man shall his blood be shed, for in the image of God has God made man." The human government and the governors that existed previously—as in the city which Cain established (4:17), or in the case of the mighty men (6:4)—existed solely on human authority. Now, however, divine authority was conferred on human government to exercise oversight over those who lived under its jurisdiction. It was

46

the responsibility of human government to curb lawlessness by punishing the evildoers.

Paul commanded, "Everyone must submit himself to the governing authorities, for there is no authority except that which God has established" (Rom. 13:1). These governing authorities include kings and all that are in authority (1 Tim. 2:2). The reason for such submission is that those in authority in the civil realm are appointed to their position by God. In Romans 13:4 and 6, they are called the ministers of God. They are not ministers of the gospel, but they are administrators in God's kingdom. Their primary function is that "we [believers] may live peaceful and quiet lives in all godliness and holiness" (1 Tim. 2:2). The peace of the kingdom would be disrupted by unrestrained lawlessness, and therefore it becomes the responsibility of those in authority to curb lawlessness.

The extent of the authority given to those in power is seen in that "he does not bear the sword for nothing. He is God's servant, an agent of wrath to bring punishment on the wrongdoer" (Rom. 13:4). The sword as an instrument of judgment reveals that lawless men may be removed from society by physical death. Since God's kingdom is to be characterized by righteousness and peace, it must be seen that human government was given authority by God to provide an atmosphere in which righteous men may live in peace without fear. The rulers, then, became theocratic administrators to exemplify God's rule in this earthly sphere.

Sign of the promise

Men who had lived so close to the awesome judgment of God through the Flood might have lived in constant fear that such a judgment would be visited upon the earth again. In order that godly men might live without fear, God made a covenant with Noah and his descendants and with all who came under the authority of these God-given rulers: "I now establish My covenant with you and with your descendants after you and with every living creature that was with you—the birds, the livestock and all the wild animals, all those that came out of the ark with you—every living creature on earth. . . . Never again will all life be cut off by the waters of a flood; never again will there be a flood to destroy the earth" (Gen. 9:9-11). Though disobedience will bring judgment, God will never again use a universal flood as a means of judgment.

This certainly would have quieted the fears of Noah and his sons. Moreover, Noah was given a reminder of the covenant God had made: "I have set My rainbow in the clouds, and it will be the sign of the covenant between Me and the earth" (v. 13). Apart from God's covenant, recurring rainstorms would have brought fear to those who remembered the Flood. The bow in the midst of the storm, however, was a reminder of God's promise to mankind.

Every appearance of a rainbow in a storm called on those who witnessed it to exercise faith in God's promise. The validity of the promise rests on the integrity of the One who made the promise. Since God is faithful, men could rest in His promise and experience peace. Faith in the God of promise would make them sons of the kingdom and they could experience the peace that God has provided for those who are subject to His authority.

Two legacies

The elimination of the human race with the exception of the eight who were in the ark might seem to suggest that God had altered His original purpose for man as revealed at Creation. But God was careful to affirm to Noah that His purpose for man to have dominion on the earth was unchanged. The right to rule was given to Noah (Gen. 9:2) and to Noah's sons after him (vv. 8-10). In spite of man's failure, God *will* accomplish His purpose in creating man.

Since Noah had three sons it was necessary to identify the one who would succeed him as theocratic administrator. Ham's response to his father's drunkenness and nakedness immediately disqualified him (vv. 20-22). On the other hand, the actions of Shem and Japheth in covering their father's nakedness signified either of them would be eligible to succeed as the administrator (v. 23). Later Noah made a prophetic announcement in which he placed judgment on the descendants of Ham (v. 24, which was fulfilled in Josh. 9:27), and he pronounced blessing on Shem, indicating that both the descendants of Ham and those of Japheth should be in subjection to the authority of Shem and his descendants (vv. 25-27). Thus the legacy of theocratic administration would pass from Noah to Shem and to Shem's descendants.

Meanwhile, though Ham had been delivered from judgment through the ark, he became the progenitor of a line through which the false kingdom of Satan was again developed in the earthly realm.

48

Ham means "the darkened one." To Ham was born Cush, which means "the blackened one," and Cush was the father of Nimrod. These names *do not* signify external skin color, but rather indicate spiritual condition. Ham had received light through the revelation that God had given through the provision of the ark, but he rejected that revelation. His spiritual darkness became even darker in succeeding generations, and it was into this line that Nimrod was born

Nimrod and Babel

Nimrod led a rebellion against God as an administrator in Satan's kingdom of darkness. As a "mighty hunter" literally *against* the Lord (Gen. 10:9), Nimrod hunted for the souls of men to lead them in rebellion and into the kingdom of darkness. He fled from the place of revelation and from the people who believed God's revelation and "they found a plain in Shinar and settled there" (11:2). Remember, it had already been said of Nimrod that "the first centers of his kingdom were Babylon [Babel in the KJV] . . . " (10:10).

Babel may be translated "the gate of God." In other words, Babel became the administrative center of the false kingdom of Satan in which Nimrod had made himself the ruling authority. As Cain had done before him (4:17), Nimrod built a fortified city (11:3-4). In the center of that city Nimrod's followers built an awesome tower "that reaches to the heavens." This tower was designed to be a symbol of strength to this people who had united together under Nimrod, as well as a symbol of a new religion Nimrod offered them.

These people were organized and unified politically as well as religiously in their rebellion against God, and thus it became evident that human government cannot and will not restrain the lawlessness of man. It will not curb the spread of Satan's false kingdom and bring man into subjection to the authority of God. Men failed under the administration of human government as they failed under the administration of conscience.

Once again God demonstrated His sovereign authority by imposing judgment on those who united in their rebellion against Him. Since they were unrestrained in their lawlessness (11:6), God confounded their language so that they could not understand one another's speech and scattered them from there over all the earth (vv. 7-8). The organized system which Nimrod had named "the gate of God" God called Babel, which means "confusion "

49

The scattering of the rebels (v. 9) meant they could not be united in their rebellion against God, though they as individuals continued to be rebels. Nor could they overrun and subjugate the chosen line of Shem. Because of the failure of human government to fulfill its function as God's administrator, God then turned to a new form of theocractic administration.

Summary

God entrusted theocratic administration to appointed administrators in the political realm, who were responsible to enforce law and punish lawless men and so curb the development of the kingdom of darkness.

However, men rebelled against this form of administration, the administrators failed to discharge their responsibilities, and lawlessness reigned. God responded to this rebellion by scattering men abroad so they were no longer united in their rebellion against Him. He then instituted a new form of theocratic administration.

5

The Kingdom Program
Developed through Abraham

When in Genesis 11:27-31 we are first introduced to Abram—who
plays such a significant role in the development of God's kingdom of
heaven on earth—we find him residing in Haran together with his
nephew Lot, both under the headship of Abram's father Terah.

The question immediately arises as to how this family that had
originated in the land of Shinar (11:2)—which originally was established by Nimrod as a center of rebellion against God—should find
themselves 500 miles from their homeland. The explanation is given
in the narrative of Genesis 12:1-3. Noah had prophesied that God's
program was to be carried on through the descendants of Shem
(9:25-27). So it was that God appeared to Abram while he was still
living in Ur of the Chaldees to give him a promise. Abram had been
brought up in a pagan household (Josh. 24:2), in a pagan culture,
and was dedicated to the worship of pagan gods. Indeed, at the time
God appeared to him Abram lived in spiritual darkness. Yet God
appeared to Abram not because he was righteous or seeking God
but rather as a revelation of His glory to prepare an instrument
through which He would work to establish His kingdom in this
earthly sphere. It is Stephen in his great message recorded in Acts 7
who stresses the fact that the God of glory appeared to Abram (v. 2).

Personal, national, universal

The promises that this glorious God gave to Abram fall into three
categories (Gen. 12:2-3). First there were *personal* promises given

51

to Abram. God said, "I will bless you; I will make your name great." Then there were *national* promises given to this childless man. "I will make you into a great nation." And finally there were *universal* promises that were to come through Abram. "You will be a blessing . . . and all peoples on earth will be blessed through you."

Further, the promise made to Abraham in Genesis 12:1-3, and confirmed and enlarged to him in Genesis 12:6-7, 13:14-17, 15:1-21, 17:1-14, and 22:15-18, included certain basic blessings. Specifically, Abram's name would be great; a great nation would emerge from his loins; all nations would be blessed through him and his seed; his physical descendants would possess the land then occupied by the Canaanites; his descendants would be as innumerable as the dust of the seashore or as the stars of heaven; whoever blessed Abram or his seed would be blessed and whoever cursed them would be cursed; he would be the father of many nations; kings would emerge from his loins; and God would be his God and his descendants would be God's people.

Conditions for receiving the promise

Any promise God gives must be appropriated by faith. God had revealed Himself to Abram as one who because of His glory was worthy to be believed (Acts 7:2). Thus God tested Abram's faith and attached certain conditions to the reception of these blessings. First, Abram would have to be separated from his country, from his kindred, and from his father's house (Gen. 12:1). The blessings God promised to Abram were not to be enjoyed in his former place of residence, for the land in which he was dwelling was the center of the kingdom of darkness. Nor were they to be enjoyed by his kindred, for they were part of the kingdom of darkness. As an idolater (Josh. 24:2), his father also was in the kingdom of darkness. God was calling Abram out of that kingdom of darkness into a new sphere in which a new kingdom would be established. Therefore God invited Abram to follow Him "to the land I will show you" (Gen. 12:1).

History tells us that Abram was leaving what was probably the most advanced culture of his day. He was evidently a man of great wealth judging from the extensive flocks and herds which he possessed and would have been a man of prominence and authority in Ur.

Even so, God did not compel Abram to leave but rather attracted him out of his homeland to seek a better country in which God's promises would be fulfilled. Abram responded in faith to God's command and journeyed to Haran. At that point he had not left his father's house nor his kindred. His father Terah was in the home, as was his nephew, Lot. Incomplete obedience could not provide a basis for the fulfillment of God's promises; therefore Abram's journey toward the land God had promised was interrupted until after the death of Terah in Haran. It was after Terah's death that "Abram left, as the Lord had told him" (v. 4). The departure spoken of here was not the departure from Ur, but rather his departure from Haran following the death of Terah.

In departing from Haran following his father's death, Abram met God's second test of obedience. He was no longer under the authority of his father nor responsible to him, but instead would become the head of the household. Still, his obedience was not yet complete because "Lot went with him."

Together they continued on their journey another 400 miles until they arrived in Canaan (v. 5), a very rich, fertile land—yet one that was occupied by a grossly depraved, pagan people. It was when they came into Canaan that "the Lord appeared to Abram and said, 'To your offspring I will give this land'" (v. 7). Since leaving Ur, Abram had been walking by faith, trusting God's guidance to bring him into the land He had promised to him. God had not revealed Himself to Abram since the momentous event in Ur. What an encouragement it must have been to Abram to have the Lord who had appeared to him in Ur reappear to reconfirm His promises.

Land and offspring

The promise God reiterated revolved around two signficant words: *offspring* and *land*. The offspring ("seed" in the KJV) referred to physical progeny who would come from Abram and who would become the "nation" God had originally promised to him. The land was that literal and physical portion that bordered the eastern coast of the Mediterranean Sea. We can only imagine how Abram's heart must have leapt with joy when he received this promise from God. Abram's response was that "he built an altar to the Lord, who had appeared to him" (Gen. 12:7).

The altar was for sacrifice, an act of worship in which Abram recognized his responsibility to God and offered worship to God who had been faithful to His promises. By this act of worship Abram claimed as his own the land God designated as his possession, and it was a sign of his anticipation of the fulfillment of the promise that a nation would come from his loins.

After that, Abram settled in Bethel which means "the house of God" and again built an altar. And Abram did what Seth had done (4:26)—"he called on the name of the Lord" (12:8). In contrast to the kingdom of darkness in Ur which Abraham had left, and in contrast to the Canaanites' kingdom of darkness where Abraham now dwelt, we find a miniature kingdom was established which recognized God's right to rule. It was a kingdom in which worship was offered to God, in which obedience was given to His commands, and in which Abram was the administrator, God's theocratic representative.

Anyone in that kingdom must walk by faith; yet when there was a famine in the land Abram failed to trust God in the midst of the famine, fleeing to Egypt to sustain himself, his flocks, and his herds (v. 10). The blessings God promised to Abram were to be enjoyed in the land God had deeded to him, not in the land of Egypt. Therefore trouble awaited Abram when he went into Egypt.

Through the circumstances that followed, God moved Pharaoh to expel Abram from Egypt (v. 20) so that he might return to the land of promise. Abram came again to Bethel and "called on the name of the Lord" (13:3-4). Restoration to the experience of blessings after disobedience depended on confession and Abram's return to the altar; it was an acknowledgment of his disobedience and a resumption of a walk by faith. The experience of the fullness of God's blessings depended on the fullness of Abram's obedience.

Remember, Abram had not yet met the condition that he separate from his family. He was still dwelling with Lot. In fact, the vast flocks and herds and tents both Abram and Lot possessed as evidences of God's blessings ultimately led to a separation between the two. Abram generously offered Lot his choice of a portion of the land that God had given to Abram. Because the plain of Jordan offered such lush pastures for his flocks and herds, Lot chose that segment in which Sodom and Gomorrah—centers of the kingdom of darkness—were located. And there Lot dwelt. Lot, by his own choice, moved out of the land of Canaan—the land of promise given by God to Abram.

The promise confirmed

The third test of Abram's obedience had been met, so once again the Lord appeared to Abram to reiterate His previous promises. Now that all the conditions for receiving the blessings of the promise had been met, God could say:

> Lift up your eyes from where you are and look north and south, east and west. All the land that you see I will give to you and your offspring forever. I will make your offspring like the dust of the earth, so that if anyone could count the dust, then your offspring could be counted. Go, walk through the length and breadth of the land, for I am giving it to you (Gen. 13:14-17).

Once again God repeated His promise concerning the land and the physical descendants that would be born in Abram's line. When Lot removed himself from Abram who was dwelling at Bethel—the house of God, the center of God's kingdom here in this earthly sphere—he moved into a sphere dominated by the kingdom of Satan. Lot was a righteous man (2 Peter 2:7-8) and could not accept the vile lifestyle of Sodom and Gomorrah. But neither did he experience the blessings of God in keeping with the promises given to Abram. Finally, when God brought judgment on that kingdom of darkness through the invasion by Kedorlaomer and his allied kings, Lot was taken captive.

By faith Abram waged war against this coalition of kings in order to deliver Lot. Abram's servants were shepherds, not soldiers, but God honored Abram's faith and gave him a great victory, delivering Lot and those who had been taken captive with him. God further honored Abram's faith and sent Melchizedek, king of Salem, who was also the priest of the Most High God (Gen. 14:18) to Abram to confer His blessing on him. This victory and the subsequent blessing vividly illustrates what God had meant when He had promised to Abram, "I will bless those who bless you, and whoever curses you I will curse" (12:3).

Abram's response to God's blessing was to give tithes to God through Melchizedek (14:20). In giving a tithe he acknowledged that all of the spoils of victory actually belonged to God and he was only a steward of them. Moreover, Abram made it clear he did not need a covenant with the king of Sodom for his protection, for God was his protector; and he did not need wealth from the king of Sodom, because God would reward him richly.

It is evident that God spoke in keeping with His original promises to Abram because Abram responded by asking about the son and heir God had promised to him. According to the custom of the day, if one died childless, a designated servant would become the administrator of his estate. Since Abram had no son, Eliezer of Damascus would have become the administrator of Abram's estate, and apparently in Abram's mind he also would have become an administrator in the kingdom in which Abram had been appointed the theocratic head.

God responded to Abram's concerns by saying, "Look up at the heavens and count the stars—if indeed you can count them. . . . So shall your offspring be" (15:5). Notice that Abram did not raise a question concerning a land, because that land had already been delivered to him and he had appropriated it by faith. But he did have questions about the descendants who would inhabit that land. Thus God promised him a physical progeny as innumerable as the stars of heaven.

Abram's response was that he "believed the Lord" (v. 6). The word translated *believed* is the Hebrew word *amen*. Abram by faith expressed his belief in the fulfillment of the promise. Moreover, Abram's faith was placed in a Person. The text does not say Abram believed *the promise,* but rather that Abram believed *the Lord.* On the basis of this evidence of Abram's faith, the Lord credited it to him as righteousness" (v. 6). Faith was not accepted as a substitute for righteousness, but on the basis of faith, God's own righteousness could be imputed to Abram. Through Abram's faith, God could make a declaration that Abram was justified in His sight. So great was Abram's faith, in fact, that he dared to ask God for a confirmation of the promise of a seed.

Blood covenant

God told Abram to prepare a sacrifice in order to enact a blood covenant. In Abram's day, contracts or covenants could be enacted in various ways. There was what was called a hand covenant in which two making a covenant would shake hands or strike the palms of their hands together (Ezra 10:19; Ezek. 17:18).

A second form of entering into a contract or covenant was what was known as the shoe covenant. Two entering into such a covenant would exchange sandals as a sign that a covenant was in effect. This covenant remained intact until the ones making the covenant reexchanged sandals to obtain their own sandal again. This is the covenant that Boaz made before the judges in order to redeem Ruth (Ruth 4:8).

The third type of covenant was the salt covenant (Num. 18:19; Lev. 2:13; 2 Chron. 13:5). Travelers would prepare for a journey by providing a pouch of salt which they would secure in the sash around their waist. Salt was essential for a traveler, preventing dehydration and enabling the body to retain moisture. Entering into a salt covenant after the terms had been agreed upon, the two making the covenant would produce their respective pouches of salt. One would dip his thumb and index finger into the other's pouch and place that pinch of salt into his own pouch. The other would do the same. This signified that the covenant was to remain in effect until each of the two could get their salt from the pouch of the other.

The fourth form of contract or covenant was the blood covenant. After the terms had been agreed on, an animal would be sacrificed and the carcass divided into two parts, with the two parts laid opposite each other on the ground. The two entering into this covenant would join hands, recite the terms of the covenant, and then walk together between the two pieces of the carcass. Thus they were bound together in covenant by blood.

This type of blood covenant signified two things. *First,* it signified that if either participant in the covenant should fail to fulfill his portion of the agreement, his blood was to be poured out like the blood of the animal that bound them in the covenant. In other words, it was a covenant that carried a death penalty for failure to fulfill its obligations. *Second,* the animal that was sacrificed was viewed as a substitute in death for the two making the covenant. The point was that while the men were living they conceivably could alter the terms of the covenant, but after their symbolic deaths the terms of the covenant were unalterable. The blood covenant, then, was viewed as an unchangeable covenant.

Returning to Genesis 15, we see that in response to Abram's request for reassurance of the fulfillment of the promises, God told Abram to prepare for a formal blood covenant. Abram would have been very familiar with the ritual, but what must have impressed him was the number of animals God asked him to sacrifice: a three-year-old heifer, a three-year-old female goat, a three-year-old ram, a turtle dove, and a young pigeon. Any one of these would have been sufficient to enact a blood covenant, but the sheer number of animals stressed the importance of what was being covenanted here.

The Abrahamic Covenant

Abram, in keeping with custom, sacrificed the animals, divided the carcasses of the three large animals, and laid those together with the two birds on the ground. It was at that point that a most significant thing took place: "Abram fell into a deep sleep" (Gen. 15:12). Normally, the two covenant-makers would agree on the terms of the covenant, with each committing himself to the fulfillment of certain promises being covenanted. They would then walk hand in hand through the pieces of the sacrifice. But on this unique occasion Abram was not a *participant in* the covenant; rather, he was a *recipient of* a covenant.

While Abram was asleep God revealed to him the destiny of his descendants: "Your descendants will be strangers in a country not their own, and they will be enslaved and mistreated four hundred years. But I will punish the nation they serve as slaves, and afterward they will come out with great possessions" (vv. 13-14). This prophecy necessitated the existence of a great nation that would spring from Abram's loins. The literal fulfillment of this portion of God's Word to Abram indicates that the covenant itself would be fulfilled literally as well.

After this revelation (which assured Abram of a seed) "the Lord made a covenant with Abram and said, 'To your descendants I give this land' " (v. 18). The covenant involved the seed—that is, the physical descendants that would be born to Abram—and the land of Canaan in which Abram was now living. From the time God had appeared to Abram in Ur up to this point, Abram had been proceeding on the basis of the promise of God. Now what God had promised He confirmed by a covenant. Abram thus had two immutable things as the basis for his faith: (1) the promise of God, and (2) the covenant of God (see Heb. 6:14-18). By *promise* the land of Canaan was given to Abraham; now by *covenant* the boundaries of that land were vastly expanded (Gen. 15:18-21).

The land Abram's descendants would ultimately possess would go from the borders of Egypt in the south; northward through Philistia, Canaan, and Syria; from the land of the Hittites (which is eastern Turkey) in the west, eastward to the River Euphrates, a territory then occupied by a multitude of tribes.

Conditional or unconditional?

Since this covenant with Abraham is the foundation for the ultimate fulfillment of the kingdom program here on the earth, it is necessary to consider it in some detail. There were two kinds of covenants into which God entered with Israel: conditional and unconditional. In a conditional covenant, that which was covenanted depended on the recipient of the covenant for its fulfillment, not on the one making the covenant. Certain obligations or conditions would need to be kept by the recipient of the covenant before the giver of the covenant would be obligated to fulfill what was promised. This type of covenant has an "if" attached to it. The Mosaic Covenant made by God with Israel is one such covenant.

In an unconditional covenant, on the other hand, that which was covenanted depended for its fulfillment solely on the one making the covenant. That which was promised was sovereignly given to the recipient of the covenant on the authority and integrity of the one making the covenant, entirely apart from the merit or response of the receiver. It was a covenant with no "if" attached to it whatsoever.

To safeguard our thinking on this point, we should observe that an unconditional covenant, which binds the one making the covenant to a certain course of action, may have blessings attached to it that are conditioned on the response of the recipient. Though these blessings grow out of the original covenant, they do not change the unconditional character of that covenant. If we fail to recognize that an unconditional covenant may have certain conditioned blessings attached to it, we might mistakenly think that conditioned blessings necessitate a conditional covenant, which could pervert our understanding of the nature of Israel's determinative covenants.

There are certain other facts we should observe concerning the covenants into which God has entered.

First, these covenants are *literal* covenants and are to be interpreted literally. Such an interpretation would be in harmony with the established literal method of interpretation.

59

Second, these covenants, according to the Scriptures, are *eternal.* All of Israel's covenants are called eternal except the Mosaic Covenant, which is declared to be temporal (i.e., it was to continue only until the coming of the promised Seed). As we will see later in our study, the Abrahamic Covenant is called "eternal" ("everlasting" in the NIV) in Genesis 17:7, 13, 19; 1 Chronicles 16:17; and Psalm 105:10; the Palestinian Covenant is called "eternal" in Ezekiel 16:60; the Davidic Covenant is called "eternal" in 2 Samuel 23:5; Isaiah 55:3; and Ezekiel 37:26; and the New Covenant is called "eternal" in Isaiah 24:5; 61:8; Jeremiah 32:40; 50:5; and Hebrews 13:20.

Third, inasmuch as these covenants are literal, eternal, and depend solely on the integrity of God for their fulfillment, they must be considered to be *unconditional* in character. This question will be considered in detail later.

Fourth and finally, these covenants were *made with a covenant people,* Israel. In Romans 9:4 Paul stated that the nation Israel had received covenants from the Lord. In Ephesians 2:11-12 he wrote, conversely, that the Gentiles have not received any such covenants and consequently do not enjoy covenant relationships with God. These two passages show us, negatively, that the Gentiles were without covenant relationships and, positively, that God had entered into covenant relationships with Israel.

One detail we do need to note here is the conditional element in the covenant program with Abram. It was not until after the death of his father (Gen. 11:32) that Abram began to realize anything of the promise God had given to him, for only after his father's death did God take him into the land (12:4) and there reaffirm the original promise to him (12:7).

It is important, therefore, to observe the relationship of obedience to this covenant program. Whether or not God would institute a covenant program with Abram depended on Abram's act of obedience in leaving the land. Once this act was accomplished, however, and Abram did obey God, God instituted an irrevocable, *unconditional* program. This obedience, which became the basis of the institution of the program, is alluded to in Genesis 22:18, where the offering of Isaac is just one more evidence of Abram's attitude toward God.

Whether there would be a covenant program with Abram depended on Abram's obedience. But once he obeyed, the covenant was instituted and depended not on Abram's continued obedience, but on the promise of the One who instituted it. The *fact* of the covenant depended on obedience; the *kind* of covenant inaugurated was totally unrelated to the continuing obedience of either Abram or his seed.

The question as to whether the Abrahamic Covenant is conditional or unconditional is recognized as the crux of the discussion relating to its fulfillment. Extensive argument can be presented to support the contention of the premillennialist as to the unconditional character of this covenant.

Dr. John F. Walvoord presents ten reasons for believing that this covenant is unconditional (John F. Walvoord, "Millennial Series," *Bibliotheca Sacra*, 109:38-40). He argues:

(1) All Israel's covenants are unconditional except the Mosaic. The Abrahamic Covenant is expressly declared to be eternal and therefore unconditional in numerous passages (see those already mentioned on p. 60).

(2) Except for the original condition of leaving his homeland and going to the Promised Land, the covenant is made with no conditions whatever.

(3) The Abrahamic Covenant is confirmed repeatedly by reiteration and enlargement. In none of these instances are any of the added promises conditioned on the faithfulness of Abraham's seed or of Abraham himself.

(4) The Abrahamic Covenant was solemnized by a divinely ordered ritual symbolizing the shedding of blood and passing between the parts of the sacrifice (Gen. 15:7-21; Jer. 34:18). This ceremony was given to Abraham as an assurance that his seed would inherit the land in the exact boundaries given to him in Genesis 15:18-21. No conditions whatever are attached to this promise in this context.

(5) To distinguish those who would inherit the promises as individuals from those who were only physical seed of Abraham, the visible sign of circumcision was given (17:9-14). One not circumcised was considered outside the promised blessing. The ultimate fulfillment of the Abrahamic Covenant and possession of the land by the seed is not hinged, however, on faithfulness in the matter of circumcision. In fact the promises of the land were given before the rite was introduced.

(6) The Abrahamic Covenant was confirmed by the birth of Isaac and Jacob to both of whom the promises are repeated in their original form (17:10; 28:12-13).

(7) Notable is the fact that the reiterations of the covenant and the partial early fulfillment of the covenant are in spite of acts of disobedience. It is clear that on several instances Abraham strayed from the will of God. . . . In the very act . . . the promises are repeated to him.

(8) The later confirmations of the covenant are given in the midst of apostasy. Important is the promise given through Jeremiah that Israel as a nation will continue forever (Jer. 31:36).

(9) The New Testament declares the Abrahamic Covenant immutable (Heb. 6:13-18; cf. Gen. 15:8-21). It was not only promised but solemnly confirmed by the oath of God.

(10) The entire scriptural revelation concerning Israel and its future as contained in both the Old and New Testaments, if interpreted literally, confirms and sustains the unconditional character of the promises given to Abraham.

Literal or figurative?

Since the Abrahamic Covenant ultimately deals with Israel's title deed to the land of Palestine, her continuation as a nation to possess that land, and her redemption so that she may enjoy the blessings in the land under her King, it is of utmost importance to determine the method of the fulfillment of this covenant.

If it is a literal covenant which needs to be fulfilled literally, then Israel must be preserved, converted, and restored. If it is an unconditional covenant, these events in Israel's national life are inevitable.

Sign of the covenant

To signify that Abram would have a vast progeny, his name was changed from Abram, which means "exalted father," to Abraham, which means "father of many nations." The birth of a son to Abraham was to be a confirmation of God's covenant. God said, "I will establish My covenant as an everlasting covenant between Me and you and your descendants after you for the generations to come, to be your God and the God of your descendants after you. The whole land of Canaan, where you are now an alien, I will give as an everlasting possession to you and your descendants after you; and I will be their God" (Gen. 17:7-8).

Again God reaffirmed His covenant that involved both a land and physical descendants to be born to Abraham. God stated this covenant to be everlasting, one that would eventually bring Abraham's descendants into a similarly intimate relationship with God. This covenant, then, determines the sphere and subjects of a kingdom over which God rules.

On this occasion God also instituted a rite which was to be a sign of that covenant. God commanded, "Every male among you shall be circumcised" (v. 10). The circumcision of a child by his father was to be a sign of the father's faith in the God who made covenant with Abraham and Abraham's descendants. Only faith could bring one within the bonds of the covenant, and circumcision became that sign of faith that identified those who were in the kingdom. In circumcising a son the father indicated that he believed the covenant would be fulfilled if not in his own day, then in his son's day, and he wanted his son to bear the sign of faith that would bring him the blessings of the covenant.

Conversely, those without faith were excluded from the benefits of the covenant. God commanded, "Any uncircumcised male . . . will be cut off from his people; he has broken My covenant" (v. 14). Without faith one could not be in God's kingdom or partake of its benefits. So in obedience to the command of God, Abraham himself was circumcised along with all the men of his house" (vv. 26-27).

Lot, along with Abraham, was an heir of the promises of the covenant. While Lot enjoyed blessings from the covenant (13:5-6), through his incestuous relationships with his daugthers (19:33-38) children were born to the daughters who became the progenitors of the Moabites and the Ammonites, persistent enemies of the covenant people throughout their history. Through this relationship a false kingdom grew up alongside the covenant kingdom, and continual conflict festered between the two. Again we see that those who rejected the revelation God gave and who refused to submit to His constituted authority became part of the kingdom of darkness and engaged in warfare against the kingdom people.

Summary

God's promise given to Abraham while he dwelt in Ur concerning a land and a progeny was confirmed to him by an eternal, unconditional, and unchangeable covenant. Enjoying the blessings of this covenant depended on the faith of the recipient of the covenant. Not all entered into the benefits of the covenant, however, and a false kingdom developed alongside the kingdom of the God of heaven.

6

The Kingdom Program through the Patriarchs

The kingdom program not only promised Abraham an heir but depended on the birth of that heir for its perpetuity. Since no heir seemed possible from Abraham and Sarah because of their age and Sarah's barrenness (Heb. 11:11-12), Sarah proposed a solution to Abraham (Gen. 16:2-3). Actually, this was an evidence of Sarah's faith in the covenant, for while God had promised Abraham an heir He had not said it must come from Sarah. But in taking Hagar as a concubine-wife Abraham resorted to human effort in order to fulfill the promises of the covenant. In doing so he did not exercise the headship that belonged to him but submitted to the headship of Sarah. It was from this union that Ishmael was born (v. 15).

As one might expect, the birth of Ishmael only engendered strife in Abraham's household (vv. 5-6). Rather than producing an heir through whom the covenant would be continued, Abraham fathered one who would further the false kingdom and whose descendants would become the chief adversary of the covenant people. Concerning Ishmael and his descendants God said, "He will be a wild donkey of a man; his hand will be against everyone and everyone's hand against him, and he will live in hostility toward all his brothers" (v. 12). His brothers in this instance refers to Abraham's descendants through Isaac, who would become the heir of the covenant.

Such was Abraham's love for Ishmael that he petitioned God to accept him as the covenanted heir (Gen. 17:18). It appears that Abraham's faith was still too weak to believe that he and Sarah would have a son, and he was willing to accept Ishmael as the fulfillment of God's promise. This solution God forthrightly rejected. He made it clear that the covenant was to continue through a child by Sarah: "Yes, but your wife Sarah will bear you a son, and you will call him Isaac. I will establish My covenant with him as an everlasting covenant for his descendants after him" (v. 19).

So, at the exact time God had predicted (Gen. 17:21), Sarah conceived and bore Isaac (Gen. 21:2-3). This birth was the result of the faith of both Sarah and Abraham (Heb. 11:11-12), and Abraham's obedience in circumcising his son (Gen. 21:4) placed Isaac in the bonds of the covenant. The feast Abraham gave at the time of Isaac's weaning (v. 8) was a public introduction of the heir to the covenant community.

Since the one born of the flesh—Ishmael—could not receive the benefits of the covenant as he would have had he remained in his father's house, Ishmael had to be put out lest he claim the inheritance for himself. Although it caused Abraham great pain, the separation was accomplished (vv. 9-11). Abraham's love for Ishmael did not diminish, but as Paul says, "The slave's son will never share in the inheritance with the free woman's son" (Gal. 4:30).

Abraham's greatest test

Since blessings from God depend on faith and faith is demonstrated by obedience, Abraham's faith was again tested when God commanded him to offer Isaac as a sacrifice. Once again Abraham's faith was demonstrated through implicit obedience. So implicit was Abraham's faith that Isaac alone could be the heir of God, he believed that God would have to raise him from the dead so that the promise could be fulfilled (Heb. 11:17-19).

As before, God responded to the obedience of faith. He said to Abraham, "I swear by Myself, declares the Lord, that because you have done this and have not withheld your son, your only son, I will surely bless you and make your descendants as numerous as the stars in the sky and as the sand on the seashore. Your descendants will take possession of the cities of their enemies, and through your offspring all nations on earth will be blessed, because you have obeyed Me" (Gen. 22:16-18). Here again God promised Abraham that he would become the recipient of the covenant blessings. The covenant was not based on obedience, nor was the perpetuity of the covenant based on obedience—but rather the reception of covenant blessings was conditioned on obedience. Remember, an unconditional covenant may have conditional blessings. Thus on the basis of faith that had produced obedience, Abraham would experience the blessings of the promises and the covenant.

Later, in sending away the sons of Keturah, his wife after the death of Sarah, and in giving all his inheritance to Isaac (Gen. 25:5), Abraham acknowledged Isaac and Isaac alone as the promised heir of the covenant. Not only did Abraham recognize Isaac as the heir but God did also, for He appeared to Isaac and confirmed His oath: "Do not go down to Egypt; live in the land where I tell you to live. Stay in this land for a while, and I will be with you and will bless you. For to you and your descendants I will give all these lands and will confirm the oath I swore to your father Abraham. I will make your descendants as numerous as the stars in the sky and will give them all these lands, and through your offspring all nations on earth will be blessed, because Abraham obeyed Me and kept My requirements, My commands, My decrees and My laws" (26:3-5). God evidenced His blessing on Isaac by providing abundant water for him and his flocks and by reaffirming His promises (vv. 17-24), and Isaac recognized God as the covenant provider by building an altar as a sign of submission to Him (v. 25). Like Seth and Abraham before him (4:26; 13:4) Isaac "called on the name of the Lord."

Isaac took Rebekah as his wife, but she like Sarah before her was barren. It is an evidence of Isaac's faith in the covenant in that he petitioned God to enable his wife to bear children (Gen. 25:21), for without a son the covenant would not be continued. God honored Isaac's faith and Rebekah conceived twins. Before Esau and Jacob were even born, God indicated His choice as heir of the covenant: "the older will serve the younger" (v. 23).

It would have been expected that Esau, the elder, would become the heir of Isaac and the administrator of the covenanted kingdom. But Esau clearly demonstrated that he was not in the kingdom of the God of heaven but rather was in the kingdom of darkness. In short, he was characterized by unbelief.

The writer of Hebrews called Esau a fornicator or profane person (Heb. 12:16). Though there was no hint of immorality in the record given in Genesis 25:27-34, a fornicator is one who lives to gratify the flesh. It was this desire to gratify his physical appetite at the expense of his heirship of the kingdom administration that characterized

Esau. Further, he was said to be profane; that is, of this world, or of the kingdom of darkness rather than of the kingdom of light.

When Esau asked Jacob for some of the food that he had prepared, Jacob replied, "Sell me your birthright" (25:31). In this request Jacob was showing faith in the promise and in the God who promised. This "birthright" represented a position as Isaac's heir and as an administrator in the kingdom. Since Esau had no faith in the God who had given promise and made covenant, he counted his birthright as worthless and willingly forfeited it for food. In spite of the fact that he was a trickster or deceiver, Jacob did believe that there was benefit to be received from that which Esau despised. (Jacob then became the rightful heir by faith to the inheritance derived from Isaac.)

Before his death, Isaac conferred a blessing on Jacob, saying, "May nations serve you and people bow down to you. Be lord over your brothers, and may the sons of your mother bow down to you. May those who curse you be cursed and those who bless you be blessed" (27:29). The faith that led Jacob to claim the birthright now brought an appointment to a position of authority in the administration of the covenant and the kingdom.

When Isaac said, "Be lord over your brothers," he was transferring to Jacob the authority of theocratic administration. When Esau belatedly asked his father to transfer the authority to him, Isaac responded, "I have made him [Jacob] lord over you and have made all his relatives his servants" (v. 37). Thus Jacob was set apart to be the administrator in the kingdom.

The appointment of Jacob and the rejection of Esau caused Esau to hold a grudge against his brother. He then became a progenitor of those in the kingdom of darkness, the Edomites, who opposed those in the kingdom of the God of heaven. Unbelief always expanded the kingdom of darkness.

Even though God had appointed Jacob as the heir of the covenant and as administrator in the kingdom, it was still necessary for Him to transform Jacob into an acceptable leader.

Jacob's transformation

God appeared to Jacob, as he fled from the wrath of Esau, and reaffirmed the Abrahamic Covenant: "I am the Lord, the God of your father Abraham and the God of Isaac. I will give you and your descendants the land on which you are lying. Your descendants will be like the dust of the earth, and you will spread out to the west and to the east, to the north and to the south. All peoples on earth will be blessed through you and your offspring. I am with you and will watch over you wherever you go, and I will bring you back to this land. I will not leave you until I have done what I have promised you" (Gen. 28:13-15).

Thus the essential truths concerning land, seed, and blessing were reconfirmed to Jacob. Jacob responded in faith to this reaffirmation of the covenant in two ways. First, he called the place Bethel" (v. 19), for the place of revelation was truly the "house of God." And second, he affirmed his faith in the God of the covenant by asserting "then the Lord will be my God" (v. 21). He set up a memorial as an evidence to his faith and anticipated the fulfillment of God's promise of blessing by declaring that he would give a tenth to the Lord. His faith would render him a member of the kingdom and make him eligible to become its administrator.

Even so, it was necessary for God to deal with Jacob once again (32:24-30). In this episode, a heavenly messenger wrestled with Jacob to bring Jacob into submission to himself and to the God of the covenant. Jacob resisted for an extended period of time, until the visitor finally touched the hollow of Jacob's thigh causing the thigh to go out of joint. Because a wrestler depends on his thigh muscles for power, Jacob became powerless and had to hold on to his visitor lest he fall to the ground. Jacob's resistance was broken, and instead of trying to attain blessing through his own efforts, he depended on the visitor for support and begged him for blessing. God had transformed Jacob from a man who sought the right thing in a wrong way to one who sought the right thing in the right way.

In response to this new attitude of dependence, God promised, "Your name will no longer be Jacob, but Israel, because you have struggled with God and with men and have overcome" (v. 28). The cheater, the trickster, the supplanter was now designated a prince. The administrative authority in the theocracy that had been given to Abraham and was transferred to Isaac fell upon Jacob

The future of Jacob's offspring

As Jacob grew older, he sought to transfer this administrative authority to his beloved son Joseph, designating him as his heir by preparing him a special coat of many colors (Gen. 37:3). But Joseph was not to be the administrator in the theocracy; instead he was to become the deliverer of God's people, the one through whom God would provide for this kingdom people in a time of destitution. Hence, Joseph was sold into slavery to be elevated to a preeminent position in the kingdom of Egypt. He was an administrator—not in the kingdom of God, but in the kingdom of Pharaoh or the kingdom of Satan.

God wonderfully used his administration in that sphere to provide for His covenant people.

God had revealed to Abraham that his descendants would be in bondage in a land that was not theirs (15:13). It was during the lifetime of Jacob that this prophecy was fulfilled. But Jacob and his family did not leave the Promised Land for Egypt apart from the promise of God, who said: "Do not be afraid to go down to Egypt, for I will make you into a great nation there. I will go down to Egypt with you, and I will surely bring you back again" (46:3-4).

It would appear that the absence of the covenant people from their land indicated that God had abandoned the covenant program or that the covenant people had forfeited the promises. However, such is not the case. God promised Jacob that his descendants would return to the land to enjoy the blessings of the covenant. Rather, God brought the people into bondage in order that they might experience the redemption that He would provide. By that redemption they would become, not only God's covenant people, but also a people for God's own possession by purchase (Isa. 43:1).

Before his death, Jacob officially designated his successor in the line of theocratic administration: "Judah, your brothers will praise you; your hand will be on the neck of your enemies; your father's sons will bow down to you. You are a lion's cub, O Judah; you return from the prey, my son. Like a lion he crouches and lies down, like a lioness—who dares to rouse him? The scepter will not depart from Judah, nor the ruler's staff from between his feet, until he comes to whom it belongs [or until Shiloh comes] and the obedience of the nations is his" (Gen. 49:8-10).

Certain things said concerning Judah foreshadow the preeminence given to the tribe of Judah: (1) Judah would be in a place of preeminence. (2) His brothers would acknowledge his superior position. (3) Judah would be victorious over all of his enemies. (4) He would be given royal authority (since the lion is the symbol of royalty. (5) The kingdom was to be administered by kings, and the kings would come, without exception, from the tribe of Judah.

And, very important, there would be a succession of kings until Shiloh comes, or until he whose right it is [to rule] shall come. This was a prophecy concerning the coming of the Blessor who, as a king, would fulfill all that had been covenanted by God to Abraham, Isaac, and Jacob. And when this Blessor should come, "the obedience of the nations [will be] his" (v. 10; compare Ezek. 21:27). This is a crucial prophetic announcement by Jacob indicating the course of the kingdom of the God of heaven on earth. It is a kingdom that will be victorious. Men will bow to its authority. And God's kingdom will, in its final form, be administered by One who is given the right to rule by the God of covenant Himself.

Jacob's belief in the ultimate fulfillment of God's covenant with him is seen in his provision that he be buried in the land of promise (Gen. 50:5). Even though he would not succeed his father as the heir (as Jacob had originally hoped), Joseph so firmly believed the promises of the covenant that he insisted that when his people returned to the land of promise, his bones be interred there (vv. 24-25).

Summary

Throughout the period of the patriarchs we see that all God had covenanted with Abraham was reaffirmed to Isaac, and again to Jacob who at the close of his life prophesied that the covenant would be fulfilled through a king arising from the tribe of Judah.

7

The Abrahamic Covenant: The Foundation of Israel's History

It becomes apparent throughout Scripture that the history of Israel and God's dealing with Abraham's descendants is founded and built on the Abrahamic Covenant. A brief survey of Israel's history supports this fact. For example, the exodus of the nation from their years of Egyptian bondage was accomplished because God remembered His covenant with Abraham, with Isaac, and with Jacob (Ex. 2:24-25; 3:15-17).

Again, when God's redeemed people sinned against Him by making a calf of gold and giving it the worship that rightfully belonged to God, He announced His intention to wipe out that generation as He had wiped out the pagans in the days of Noah; and He would constitute Moses as the head of a new nation through whom the covenant promises to Abraham would be fulfilled. But Moses begged God to remember His covenant as given to Abraham and reconfirmed to Isaac and Jacob (32:12-13). Moses' prayer that God would deal with that guilty generation in grace rather than in judgment was based on the Abrahamic Covenant.

In Israel's history we also see that the unconditional Abrahamic Covenant definitely had conditional blessings. Faith that produces obedience was always a precondition to blessing. Disobedience did not nullify the covenant or bring it to an end, but it did cause God to withhold His blessing or even institute discipline. In Leviticus 26 God outlined chastisement that would come upon a disobedient people. The final discipline would be dispersion from the land that God had given to them through the Abrahamic Covenant (vv. 32-

39). But God also promised that the covenant people would be restored to blessing after they confessed their sin and returned to a life of obedience, based again on His covenant with Abraham: "I will remember My covenant with Jacob and My covenant with Isaac and My covenant with Abraham, and I will remember the land" (v. 42). Restoration to blessing after disobedience was because of God's faithfulness to His covenant with Abraham.

A little later in Israel's history, the generation that had been redeemed from bondage in Egypt was prevented from entering the land of promise because of their unbelief that led to rebellion at Kadesh Barnea. Joshua and Caleb's exhortation to the people to enter the land as God had commanded was based on their expectation that God would fulfill the Abrahamic Covenant (Num. 14:8, 16, 23, 30-31). While they were not unmindful of the power of their adversaries or the strength of the city walls, they expected God to be faithful to His covenant and thus believed they would conquer the land. Indeed, when the new generation was about to enter the land, the boundaries of the land they were to possess as outlined in Numbers 34:3-12 are in keeping with the boundaries of the land God first promised to Abraham (Gen. 15:18-21).

When Moses—at the close of his term as theocratic administrator—reviewed God's dealing with the nation, he reminded the new generation that the land to which they were going was theirs because of the Abrahamic Covenant (Deut. 1:8). He proclaimed, "Hear, O Israel: the Lord our God is one," reminding them that this was the God who had redeemed them and who ruled over them. Thus they were responsible to "love the Lord your God with all your heart and with all your soul and with all your strength" (6:4-5).

The revelation God had given to Israel through Moses was a revelation for which the people were responsible. God was to be preeminent in their affections: "These commandments . . . are to be upon your hearts" (Deut. 6:6). Their knowledge of God was to control all of their actions: "Tie them as symbols on your hands" (v. 8). That knowledge was to control their thinking: "Bind them on your foreheads" (v. 8). Their responsibility to God was because of God's faithfulness to the covenant which He made with Abraham, Isaac, and Jacob (v. 10). They as a redeemed people had been constituted a kingdom over which God ruled through appointed theocratic administrators, and as a result they were to "be careful that you do not forget the Lord, who brought you out of Egypt, out of the land of slavery. Fear the Lord your God, serve Him only and take your oaths in His name" (vv. 12-13). These would be the responsibilities—the instructions for living—of those *in* the kingdom to the Ruler *of* the kingdom.

And lest the people be lifted up in pride because of the blessings that they would shortly experience in the land, Moses reminded them:

> The Lord did not set His affection on you and choose you because you were more numerous than other peoples, for you were the fewest of all peoples. But it was because the Lord loved you and kept the oath He swore to your forefathers that He brought you out with a mighty hand and redeemed you from the land of slavery, from the power of Pharaoh king of Egypt. Know therefore that the Lord your God is God; He is the faithful God, keeping His covenant of love to a thousand generations of those who love Him and keep His commands (Deut. 7:7-9).

Therefore Israel's forthcoming victories under Joshua would occur only because of God's faithfulness to His covenant (9:5, 26-28).

When Moses, just before his death, went to the mountains of Nebo to the top of Pisgah and viewed the land of promise, northward to the slopes of Mount Hermon, "The Lord said to him, 'This is the land I promised on oath to Abraham, Isaac and Jacob when I said, "I will give it to your descendants." I have let you see it with your eyes, but you will not cross over into it'" (34:4). The land of promise was the same land that God had given to Abraham and his descendants, as reaffirmed by God to Moses.

Possession, preservation

When Joshua assumed the role of theocractic administrator from Moses, he commanded the people to follow him across the River Jordan into the land God had given to Abraham. It extended from the wilderness on the south, through the land of the Hittites, to the Euphrates on the north, as defined in Genesis 15:18-21. Thus Israel's history from the Exodus to their actual occupation on the land of Canaan under Joshua was based entirely on the Abrahamic Covenant.

Continuing on from there, the Abrahamic Covenant became the basis of Israel's protection and deliverance during invasions in the period of the monarchy. We read, for instance, that "Hazael king of Aram oppressed Israel throughout the reign of Jehoahaz. But the Lord was gracious to them and had compassion and showed concern for them because of His covenant with Abraham, Isaac, and Jacob. To this day He has been unwilling to destroy them or banish them from His presence" (2 Kings 13:22-23).

Again, when David restored the ark to Israel, he delivered a psalm of thankful praise to the Lord:

Give thanks to the Lord, call on His name; make known among the nations what He has done. Sing to Him, sing praise to Him; tell of all His wonderful acts. Glory in His holy name; let the hearts of those who seek the Lord rejoice. Look to the Lord and His strength; seek His face always. Remember the wonders He has done, His miracles, and the judgments He pronounced, O descendants of Israel His servant, O sons of Jacob, His chosen one. He is the Lord our God; His judgments are in all the earth. He remembers His covenant forever, the word He commanded, for a thousand generations, the covenant He made with Abraham, the oath He swore to Isaac. He confirmed it to Jacob as a decree, to Israel as an everlasting covenant: "To you I will give the land of Canaan as the portion you will inherit" (1 Chron. 16:8-18).

David recognized that all that God had done for His people was because of His covenant with Abraham.

When Jehoshaphat, king of Judah, was attacked by the combined forces of Moab and Ammon he turned to the Lord and asked for God's protection, saying, "Did You not drive out the inhabitants of this land before Your people Israel and give it forever to the descendants of Abraham Your friend? They have lived in it" (2 Chron. 20:7-8). Jehoshaphat's appeal was based on his confidence that God would fulfill that which He covenanted to Abraham.

Israel's possession of the land was a partial fulfillment of the Abrahamic Covenant, and their preservation in the land could be expected because of God's faithfulness to His covenant. Even after the Babylonian captivity, the Abrahamic Covenant became the basis for Nehemiah's prayer, "O Lord, God of heaven, the great and awesome God, who keeps His covenant of love with those who love Him and obey His commands, let Your ear be attentive and Your eyes open to hear the prayer Your servant is praying before You" (Neh. 1:5-6). Nehemiah dared approach God because God had proved Himself faithful to His covenant and merciful to those who trust Him. Those who labored with Nehemiah to rebuild the wall did so because of their confidence that God was a God who would keep His covenant with Abraham: "You are the Lord God, who chose Abram and brought him out of Ur of the Chaldeans and named him Abraham. You found his heart faithful to You, and You made a covenant with him to give to his descendants the land of the Canaanites. . . . You have kept Your promise because You are faithful" (9:7-8).

In short, all that God had done throughout Israel's history was based on His original covenant with Abraham. Thus throughout the period of the monarchy the Abrahamic Covenant was the foundation of the nation's relationship to God.

The prophetic books

When we turn to the prophetic books of the Old Testament we find that the Abrahamic Covenant likewise was the foundation for the message the prophets proclaimed. The prophets were God's messengers with God's twofold message to His covenant people. First, the prophets called a guilty people to repentance and warned of judgment if the people did not repent. Second, they brought a message of comfort and hope to the nation that was distressed, oppressed, and even exiled from their land. The hope given to the people was based on God's faithfulness to His covenant with Abraham.

Isaiah brought comfort to a nation that was to suffer at the hands of Babylon. But he also predicted the overthrow of Babylon (Isa. 13:17-22), and then promised the restoration of the nation to their land because of God's mercy on Jacob and on Israel (14:1). Thus the hope of restoration that Isaiah promised was ultimately based on the Abrahamic Covenant.

Isaiah's message of comfort is very clear (40:1-2). This comfort was based on the pledge of God who said, "But you, O Israel, My servant, Jacob, whom I have chosen, you descendants of Abraham My friend, I took you from the ends of the earth, from its farthest corners I called you. I said, 'You are My servant; I have chosen you and have not rejected you. So do not fear, for I am with you; do not be dismayed, for I am your God. I will strengthen you and help you; I will uphold you with My righteous right hand' " (41:8-10). Isaiah reminded the nation that they were a redeemed people (43:1), a redemption based on the Abrahamic Covenant (Ex. 2:24; 3:8). That historical redemption gave assurance that God would complete that which He had covenanted.

Isaiah also reminded Israel that they were chosen to be God's servant (Isa. 49:3). While Israel was disobedient they could not function as a servant; but the Lord promised that because of His covenant, they as God's servants eventually would proclaim a message of salvation to the world (Gen. 49:8-10). The blessings that a restored nation, Israel, could anticipate were based on the covenant God had given to Abraham (Isa. 51:1-5).

The original Abrahamic Covenant had promised the coming of a Blessor who would bring blessing not only to Israel but to the whole world (Gen. 12:3). Isaiah brought Israel hope by promising, " 'The Redeemer will come to Zion, to those in Jacob who repent of their sins,' declares the Lord. 'As for Me, this is My covenant with them,' says the Lord. 'My Spirit, who is on you, and My words that I have put in your mouth will not depart from your mouth, or from the mouths of your children, or from the mouths of their descendants from this time on and forever,' says the Lord" (Isa. 59:20-21).

God considered Himself bound by a covenant to provide a redeemer for Israel. Isaiah's prophecy closed with a guarantee of the perpetuity of the nation (66:22) based on the unconditional character of God's covenant with Abraham.

Another prophet, Jeremiah, conveyed God's message concerning the dispersion of Judah to a guilty people (Jer. 16:13). But God promised a restoration to the land (v. 15) that was as certain as the past restoration from Egypt (v. 14). God thus revealed that He considered Himself bound by the terms of the Abrahamic Covenant. The same fact is seen in Jeremiah 30:10-11 and 31:8, 35-37, where restoration to the land is also promised. The restoration is not only physical restoration, but a restoration to an intimate fellowship with God, for God promised, "You will be My people and I will be your God" (Jer. 30:22; see also 32:38).

Jeremiah's hope given to a people passing into captivity was based on an appeal to the terms of the Abrahamic Covenant. Israel's existence as a nation is shown to be as enduring as the sun and the moon (31:35-36).

Ezekiel gave the deportees the same confident hope of restoration that Jeremiah had given (Ezek. 11:17-21; 20:33-38, 42; 34:11-16, 24, 30-31; 36:28; 37:21-28; 39:28). This hope of restoration was woven throughout Ezekiel's message to the captives and is the outworking of the promises which God gave to Abraham by covenant.

Hosea promised that the disobedient people would be restored to their land after dispersion. The reference to Israel as "the sand of the sea" (Hos. 1:10) seems to have in mind God's promises in Genesis 13:14-17 and 28:13-14. Amos' concluding message (Amos 9:14-15) concerned release from captivity and return to the land.

Micah gave the same hope (Micah 4:6-7). So did Zephaniah (Zeph. 3:17-20). Zechariah promised not only a restoration to the land but also restoration to intimate fellowship with God (Zech. 8:7-8; 13:9). This hope of restoration was based on the character of God who said, "I will strengthen the house of Judah and save the house of Joseph. I will restore them because I have compassion on them" (10:6).

The covenant program continued

It must be concluded from this brief survey of the Old Testament that the Lord God—who chose Abraham to be the father of a nation in which the kingdom of the God of heaven on earth would be developed—deals with that covenant nation on the basis of the Abrahamic Covenant, and considers Himself bound to fulfill the terms of that covenant. That's why the comfort and hope given to Israel is so certain—because God is faithful.

As the New Testament opens, we find that great prominence again is given to the Abrahamic Covenant. Jesus Christ is introduced in Matthew 1:1 as the son of Abraham, the author's indication that He had come to fulfill the promises of the Abrahamic Covenant. Mary in her hymn of praise (Luke 1:45-55) stated that the blessings anticipated through the coming of the Messiah were based on the Abrahamic Covenant (vv. 54-55).

Zechariah, the father of John the Baptist, prophesied that God intended through the coming of Messiah (of whom his son was to be the forerunner) "to show mercy to our fathers and to remember His holy covenant, the oath He swore to our father Abraham" (Luke

1:72-73). Simeon was "waiting for the consolation of Israel" (2:25) based on the covenant promises God had made. This also was the basis for Anna's hope (vv. 36-38).

Paul, in expounding the great doctrine of justification by faith, referred to Abraham's response to the promises which God had given to him. Abraham was "fully persuaded that God had power to do what He had promised. This is why 'it was credited to him as righteousness'" (Rom. 4:21-22). Apart from the promises there could have been no such response and no justification by faith for Abraham. Paul recognized the legitimacy of the promises given to Abraham which were confirmed by a covenant.

In Galatians 3:13-16 Paul argued that God's covenant with Abraham was unchangeable and permanent. And since that covenant provided for universal blessings as well as blessings on Abraham's descendants, Gentiles today may have hope and salvation. If the Abrahamic Covenant were not a continuing covenant, there would be no basis for the Gentiles' hope. But since the covenant is an eternal, unchangeable covenant, the Gentiles can have confidence.

Elsewhere in the New Testament, the writer to the Hebrews in 6:13-20 gives believers today a basis for their hope of salvation. The God who provides salvation for us is the same God who gave promise and covenant to Abraham. If God is unfaithful to His promise to Abraham, argues the writer, He may likewise be unfaithful to us. But if God is faithful to His promise to Abraham, then He will be faithful to His promise to us. This means our assurance and security as Christians depends on whether God is faithful to His covenants. And since the covenant with Abraham is viewed as immutable and confirmed, "a better hope is introduced" (6:18).

Who is "the seed of Abraham"?

Since those who are the "seed of Abraham" would constitute the subjects of the kingdom of the God of heaven on earth, it is important to take a moment to observe how that term is used in Scripture.

(1) In the Old Testament that term always refers to *the literal physical descendants of Abraham*. Those who sprang from Abraham's loins and in whose bodies the blood of Abraham flowed were considered the seed of Abraham. They were referred to as Israel or as the Jews. In the New Testament Paul referred to those "who are

Jews by birth" (Gal. 2:15) or those who are "my brothers, those of my own race" (Rom. 9:3). Paul was referring to those who are physical descendants of Abraham and, as such, would be considered the seed of Abraham.

(2) In Romans 9:6-7, Paul drew a distinction between those who are related to Abraham by physical descent and those who are related to Abraham by faith. He wrote, "For not all who are descended from Israel are Israel. Nor because they are his descendants are they all Abraham's children." The term *Israel*, then, can refer to those who are the physical descendants of Abraham—but God reckons as Israel only those who are related to Abraham *by faith as well as by physical descent.* They are "spiritual Israel" and would be considered seed of Abraham, but this spiritual seed would be distinct from the physical seed.

(3) Paul referred to a third seed of Abraham in Galatians 3:29 and Romans 4:11. There he made reference to Gentiles who were not physical seed of Abraham but possessed Abraham's faith. Consequently, by faith they were considered seed of Abraham. Based on that, in this present age (as opposed to the time of the Old Testament) *those physical descendants of Abraham who possess Abraham's faith* are seed of Abraham, and *those who are not physically descended from Abraham but who possess Abraham's faith* are also considered seed of Abraham. Both then would be in the kingdom.

This recognition of two distinct seeds of Abraham is seen in Galatians 6:16. Paul had Gentiles in view when he referred to those "who follow this rule," but had saved Jews in view when he refers to "the Israel of God." It is very important to recognize that *in no place in the New Testament is a Gentile ever referred to as Israel,* for to be included in the nation of Israel one must be a physical descendant of Abraham.

Many applications

The covenant into which God entered with Abraham has its application in many different realms. For one, this covenant has an important bearing on the doctrine of soteriology. Paul, in writing to the Galatians, showed that Christian believers enter into the blessings promised to Abraham (Gal. 3:14, 29; 4:22-31). The argument of Paul in Romans was based on this same covenant promise made with Abraham (Rom. 4:1-25). He argued that immediately after the fall of man, God revealed His purpose to provide salvation for sinners. This program was gradually unfolded by God to man, and the promise made to Abraham represented a progressive step in that revelation.

The Abrahamic Covenant has an important bearing on the doctrine of resurrection. In fact, the promise detailed in the covenant was the basis of Christ's refutation of the Sadducees' unbelief in the resurrection (Matt. 22:23-32). To those who denied the possibility of resurrection, the Lord affirmed that resurrection was not only possible but necessary. Since God had revealed Himself as the God of Abraham, Isaac, and Jacob (Ex. 3:15), with whom He had entered into covenant relationships; since these men had died without receiving the fulfillment of the promises (Heb. 11:13); and since the covenants could not be broken, it was necessary for God to raise these men from the dead in order to fulfill His word. In addition, Paul (before Agrippa in Acts 26:6-8) united "the promise to the fathers" with the resurrection of the dead in his defense of the doctrine. Consequently the fact of the believer's resurrection is founded on the kind of covenant made with Abraham.

Finally, the Abrahamic Covenant has a most important bearing on the doctrine of eschatology. The eternal aspects of this covenant, which guarantee Israel a permanent national existence, perpetual title to the land of promise, and the certainty to material and spiritual blessing through Christ—and guarantee Gentile nations a share in these blessings—determine the whole eschatological program of the Word of God. And this covenant becomes the seed from which later covenants with Israel issue. As we will see in the chapters that follow, the essential aspects of the Abrahamic Covenant—the land, the seed, and the blessing—are enlarged in the subsequent covenants made with Israel.

Summary

Thus we see that the Abrahamic Covenant becomes the foundation of the message the Old Testament writers and prophets delivered to the nation Israel. It gave hope to the persecuted and the dispersed. Reference to it in the New Testament—as we will see further— reveals that it continues as the basis for the development of God's plan to establish on earth the kingdom of the God of heaven.

81

8

The Abrahamic Covenant
and the Mosaic Law

In the kingdom of darkness

As we have seen, it was God's purpose to establish His theocracy on earth through the descendants of Abraham, and through them also to extend that kingdom to the whole world. But at the same time God instituted the Abrahamic Covenant He also revealed that Abrahams' descendants would become slaves in a foreign land where they would remain for 400 years.

And so, as recorded at the close of the Book of Genesis, Jacob and his descendants settled in Egypt for what they thought would be a temporary stay—because of a famine in Canaan—but their descendants remained there for 400 years. Spiritually, the people were living in the realm of the kingdom of darkness. In that extended interval Abraham's descendants lost their knowledge of the God of Abraham and no longer harbored the hope of blessing given to their forefathers. They had thoroughly settled into the culture of Egypt.

While the people had lost their covenanted promises, God had not forgotten them. The Bible tells us, "God heard their groaning and He remembered His covenant with Abraham, with Isaac and with Jacob. So God looked on the Israelites and was concerned about them" (Ex. 2:24-25). In a special revelation of Himself to Moses at the burning bush (3:1-5), God identified Himself as "the God of Abraham, the God of Isaac, and the God of Jacob" (v. 6). He declared, "I have come down to rescue them from the hand of the Egyptians and to bring them up out of that land into a good and spacious land, a land flowing the milk and honey" (v. 8) And Moses was appointed as the executor of God's program and the administrator of the theocracy which would be established once the people had been redeemed from bondage in Egypt (v. 10).

Moses' authority as an administrator in the theocracy was demonstrated to God's people by the miracles God gave him to perform (4:1-9). Likewise, Moses was authenticated before Pharaoh as God's messenger with God's message by the miracles he performed in Pharaoh's sight. These miracles were further intended to reveal the Lord to the Egyptians so that they would have an opportunity to submit to His authority (7:5). What we refer to as the ten "plagues" were actually judgments designed to authenticate Moses as God's messenger and his message as God's message. Their ultimate purpose was to reveal the greatness of the power and authority of God to the Egyptians (7:10–12:36) in order to bring Pharaoh and the Egyptians into subjection to God.

Redemption by faith

From the inception of the first form of the theocracy in the Garden of Eden, faith was the basis for entrance into the kingdom of the God of heaven on earth. Therefore the kingdom God would establish in and through Israel would have to be based on faith—faith that would be evidenced by obedience and would bring redemption.

Thus the tenth plague in Egypt was designed to provide Israel an opportunity to demonstrate faith that produced obedience that would in turn produce redemption. God demonstrated the extent of His sovereign authority over all of His creation by passing judgment on all of the firstborn in Egypt—the firstborn of the Egyptians, the firstborn of the Israelites, and the firstborn of the cattle.

But God also demonstrated He was a gracious and merciful God by providing a way of escape from the impending judgment— through a blood sacrifice. The point was that God's judgment would either be carried out on the firstborn or executed on an innocent substitute for the firstborn.

The blood of the animal sacrifice was to be applied to the top and both sides of the entrance to the house (Ex. 12:7). Then those for whom the sacrifice was offered were to enter—literally—through blood into the security of the house. This act of obedience would demonstrate personal faith in the provision God had made, and the peace those within experienced was the result of their faith in the God who promised that "the blood will be a sign for you on the houses where you are; and when I see the blood, I will pass over you. No destructive plague will touch you when I strike Egypt" (v. 13). And again, "When the Lord goes through the land to strike down the Egyptians, He will see the blood on the top and sides of the doorframe and will pass over that doorway, and He will not permit the destroyer to enter your houses and strike you down" (v. 23).

The word *passover* in verses 13 and 23 can be translated to *hover over*. Thus the Sovereign who passed judgment is seen in the position of a protector of those who have placed their faith in Him, and who by faith availed themselves of His provision to escape the judgment He had decreed.

A redeemed nation

The ten miracles accomplished exactly what God had designed them to accomplish. Pharaoh's initial response to God's command to liberate His covenant people was, "'Who is the Lord, that I should obey Him and let Israel go? I do not know the Lord and I will not let Israel go'" (Ex. 5:2). The miracles, however, revealed who God is and the authority that rightfully belongs to Him. So at the conclusion of the tenth miracle, "Pharaoh summoned Moses and Aaron and said, 'Up! Leave my people, you and the Israelites! Go, worship the Lord as you have requested. Take your flocks and herds, as you have said, and go. And also bless me'" (12:31-32). Pharaoh had come to a point where he acknowledged the authority of God and recognized Moses as God's administrator for he sought a blessing from God through Moses.

That very night, the Bible tells us, the Children of Israel left the bondage of Egypt behind them. They became a redeemed people and began a journey by faith that was to take them into the land of promise where they would receive the covenanted blessings. By redemption the people became God's people. That's why Isaiah could convey God's message, "But now, this is what the Lord says— He who created you, O Jacob, He who formed you, O Israel: 'Fear not, for I have redeemed you; I have called you by name; you are Mine'" (Isa. 43:1).

It is crucial to understand at this point that the nation as a nation was redeemed. They were taken out of the kingdom of darkness and were designated as the kingdom over which God ruled through His delegated ruler, Moses. We must also understand the distinction between individual salvation—which was based on faith through blood—and the redemption of the nation as a nation. By way of the first Passover and the Exodus, the redeemed nation became the people through whom God's theocracy would be established here on this earth.

Protection, provision, worship

God further demonstrated His power to preserve the infant nation by destroying the armies of Pharaoh who sought to return the people to bondage (Ex. 14:13-28).

Moreover, in redeeming His people God not only provided for their protection but also made provision for their daily needs. He provided water to satisfy their thirst (15:23-26; 17:5-6) and the bread of heaven to satisfy their hunger (16:1-6). In this provision God revealed that physical blessings and spiritual blessings both were benefits that would come to the covenant people based on the covenant God had established with Abraham.

The redeemed people also became a worshiping people (15:1-21). God's redemption of Israel had in view the fulfillment of His covenant promises to Abraham (Gen. 15:18), thus all God had done to redeem His people was an evidence that "the Lord will reign for ever and ever" (Ex. 15:18).

The conditional nature of the Law

After redeeming His people, God gave them at Sinai a covenant for their guidance and protection. A redeemed people have an obvious obligation to their Redeemer, but because of their immaturity and the influence of Egyptian culture on them, the redeemed generation had no concept of how to fulfill their obligation. Thus God graciously gave them the Mosaic Covenant, or the Law.

To understand the nature of the Law, we need to remember that the entire Mosaic revelation is viewed as a covenant (Ex. 34:27-28), but in contrast to the Abrahamic Covenant, which was *unconditional*, the Mosaic Covenant was *conditional* (15:25-26; 19:4-5; 26:3-46).

That brings up the question, what relationship can exist between an unconditional covenant and a conditional covenant?

Quite simply, the unconditional Abrahamic Covenant had conditional blessings attached to it. Those blessings would be obtained by faith that evidenced its genuineness through obedience. But obedience to what? Obedience to the Mosaic Covenant. In other words, the Mosaic Covenant was added *alongside* the Abrahamic Covenant (Gal. 3:19) in order to define and delineate the obedience that was required in order to obtain the blessings promised by the Abrahamic Covenant.

The Abrahamic Covenant—not the Mosaic Covenant—was the source of blessings, and the Abrahamic Covenant was still unconditional. It was entirely dependent on God for its eventual fulfillment. But faith in the promises of the Abrahamic Covenant would produce obedience to the guidelines offered by the Mosaic Covenant. Conversely, a lack of faith in the covenant promises would produce a lack of obedience. And though a lack of faith resulting in disobedience would not nullify the Abrahamic Covenant, the covenanted blessings would not be extended to those who lacked faith in the unconditional covenant.

Israel's need for the Law

We might well ask the question: *What exactly was the function of the Law?* This is the question Paul addressed in Galatians 3 as he taught the doctrine of sanctification by faith in Jesus Christ.

Paul was dealing with the problem of how a person is sanctified (made perfect) or how he experiences the promises and blessings that are his in Christ. The Galatians had been led to believe that sanctification was by the Law; that through keeping the Law believers will obtain the promises given to them by God. In order to show the fallacy of this interpretation, the apostle cited the experience of Abraham.

Abraham was given promises by God (Gen. 12) which were repeated (Gen. 13) and ratified by a blood covenant (Gen. 15). All that Abraham obtained he obtained by faith, since no Law had been given in Abraham's time. Therefore, all that Abraham realized he realized by faith in the promise of God. The error that had been taught among the Galatians was that although Abraham attained the promises of God by faith alone, the giving of the Law altered the basic plan by which God dealt with men. Therefore (it was argued) Abraham's children subsequent to the giving of the Law must attain blessing by keeping the Law rather than by faith in the promise of God.

To dispel this error, Paul showed in Galatians 3:17-18 that, "That Law, introduced 430 years later, does not set aside the covenant previously established by God and thus do away with the promise. For if the inheritance depends on the Law, then it no longer depends on a promise; but God in His grace gave it to Abraham through a promise." Paul added in verse 19 that rather than disallowing or nullifying the promise, the Law was added, or better, added *alongside* the existing promise in order to perform a specific function. He further explained in verse 21 that there was no basic conflict between the Law and the promises of God and that the two could coexist.

Anticipating certain objections or questions in the minds of his readers, Paul faced the question specifically: "What, then, was the purpose of the Law?" (v. 19) Let's consider that question in detail.

We need to remember that many who lived under the Law had the deepest reverence, respect, and love for it. In writing Psalm 119 David frequently reflected this attitude:

Your Law is my delight (v. 77).

Oh, how I love Your Law! I meditate on it all day long (v. 97).

How sweet are Your promises to my taste, sweeter than honey to my mouth! I gain understanding from Your precepts (vv. 103-104).

See how I love Your precepts (v. 159).

In contrast to much current teaching which treats the Law as a worthless, worn-out garment to be discarded, the Apostle Paul in Romans 7:12 wrote, "The Law is holy, and the commandment is holy, righteous and good." It stands to reason, then, that something which is loved and revered by Old and New Testament writers must have served a worthy function—but it was not to save souls.

It is extremely important to remember that the Law of Moses was given to *a redeemed people*, not to *redeem a people*. The writer to the Hebrews said of Moses, "By faith he kept the Passover and the sprinkling of blood, so that the destroyer of the firstborn would not touch the firstborn of Israel. By faith the people passed through the Red Sea as on dry land" (Heb. 11:28-29). Israel, on the night of the Passover in Egypt, was redeemed by blood, and by faith they began a walk through the wilderness toward the land of promise.

Although the nation as a nation had been redeemed, it was nevertheless a nation that was viewed as spiritually immature. As stated earlier, though they recognized a responsibility to the Redeemer, they did not know how to carry out that responsibility.

Israel's infancy at the time of the giving of the Law was recognized by the Apostle Paul who wrote in Galatians 3:23-26:

> Before this faith came, we were held prisoners by the Law, locked up until faith should be revealed. So the Law was put in charge to lead us to Christ that we might be justified by faith. Now that faith has come, we are no longer under the supervision of the Law.

Again in Galatians 4:1-5, Paul wrote:

> What I am saying is that as long as the heir is a child, he is no different from a slave, although he owns the whole estate. He is subject to guardians and trustees until the time set by his father. So also, when we were children, we were in slavery under the basic principles of the world. But when the time had fully come, God sent His Son, born of a woman, born under Law, to redeem those under Law, that we might receive the full right of sons.

Paul saw those living under the Law as immature children, and he viewed the Law as a "pedagogue," a child trainer or overseer, whose responsibility it was to supervise every area of the life of the child committed to its care. Because of immaturity Israel needed the Law, and because God is gracious, He provided it.

The purposes of the Law

As the Scriptures are studied, a number of reasons why the Mosaic Law was given to the nation Israel become apparent.

First, the Law was given *to reveal the holiness of God.* In 1 Peter 1:15-16 Peter wrote, "But just as He who called you is holy, so be holy in all you do; for it is written: 'Be holy, because I am holy.'"

The fact that God is a holy God was made very clear to Israel in the Law of Moses. Perhaps the primary function of the Law was to educate the people concerning the character of the God who had redeemed them from Egypt. All the requirements laid on the nation Israel had in view the holy character of God as revealed in the Mosaic Law.

Second, the Mosaic Law was given *to reveal or expose the sinfulness of man.* Paul wrote, "It [the Law] was added because of transgressions, until the Seed to whom the promise referred had come. The Law was put into effect through angels by a mediator. . . . But the Scripture declares that the whole world is a prisoner of sin, so that what was promised, being given through faith in Jesus Christ, might be given to those who believe" (Gal. 3:19, 22).

In other words, the holiness of God as revealed in the Law became the test of man's thoughts, words, and actions; and anything that failed to conform to the revealed holiness of God was sin. This is exactly what Paul had in mind when he wrote, "For all have sinned, and fall short of the glory of God" (Rom. 3:23).

That in which God finds His highest glory is His own holiness. Sin is not only a lack of conformity to the Law, but it is also a lack of conformity to the holiness of God of which the Law is a revelation. Consequently the holiness of God—not the Law itself—becomes the final test of sin. Because all Abraham's seed were born in sin, the Law was given so that the people of Israel might readily determine their sinfulness before a holy God. And the Law was so specific in the requirements of divine holiness, even children in spiritual infancy could determine whether their conduct was acceptable to a holy God.

A *third* function of the Law, related to the preceding, was *to reveal the standard of holiness required of those in fellowship with a holy God.* Israel had been redeemed as a nation in order to enjoy fellowship with God. As these redeemed ones faced the question of what kind of life was required of those who walk in fellowship with their Redeemer, the Law was given to reveal the standard that God required.

The psalmist recognized this when he wrote, "Who may ascend to the hill of the Lord? Who may stand in His holy place? He who has

89

clean hands and a pure heart, who does not lift up his soul to an idol or swear by what is false. He will receive blessing from the Lord and vindication from God His Saviour" (Ps. 24:3-5).

Those who were redeemed were redeemed to enjoy the Redeemer, and the Law made it very clear the kind of life that was required if they were to walk in fellowship with Him.

A *fourth* function of the Law is stated in Galatians 3:24: "The law was put in charge *to lead us to Christ* that we might be justified by faith." The word *schoolmaster* used here in many translations refers to the household slave whose responsibility it was to supervise the total development of the child—physically, intellectually, and spiritually. The child was under this pedagogue's constant supervision until such time that he should move out of infancy into adulthood. Every area of the child's life was under the supervision of the pedagogue until he came to maturity.

It is the teaching of the Apostle Paul, then, that the Law served to supervise physical, mental, and spiritual development of the redeemed Israelite until he should come to maturity in Christ. The psalmist reflected this same concept in Psalm 119:71-72, writing, "It was good for me to be afflicted so that I might learn Your decrees. The Law from Your mouth is more precious to me than thousands of pieces of silver and gold." David confessed that through the Law he learned of God's requirements.

A *fifth* function of the Law was *to be the unifying principle that made possible the establishment of the nation.* In other words, the Law was given by God as the national constitution for Israel.

In Exodus 19:5-8 we read:

> "'Now if you obey Me fully and keep My covenant, then out of all nations you will be My treasured possession. Although the whole earth is mine, you will be for Me a kingdom of priests and a holy nation.' These are the words you are to speak to the Israelites." So Moses went back and summoned the elders of the people and set before them all the words the Lord had commanded him to speak. The people all responded together, "We will do everything the Lord has said." So Moses brought their answer back to the Lord.

In response to the instruction given by Moses concerning the things God had revealed, the nation voluntarily submitted themselves to the authority of the Law. Apart from voluntary submission to a unifying principle there could have been no nation. The people redeemed out of Egypt by blood—who had begun a walk by faith—were constituted a nation when they as a people voluntarily submitted themselves unto the Law. This was reaffirmed in Deuteronomy 5:27-28: "Go near and listen to all that the Lord our God says. Then tell us whatever the Lord our God tells you. We will listen and obey."

From the divine viewpoint, Israel became a nation at the time the people voluntarily submitted themselves to the Law. But in Deuteronomy 28 Moses had made it very clear that if the people abandoned the Law, God would deliver them into the hands of the Gentiles. The Prophet Jeremiah warned the people of the same consequences, and thus the Babylonian captivity by which Israel lost her national identity became a sad reality. And as we will see later in our study, it is equally significant that until Israel submits to the authority of the law of her Messiah-King, she will not be recognized by God as a nation again.

A *sixth* function somewhat related to the fifth is that the Law was given *to separate Israel from the nations in order that they might become a kingdom of priests.* In Exodus 31:13 we read, "Say to the Israelites, 'You must observe My Sabbaths. This will be a sign between Me and you for the generations to come, so you may know that I am the Lord, who makes you holy." Israel was sanctified or set apart, according to Exodus 19:5-6, to become a kingdom of priests, that is, a nation that mediated the truth of God to the other nations of the earth. The Law became a hedge that separated and preserved Israel from these nations. In order that Israel might serve the function of a light to the world, the people were given the Law to make them distinct from all the other nations.

A *seventh* reason the Law was given to a redeemed people was *to make provision for forgiveness of sins and restoration to fellowship.* Leviticus 1–7 describes five offerings God instituted for the nation. While the nation as a nation was preserved before God because of the annual offering of the blood of atonement, individuals in the nation were restored to fellowship and received forgiveness for specific sins through the various offerings that God provided. The God who had redeemed the nation by faith through blood provided a way the redeemed could walk in fellowship with Him and with each other. The same Law that revealed their unworthiness for fellowship also provided for restoration to the fellowship. This was one the primary functions of the Law.

Eighth, the Law was given *to make provision for a redeemed people to worship.* A redeemed people will be a worshiping people and a people who walk in fellowship with God will worship the God with whom they enjoy fellowship.

In Leviticus 23 the Law revealed a cycle of feasts the nation was expected to observe annually. These feasts were the means by which the nation as a redeemed nation worshiped God. In the cycle of feasts, Israel's attention was directed backward to their redemption from Egypt, and also directed forward to the final redemption that would be provided through the promised Redeemer.

Ninth, the Law was given *to provide a test as to whether one was in the kingdom over which God ruled.* In Deuteronomy 28, as Israel stood on the border of the Promised Land, Moses revealed the principle by which God would deal with the nation. The first portion of that chapter outlines the blessings that would come to the nation for obedience. But a great portion of the chapter also deals with the curses that would come on the nation because of disobedience.

Even though the nation as a whole entered the Promised Land, because not all believed God, not all were eligible to receive the blessings promised to those in the land. The Law, then, became the standard that revealed whether or not a person was rightly related to God. Those who submitted to and obeyed the Law did so because of their faith in God which resulted in obedience. Conversely, those who disobeyed the Law did so because they were without faith in God, and their lack of faith produced disobedience. Whether or not a person obeyed the Law, then, became the test as to whether he was rightly related to God or in God's kingdom. It measured whether an individual was participating in God's covenant promises by faith, or was a Jew in name only.

Tenth and finally, it becomes clear from the New Testament that the Law was given *to reveal Jesus Christ.* Great truths concerning the person and work of the Lord Jesus Christ are woven throughout the Law, and the Law was given in order that it might prepare the nation for the coming Redeemer King. It was because of this that Christ on the Emmaus road could expound to His companions great truths concerning the Messiah. They had been revealed in the Law and the Prophets.

Revelatory and regulatory

Israel, through the Law's revelation, was being prepared for the coming Messiah. And as we look back over these reasons for the giving of the Law, we can see that there was in the Law that which is *revelatory* of the holiness of God.

This revelatory aspect of the Law is permanent. Holiness does not change from age to age, and that which revealed the holiness of God to Israel may still be used to reveal the holiness of God to men today. That which reveals the holiness of God also reveals the unholiness of men. It is this revelatory aspect of the Law that Paul referred to as holy, just, and good.

But there was also that in the Law which was *regulatory*. The Law regulated the life and the worship of the Israelite. It is this regulatory aspect of the Law that was temporary and that has since been done away with. Paul in 1 Timothy 1:8 wrote, "We know that the Law is good if one uses it properly." But how can the Law be used properly or lawfully in an age in which the Law has been done away?

If the Law is used to reveal the holiness of God, the unholiness of man, the requirements of those who would live in fellowship with the holy God, or to learn of the person and work of Christ, it is used lawfully. On the other hand, someone who attempts to use the regulatory portions of the Law which were "only until Christ" is using the Law unlawfully. While we may sing, "Free from the Law, Oh happy condition," we must still recognize that the Law is "holy, just, and good."

Deficiencies of the Law

There were certain deficiencies in the Law. The Law could not justify (Gal. 2:16; 3:11, 21; Heb. 10:4). The Law confined those who were under it to a state of infancy (Gal. 3:23-24). The Law could not perfect, that is, bring one to maturity (Heb. 10:1). Those who were under the Law were under bondage (Gal. 4:1-4). The law could not cleanse the conscience permanently (Heb. 10:2).

On the other hand, the Law was designed to make sin transparent or evident (Gal. 3:19). It was designed to shut men up in a state of sin (v. 22) so that God might deal with sinners by grace through faith. And it was designed to be a schoolmaster (v. 24).

93

As we briefly noted earlier, in Greek society the schoolmaster was responsible for the oversight of the family heir in every area of his life. The Law was designed to be a schoolmaster for Israel to control every area of the people's lives. They as God's children were not responsible to make decisions—their decisions were made for them by the Law. Their only responsibility then was to put themselves under its authority as a schoolmaster and to obey.

In spite of its deficiencies and in the light of its purposes, Paul could say that "the Law is holy, and the commandment holy, righteous and good" (Rom. 7:12). The Law was holy in that it revealed the holiness of God and the demands a holy God makes on those who walk in fellowship with Himself. The Law was righteous, or just, because it passed a just sentence on those who fall short of the holiness of God. The Law was good in that it did what it was designed to do.

Now, had it been designed as means of salvation, the Law would have been a total failure and never could have been called good. Yet Paul never disparaged the Law. Through it he had come to a knowledge of God and he had received personal benefit (Gal. 1:14). Indeed, in Philippians 3:7 Paul referred to his Hebrew upbringing as "profit." Paul did not give up what he considered to be bad for what was good, but he gave up what was good for that which was better; namely the superior worth there is in knowing Christ Jesus as Lord (Phil. 3:8).

The "mixed multitude"

While the nation as a nation was redeemed and those who evidenced true faith constituted the kingdom of the God of heaven on earth, not all who left Egypt were in that kingdom. According to Numbers 11:4 a "mixed multitude" (KJV; "rabble" in the NIV) accompanied Moses. And as has always been true, those who were in the false kingdom rejected the authority of Moses as God's theocratic administrator and rebelled against God.

According to the biblical account of the Exodus, within three days after the destruction of the Egyptians in the Red Sea and the corporate worship by the redeemed people that followed, "The people grumbled against Moses" when they tasted the bitter waters of Marah (Ex. 15:24). Despite such complaining, God revealed His faithfulness to His people by making the bitter water sweet and bringing them to an oasis in Elim where they found an abundance of water.

But apparently they learned little of God's faithfulness, because a month later "the whole community grumbled against Moses and Aaron" (16:2), this time because there was no bread. The Israelites recognized that it was by the leadership of Moses they had been brought out of Egypt, but they incorrectly concluded that Moses had led them into the wilderness to die. God responded to this rebellion by providing manna from heaven.

Again, when there was no water for the multitude at Rephidim "they quarreled with Moses" (17:2). God responded to this rebellion by bringing water out of the rock through the staff of Moses. By this miracle God validated the authority of Moses as His theocratic administrator.

But after leaving Sinai on their way to the Promised Land "the people complained about their hardships" (Num. 11:1). To warn the people of the danger of rebellion, instead of responding with a miracle as He had in previous instances of rebellion, "Fire from the Lord burned among them and consumed some of the outskirts of the camp." The people were compelled to turn to Moses to alleviate the judgment, and when in response to Moses' intercession the fire was quenched, God had again proven the authority of Moses.

The mixed multitude that lusted for the fish, the cucumbers, the melons, the leeks, the onions, and the garlic of Egypt not only rebelled against Moses and against God, but they also incited the Children of Israel to follow them in their rebellion (vv. 4-6). Moses was so distressed by the unstoppable rebellion that he cried out to God, "I cannot carry all these people by myself; the burden is too heavy for me. If this is how You are going to treat me, put me to death right now—if I have found favor in Your eyes—and do not let me face my own ruin" (vv. 14-15).

Moses had been given responsibility to lead this people as God's theocratic administrator, but the burden was too great for him to bear. God responded to Moses' distress saying, "I will take of the Spirit that is on you and put the Spirit on them [seventy elders]. They will help you carry the burden of the people so that you will not have to carry it alone" (v. 17). As long as the people walked in obedience to God and recognized His authority, Moses was able to discharge the responsibilities of theocratic administration under the Law. But when the people rebelled, he could not bear the task alone. Thus God appointed seventy administrators under Moses who would share the load of controlling lawlessness and punishing evildoers: "Then the Lord came down in the cloud and spoke with him, and He took of the Spirit that was on him and put the Spirit on the seventy elders. When the Spirit rested on them, they prophesied, but they did not do so again" (v. 25). The Spirit placed upon the seventy was not only divine enablement but also was the authority to administer or oversee the kingdom.

Later, God satisfied the desire of the multitude by sending them quail to eat—but in gratifying the lust of the flesh "the anger of the Lord burned against the people, and He struck them with a severe plague" (v. 33). Still later, Miriam and Aaron resented the authority God had given Moses and they coveted that authority for themselves (12:2). That covetousness led to their criticism of Moses because of his marriage. In response, God once more vindicated Moses as His representative. God declared Moses to be His prophet (v. 6)—that is, God's messenger with God's message—and He rebuked those who rejected Moses' unique authority (vv. 8-9). Judgment immediately fell on Miriam, who became leprous and consequently would have been excluded from the people. It was only through the intercession of Moses that the leprosy was removed.

In each of these situations, God authenticated the authority that belonged to Moses under the terms of His covenant.

Failure at Kadesh Barnea

When the Children of Israel came to Kadesh Barnea along the southern border of the land God had covenanted to give to Abraham and to Abraham's descendants, twelve spies were sent into the land at God's command (Num. 13:1-2). But when ten of those twelve brought back an adverse report, "That night all the people of the community raised their voices and wept aloud. All the Israelites grumbled against Moses and Aaron, and the whole assembly said to them, 'If only we had died in Egypt! Or in this desert!'" (14:1-2)

As a result of this crisis of faith, the congregation openly rejected the authority of Moses and decided to appoint a new captain who could lead them back to Egypt (v. 4). But Joshua and Caleb reminded the people of God's past faithfulness and called them to believe that God would bring them safely into the land (v. 8). They exhorted the people not to rebel against the Lord by 'disobeying His command to occupy the land (v. 9). Unfortunately, in response to this exhortation "the whole assembly talked about stoning them" (v. 10). This was a willful, deliberate act of disobedience that originated in a lack of faith in the covenant promises of God.

The writer to the Hebrews says of this decision, "'Their hearts are always going astray, and they have not known My ways. . . . ' See to it, brothers, that none of you has a sinful, unbelieving heart that turns away from the living God" (Heb. 3:10-12). So serious was this rebellion that sprang from unbelief that God pronounced a severe judgment on that entire generation, with the exception of Joshua and Caleb:

> As surely as I live and as surely as the glory of the Lord fills the whole earth, not one of the men who saw My glory and the miraculous signs I performed in Egypt and in the desert but who disobeyed Me and tested Me ten times—not one of them will ever see the land I promised on oath to their forefathers. No one who has treated Me with contempt will ever see it. But because My servant Caleb has a different spirit and follows Me wholeheartedly, I will bring him into the land he went to, and his descendants will inherit it (Num. 14:21-24).

Up to this point God had graciously tolerated the rebellion of the people against His delegated administrator and against Himself, and He had sought to bring the people to faith and to obedience. But now God determined to bring judgment upon the rebels, and thus none of them would inherit the blessings of the covenanted land (vv. 29-33).

Further rebellion against Moses

Another rebellion against the authority of Moses was led by Korah and several others. "With them were 250 Israelite men, well-known community leaders who had been appointed members of the council. They came as a group to oppose Moses and Aaron and said to them, 'You have gone too far! The whole community is holy, every one of them, and the Lord is with them. Why then do you set yourselves above the Lord's assembly?'" (Num. 16:2-3) They repudiated the authority God had conferred on Moses to be His theocratic administrator and claimed that Moses was self-appointed. They further charged that Moses had made himself a prince over them (v. 13). Referring to Moses as a prince they recognized that he had a right to rule, but they falsely claimed it was by self-appointment instead of by divine appointment. God, however, vindicated the authority of Moses by causing the earth to open up and swallow the rebels (vv. 32-35).

In spite of all the warnings that had been given against rebellion, the carnality of the people again manifested itself in rebellion because of a lack of bread and of water. God had provided manna from heaven, but the rebellious people had no taste for heavenly bread. This time God judged their rebellion by sending "venomous snakes among them; they bit the people and many Israelites died" (21:6). God again graciously provided a means of deliverance from judgment—but deliverance depended on the faith of the people under judgment.

In this case the Lord instructed Moses to fashion from bronze a replica of that which had brought judgment on the people, and He gave the promise that *"anyone* who is bitten can look at it and live" (v. 8). From our Lord's reference to this incident in John 3, we discover that the look was to be a look of faith. In other words, the *looking* of Numbers 21 is the *believing* of John 3:15. And it was that *looking* in faith that was necessary in order to live. God would be faithful to His covenant promises for those who placed their faith in Him.

Episode with Balaam

The faithfulness of God to His covenants that will eventually bring about their complete fulfillment is seen through the utterances of that enigmatic prophet Balaam. While Balak viewed him as a diviner (Num. 22:7), Balaam considered himself a servant of the true God (v. 18). Eager for the rich rewards for cursing Israel, Balaam instead reaffirmed God's purposes for the nation Israel as defined in the covenant: "How can I curse those whom God has not cursed? How can I denounce those whom the Lord has not denounced? From the rocky peaks I see them, from the heights I view them. I see a people who live apart and do not consider themselves one of the nations. Who can count the dust of Jacob or number the fourth part of Israel? Let me die the death of the righteous, and my end be like theirs!" (vv. 8-10)

Or again:

> God is not a man, that He should lie, nor a son of man, that He should change His mind. Does He speak and then not act? Does He promise and not fulfill? I have received a command to bless; He has blessed, and I cannot change it. No misfortune is seen in Jacob, no misery observed in Israel. The Lord their God is with them; the shout of the King is among them. God brought them out of Egypt; they have the strength of a wild ox. There is no sorcery against Jacob, no divination against Israel. It will now be said of Jacob and of Israel, "See what God has done!" The people rise like a lioness; they rouse themselves like a lion that does not rest till he devours his prey and drinks the blood of his victims (vv. 19-24).

Balaam, who had been seeking a message from God through enchantments, went to view the encampment of Israel and God gave him a revelation (24:1-4) and made the prophetic announcement found in Numbers 24:5-9. Later a final revelation was given to Balaam who declared: "I see him, but not now; I behold him, but not near. A star will come out of Jacob; a scepter will rise out of Israel. He will crush the foreheads of Moab, the skulls of all the sons of Sheth. Edom will be conquered; Seir, his enemy, will be conquered, but Israel will grow strong. A ruler will come out of Jacob and destroy the survivors of the city" (vv. 17-19).

Balaam was only reaffirming what Jacob had predicted earlier in Genesis 49:10, that the one who would ultimately have the right to rule in the kingdom of the God of heaven on earth would come from the descendants of Jacob. Through Balaam God reiterated blessings of the promises and covenants given to Abraham, and revealed that the ultimate form of the theocracy would come to its fulfillment in one of Jacob's sons.

Summary

This survey reveals that throughout the length of Moses' theocratic administration two kingdoms were developing side by side. There was on the one hand a small remnant who believed God and demonstrated their faith through their obedience, thus revealing that they were subjects of the kingdom of the God of heaven on earth.

Over against that is an almost unbroken line of unbelief, lawlessness, and rebellion. Those who rebelled lost the covenanted blessings. They came into judgment because of their rebellion, though God always provided a way of escape from judgment. That way of escape always involved faith that would demonstrate itself in obedience.

Thus throughout Moses' long reign as a theocratic administrator it is seen that God dealt with Israel as His covenant people. Blessings would come on the obedient and discipline would fall on the disobedient. The standard for obedience or disobedience would be the Law that gave to Israel through Moses. A kingdom program was being developed which included in it those who believed and validated their faith by obedience. But this kingdom was constantly being attacked by rebels whose real citizenship was in the kingdom of darkness.

9

The Palestinian Covenant

In the closing chapters of the Book of Deuteronomy, we find that the Children of Israel—the physical seed of Abraham—are facing a crisis in their national existence. They are about to pass from the proven leadership of Moses into the unproven leadership of Joshua, as they are standing at the entrance to the land that was promised to them by God in such terms as:

> To your offspring I will give this land (Gen. 12:7).

> All the land that you see I will give to you and your offspring forever (Gen. 13:15).

> I will establish My covenant between Me and you and your descendants after you for the generations to come, to be your God and the God of your descendants after you. The whole land of Canaan, where you are now an alien, I will give as an everlasting possession to you and your descendants after you; and I will be their God (Gen. 17:7-8).

The Promised Land, however, was occupied by Israel's enemies, who had shown they would resist any attempt by Israel to enter. It was impossible for them to return to their former status as a slave nation, and the land to which they were journeying as "strangers and pilgrims" seemed shut before them. As a result, certain important considerations had to be faced by the nation. Was the land of Palestine still their possession? Did the inauguration of the Mosaic

Covenant (which all agree was conditional) set aside the unconditional Abrahamic Covenant? Could Israel hope to enter into permanent possession of their land in the face of pagan opposition?

The covenant given

To answer these important questions God again stated His covenant
promise concerning Israel's possession and inheritance in the land.
In Deuteronomy 30:1-10 we find the Palestinian Covenant, which
answers the question of Israel's relation to the land promises of the
Abrahamic Covenant. During the forty years of the nation's wilderness wanderings because of its rebellion at Kadesh Barnea, Moses
had served as the theocratic administrator. Then, before turning
that administration over to Joshua, Moses discharged his responsibilities as theocratic administrator by teaching the Law to the new
generation which would enter the land.

Moses' instruction to the nation is found in the Book of Deuteronomy, which means *the second law*. This was not an alteration of the
Law found in Exodus and Leviticus; rather, it was a restatement of
the Law for the new generation. At the heart of Moses' instruction
was the covenant God made with the Children of Israel found in
Deuteronomy 28-30.

The important principal given in Leviticus 26:3-46 as a precondition to blessing is now formalized by God in a covenant. Because it
determines the principal upon which God will deal with His people
when they come into the land of Palestine (given to them through
the Abrahamic Covenant), we refer to it as the Palestinian Covenant.

Important distinctions

Though many similarities exist between Leviticus 26 and these
chapters, a distinction must be made for this covenant which was
given *in addition* to the God made with Israel at Horeb (Deut.
29:1). Great importance is attached to this covenant because:

(1) It reaffirmed to Israel, in no uncertain terms, their title deed
to the land of promise. In spite of unfaithfulness and unbelief—as
had occurred so frequently in Israel's history from the time of the
promise to Abraham until the conquest—the covenant was not
nullified or abrogated. The land was still theirs by promise.

(2) Further, the introduction of a conditional covenant, under which Israel was then living, could not and did not set aside the original gracious promise concerning the purpose of God. This was the basis of Paul's argument when he wrote, "The Law, introduced 430 years later, does not set aside the covenant previously established by God and thus do away with the promise" (Gal. 3:17).

(3) This covenant was a confirmation and enlargement of the original Abrahamic Covenant, which promised land, seed, and blessing. The Palestinian Covenant, in fact, amplified the *land* features of the Abrahamic Covenant. And the amplification, coming after willful unbelief and disobedience in the life of the nation, strongly proves that the original promise was given to be fulfilled in spite of disobedience.

Seven features

The Palestinian Covenant is stated in Deuteronomy 30:1-10, where we read:

> When all these blessings and curses I have set before you come upon you and you take them to heart wherever the Lord your God disperses you among the nations, and when you and your children return to the Lord your God and obey Him with all your heart and with all your soul according to everything I command you today, then the Lord your God will restore your fortunes and have compassion on you and gather you again from all the nations where He scattered you. . . . He will bring you to the land that belonged to your fathers, and you will take possession of it. . . . The Lord your God will circumcise your hearts and the hearts of your descendants, so that you may love Him with all your heart and with all your soul, and live. The Lord your God will put all these curses on your enemies who hate you and persecute you. . . . You will again obey the Lord and follow all His commands. . . . The Lord will again delight in you and make you prosperous. . . .

A careful analysis of this passage reveals seven main features in God's timetable:

(1) The nation will be plucked off the land for its unfaithfulness (Deut. 28:63-68; 30:1-3).

103

(2) There will be a future repentance of Israel (Deut. 28:63-68; 30:1-3).

(3) Israel's Messiah will return (Deut. 30:3-6).

(4) Israel will be restored to the land (Deut. 30:5).

(5) Israel will be converted as a nation (Deut. 30:4-8; cf. Rom. 11:26-27).

(6) Israel's enemies will be judged (Deut. 30:7).

(7) The nation will then receive her full blessing (Deut. 30:9).

Surveying the breadth of this one passage that sets forth the covenant program, we are compelled to recognize that God considers Israel's relation to the land vitally important. Not only did God guarantee its possession to them, but He also obligated Himself to judge and remove all Israel's enemies, and to give the nation a new heart—or conversion—prior to placing them in the land.

This same covenant was confirmed again later in Israel's history. In Ezekiel's prophecy God affirmed His love for Israel in the time of her infancy (Ezek. 16:1-7); He reminded her that she was chosen and related to Jehovah by marriage (vv. 8-14); but she played the harlot (vv. 15-34); therefore, revealed God, the punishment of dispersion was meted out to her (vv. 35-52). However, this was not a final setting aside of Israel, for a restoration would take place (vv. 53-63), based on the promise:

> Yet I will remember the covenant I made with you in the days of your youth, and I will establish an everlasting covenant with you. Then you will remember your ways and be ashamed when you receive your sisters, both those who are older than you and those who are younger. I will give them to you as daughters, but not on the basis of My covenant with you. So I will establish My covenant with you, and you will know that I am the Lord (vv. 60-62).

Thus the Lord reaffirmed the Palestinian Covenant and called it an eternal covenant by which He is bound.

Why this covenant is unconditional

This covenant made by God with Israel in regard to the land must be seen also as an unconditional covenant. Several evidences support this.

First, it was called by God an eternal or everlasting covenant in Ezekiel 16:60. Remember, a covenant can be eternal only if its fulfillment is entirely divorced from human responsibility and rests on the reliability of God alone.

Second, it is merely an amplification and enlargement of parts of the Abrahamic Covenant, which itself is an unconditional covenant. Therefore, this amplification must be eternal and unconditional also.

Third, this covenant has God's guarantee that He will bring about the conversion necessary for its fulfillment. Such passages as Romans 11:26-27, Hosea 2:14-23, Deuteronomy 30:6, and Ezekiel 11:16-21 all make this very clear. This conversion is viewed by Scripture as a sovereign act of God, and it must be acknowledged as certain because of His integrity.

Fourth, portions of this covenant have already been fulfilled literally. Israel has experienced its historic dispersions as judgments for unfaithfulness. Israel also has experienced restorations to the land and now awaits its final restoration. And Israel's history abounds in examples of her enemies who have been judged. These partial fulfillments—all of which were literal fulfillments—indicate a future literal fulfillment of the unfulfilled portions in the same way.

Some argue that this covenant is conditional because of the statements of Deuteronomy 30:1-3: "when . . . then." We need to observe, however, that the only conditional element here is the *time* element. The program itself is certain; but the time when this program will be fulfilled depends on the conversion of the nation. A conditional time element does not make the whole program conditional.

A historic principle

For understanding and explaining Israel's history as recorded throughout the Old Testament, there are perhaps no more important chapters than Deuteronomy 28–30. Everything we read of Israel's history and God's plan for Israel is related to what was included in the Palestinian Covenant.

The principle that has governed Israel's history and its relationship to God is very simple: *Obedience will bring blessing, while disobedience will bring discipline and possibly even disaster.*

God stated at the outset, "If you fully obey the Lord your God and carefully follow all His commands . . . the Lord your God will set you high above all the nations on earth. All these blessings will come upon you and accompany you if you obey the Lord your God" (Deut. 28:1-2). That which the nation was called upon to obey was the Mosaic Law. The blessings of obedience are enumerated in verses 3–14; all are material blessings and promise Israel prosperity as a nation and peace in their land.

By contrast, in verses 15-68 God announced that disobedience would bring discipline, which in turn could lead to disaster. As with the blessings, so all the curses are in the physical and material realm (vv. 16-18). If Israel chose to disobey, her people would be afflicted with incurable diseases (vv. 21-22, 27, 35). The Lord would withhold rain (vv. 23-24) so that their fields could produce no food. God would send locusts and worms that would devour what grew in the fields and in the vineyards (vv. 38-39, 42). And lawlessness would erupt throughout the land (vv. 30-31).

These curses were not viewed as punishment for disobedience as much as disciplines to bring a guilty people back to obedience to God. If these disciplines did not accomplish obedience, God would climax His disciplines with dispersion and exile from the land (vv. 36-37). Anticipating the disobedience of the people (v. 48) Moses then described the ultimate discipline in detail (vv. 49-68). The disciplinary instrument would be a Gentile nation (v. 49) who would deal very severely with the disobedient people (vv. 50-52). Against these Gentile armies there would be no defense and no escape (v. 52). The people would sink to almost unbelievable levels because of their distress (vv. 53-57) and only a remnant would survive the invasions (v. 62). The remnant that did survive would be "uprooted from the land you are entering to possess. Then the Lord will scatter you among all nations, from one end of the earth to the other" (vv. 63-64). Even in their dispersion the remnant would find no peace but would live in abject terror (vv. 65-67).

It must be observed that both the blessings and the curses were promised to the seed of Abraham as a nation. Both were national, not individual.

The means of restoration

Moving on to Deuteronomy 30, we find that Moses revealed the basis upon which a guilty and disciplined people might be restored to the land and the blessings of the covenant. He stated, "When all these blessings and curses I have set before you come upon you and you take them to heart wherever the Lord your God disperses you among the nations, and when you and your children return to the Lord your God and obey Him with all your heart and with all your soul according to everything I command you today, then the Lord your God will restore your fortunes and have compassion on you and gather you again from all the nations where He scattered you" (Deut. 30:1-3).

In order to be restored to the land and to the blessings of the covenant, the guilty people must *repent.* Repentance would involve a remembrance of the principle that had brought about the discipline. It would involve returning to the Lord, that is, acknowledging their sin. It would also involve walking in obedience to the commands of God. This would have to be more than mere words; it would have to be "with all your heart and with all your soul" (v. 2).

On the basis of this repentance God lovingly promised to reverse their captivity and to regather them to the land from which they had been scattered. Moreover, on the basis of the faith that brought about this true repentance God would give them a new heart so that they would "love Him with all [their] heart and with all [their] soul, and live" (v. 6). And as a result they would experience all the blessings promised in Deuteronomy 28:1-14 (v. 9).

This was God's continuing principle by which He would deal with His people, as seen in His word to Solomon at the time of the dedication of the temple.

> When I shut up the heavens so that there is no rain, or command locusts to devour the land or send a plague among My people, if My people, who are called by My name [because I redeemed them (Isa. 43:1)] will humble themselves and pray and seek My face and turn from their wicked ways, then will I hear from heaven and will forgive their sin and will heal their land (2 Chron. 7:13-14).

After mentioning the curses (the same ones mentioned in Deut. 28) that Israel would experience because of disobedience, God reminded Solomon that repentance would bring restoration and blessing.

It is important for us to notice that four things were involved in repentance. *First,* the people must humble themselves. This has to do with the acknowledgment of the sins committed. *Second*, they must pray. Prayer is an attitude of dependence on or trust in God. *Third*, they must seek His face. This would have to do with walking in obedience to the command of God. *Fourth* and finally, they must turn from their wicked ways, which would mean forsaking their sins. Repentance was not merely a mental acknowledgment of wrong done. It involved all four things God demanded here. Repentance then becomes a vital part of the message of the prophets to the nation throughout its history.

Summary

God made it very clear to the new generation about to enter the Promised Land that He would deal with the covenant nation on the basis of the principle that obedience would bring blessing and disobedience would bring discipline and possibly even disaster. If the nation did disobey, the people would not experience the covenanted blessings apart from repentance which produced obedience.

10

Understanding Israel's History in Light of the Palestinian Covenant

If a Bible novice or non-Christian were to survey Israel's history as recorded in the Old Testament, he might begin to wonder about the Lord's faithfulness. When Israel fell on hard times and experienced famine, drought, and hunger, it might seem that God had forgotten His people. When Israel was beset by foreign enemies, it appears as though God had abandoned His people. When Israel eventually suffered dispersion and captivity, it seems as though God had either forgotten His covenants or was too weak to defend His people. The Palestinian Covenant, however, enables us to understand these afflictions in the light of the one overriding principle: Obedience would bring blessing while disobedience would bring discipline.

The principle of the Palestinian Covenant in Israel's history is vividly illustrated in the Book of Judges. No sooner had the land been conquered and settled, as God had promised through Moses, than the people turned from obedience to disobedience. Therefore God allowed an outside people to enter and suppress a portion of the land. This oppression brought the people to repentance and confession, which in turn caused God to mercifully raise up a deliverer who in miraculous ways expelled the invaders and restored peace to the land. Overall, Judges records the repetitious cycle of disobedience, discipline, repentance, and then deliverance so the people could again enjoy covenant blessings.

The same principle was demonstrated again in the days of David and Solomon. Saul's disobedience as king brought a three-year famine (2 Sam. 21:1)—obviously one of the disciplines God forewarned in Deuteronomy 28. Not until the matter was rectified by David was the famine lifted.

Thereafter the days of David and Solomon were days of unprecedented blessing on Israel. The nation as a nation enjoyed great material prosperity as seen in the vast amount of the materials David was able to gather together for the construction of the temple (2 Sam. 8:7-11). Solomon's lavish wealth was described in 1 Kings 10:14-29 and 2 Chronicles 9:13-28. These kings expanded their borders to occupy more of the Promised Land than at any time in Israel's history. And they enjoyed the blessing of peace, all of which can be attributed to their righteous obedience.

As Solomon looked back over David's life and the great blessings God had given him, he said, "You have shown great kindness to Your servant, my father David, because he was faithful to You and righteous and upright in heart" (1 Kings 3:6). Moreover, God promised Solomon, "If you walk in My ways and obey My statutes and commands as David your father did, I will give you a long life" (v. 14). The necessity of obedience in order to continue in God's blessings is further seen in Solomon's prayer at the dedication of the temple (8:56-61).

The northern kingdom

Following Solomon's death the kingdom was divided. Ten of Israel's twelve tribes formed the northern kingdom of Israel, while the other two tribes—Judah and Benjamin—formed the southern kingdom of Judah. The northern kingdom of Israel had an unbroken succession of godless kings—none of whom were of Davidic descent—while the southern kingdom was ruled by David's descendants from the tribe of Judah. The succession of prophets God sent to Israel condemned its apostasy and disobedience, warned of coming judgment, and called the people to repentance.

The Prophet *Hosea* pictured Israel as an adulterous wife because it had turned from the Lord—who had been as a faithful husband to them—and had joined itself to idols. The prophet warned of judgment to come (Hosea 12:2) and exhorted them to return to God (12:6; 14:1-2), noting that blessing would follow repentance (14:4-9).

Amos delivered a message to the northern kingdom warning of judgment to come because of the disobedience of the people (Amos 2:6-8; 3:2, 11, 14-15). The prophet reminded them of the principle

that disobedience brings discipline and referred to God's past deal-
ings with Israel to prove his point (4:6-13). The prophet warned that
the nation would fall (5:1-3). He also invited them to turn to the
Lord in repentance (5:4, 6, 14-15). But because there was no repentance, judgment was inescapable (8:1-3). And having rejected the
exhortation of the prophet there would be no further message from
God, who said:

> The days are coming . . . when I will send a famine through
> the land—not a famine of food or a thirst for water, but a
> famine of hearing the words of the Lord. Men will stagger
> from sea to sea and wander from north to east, searching for
> the word of the Lord, but they will not find it (vv. 11-12).

The disobedient nation would be consigned to discipline (9:1-4) just
as had been predicted in Deuteronomy 28:48-52.

Micah likewise pictured God descending on the guilty nation in
judgment (Micah 1:1-5) with the northern kingdom being destroyed
(v. 6). The judgment was coming because they "hate good and love
evil" (3:2). The prophet recognized that he was empowered by the
Spirit of the Lord to speak "with justice and might, to declare to
Jacob his transgression, to Israel his sin" (3:8). The sacrifices of the
guilty were rejected by God (6:6-7) because of their disobedience.
The prophet reminded the people that obedience was a prerequisite
to blessing when he said, "He has showed you, O man, what is
good. And what does the Lord require of you? To act justly and to
love mercy and to walk humbly with your God" (6:8). In fact, the
prophet seemed to be quoting from Deuteronomy 28 when in
verses 13-16 of that same chapter he spoke of the disciplines that
would fall on that disobedient generation.

Despite all the prophets God sent to the northern kingdom, there
was no repentance. The people refused to humble themselves and
pray and seek God's face and turn from their sin. So in 722 B.C. God
brought the Assyrians into the land to conquer it and to take the
people into exile (2 Kings 17:7-41). This invasion occurred because
"the Israelites had sinned against the Lord their God . . . the Israelites secretly did things against the Lord their God that were not
right . . . they worshiped idols" (vv. 7-12). The nation was reminded
of the ministry of the prophets whom God had sent, and that thus it
was without excuse (vv. 13-18).

The southern kingdom

The same course of history occurred in the southern kingdom of Judah. Even though this small nation was ruled over by Davidic descendants, not all the kings walked in the ways of their father David.

The Prophet *Joel* (Joel 1:4-20) described conditions in the lana that were strangely similar to the disciplines of Deuteronomy 28, and went on to describe an invasion by an irresistible army. In light of this the Lord exhorted the people through Joel: "Even now, return to Me with all your heart, with fasting and weeping and mourning. Rend your heart and not your garments. Return to the Lord your God, for He is gracious and compassionate, slow to anger and abounding in love, and He relents from sending calamity. Who knows? He may turn and have pity and leave behind a blessing. . . Call a sacred assembly. Gather the people. . . . Let the priests, who minister before the Lord, weep between the temple porch and the altar. Let them say, 'Spare Your people, O Lord. Do not make Your inheritance an object of scorn, a byword among the nations'" (2:12-17). The nation was called on to repent in order to escape or to alleviate the disciplines that must fall on the disobedient.

Habakkuk was moved by the iniquity of Judah, about which Goa seemed indifferent. But God responded by revealing, "I am raising up the Babylonians, that ruthless and impetuous people, who sweep across the whole earth to seize dwelling places not their own. They are a feared and dreaded people; they are a law to themselves ana promote their own honor" (Hab. 1:6-7). The description of the judgment wrought by these Babylonians is amazingly similar to the description of the invading forces of Deuteronomy 28:49-52.

The Prophet *Zephaniah* relayed God's announcement, "I will sweep away everything from the face of the earth. . . . I will sweep away both men and animals; I will sweep away the birds of the air and the fish of the sea. The wicked will have only heaps of rubble when I cut off man from the face of the earth" (Zeph. 1:2-3). But the prophet, like his predecessors, called the people to repentance with the words, "Seek the Lord, all you humble of the land, you who do what He commands. Seek righteousness, seek humility; perhaps you will be sheltered on the day of the Lord's anger" (2:3). The sins of the people are described in 3:1-4, and it is because God is just that He will bring judgment upon the guilty (3:5).

Jeremiah, over the span of a generation, condemned sin in the nation, warned of coming judgment, and called the nation to repentance. His announcement of forthcoming invasion and captivity was very clear (Jer. 18:15-17; 21:5-10; 25:9-13). And his call to repentance was equally clear (3:12-18, 22; 7:3-7; 18:7; 25:5; 32:1-5).

Lest the people conclude that God had forgotten His covenants and that the nation would not inherit the promised blessings, the prophets were careful to prophesy a restoration of a repentant people to the land. Jeremiah illustrated this vividly when he purchased a field and secured it with a title deed so that after the restoration his descendants could claim property in the land (32:6-15). Restoration as a blessing was described in Jeremiah 23:7-8 and 33:6-26. The people would be brought back from captivity, the land would enjoy the bountiful blessings of Deuteronomy 28:1-14, and restoration would occur because of God's faithfulness to His covenants.

Specifically, from David's line would come a theocratic administrator who shall "do what is just and right in the land" (Jer. 33:15). This prophetic proclamation assured the nation of ultimate fulfillment of the Palestinian Covenant. The people will one day dwell in their land in righteousness and will experience the multiplied blessings promised to those who are in the kingdom of the God of heaven on earth.

Ezekiel joined Jeremiah in promising a restoration of the dispersed people to their land and covenanted blessings to follow (Ezek. 34:11-16; 36:8-12; 37:12, 21, 25; 39:25-28).

Amos likewise was anticipating the enjoyment of the blessings of the Palestinian Covenant when he wrote: "I will bring back My exiled people Israel; they will rebuild the ruined cities and live in them. They will plant vineyards and drink their wine; they will make gardens and eat their fruit. I will plant Israel in their own land, never again to be uprooted from the land I have given them" (Amos 9:14-15).

The ministry of Daniel

We can clearly see as we consider the message of the prophets that every denunciation of sin, every warning of discipline, every call to repentance is an outworking of the Palestinian Covenant found in Deuteronomy 28–30.

The fact that repentance on the part of a disobedient, disciplined people is a prerequisite for restoration of blessings is obvious in the experience of *Daniel*. Though burdened with administrative duties in a kingdom under Darius, Daniel found time to study the Scriptures. There he learned through Jeremiah's writing (Jer. 25:11-12) that his people were to be held in captivity in Babylon for seventy years. When Daniel realized that these seventy years were coming to a close, as a representative of the nation, he prayed to the Lord and confessed Israel's sin (Dan. 9:4).

Daniel recognized that it was sin that had brought about the discipline of the Babylonian captivity and he freely acknowledged the sin of the nation to the Lord (v. 5). He acknowledged that Israel had ignored the warnings of the prophets and their calls to repentance (v. 6), and what's more, that God was righteous in bringing this discipline on a sinful people (v. 7). At last he confessed, "We have not obeyed the Lord our God or kept the laws He gave us through His servants the prophets. All Israel has transgressed Your law and turned away, refusing to obey You" (v. 10-11). After this confession, Daniel interceded for his people and on behalf of the nation he offered true repentance to God (vv. 16-19).

God proved Himself true to His covenant, and eighteen months after this prayer of repentance, Cyrus (now on the Babylonian throne) issued his decree permitting captives to return to Jerusalem if they desired (Ezra 1:1-4).

But let's back up for a few moments to the Captivity itself. To execute His discipline on Jerusalem and Judah, God brought Nebuchadnezzar into the land. The vivid description of invasion in Deuteronomy 28:47-52 might well have the invasion of Nebuchadnezzar in view, though that invasion does not exhaust the prophecy. Nebuchadnezzar came first in 605 B.C. and carried a number of the royal princes as captives into Babylon (Daniel 1:1-4). He returned the second time in 597 B.C. when Ezekiel the prophet-priest was taken captive and with him a large portion of the inhabitants of Jerusalem (2 Kings 24:11-16). Finally Nebuchadnezzar returned the third time in 586 B.C. and set siege against the city, bringing about its downfall and destruction (2 Kings 25:1-21; 2 Chron. 36:17-20; Jer. 39:8-10).

The "times of the Gentiles"

The city was left without a temple and without a throne. Thus Nebuchadnezzar's invasions marked the beginning of a very significant prophetic time period which Christ later referred to as "the times of the Gentiles" (Luke 21:24). The times of the Gentiles is that extended period of discipline on God's covenant people during which time no Davidic descendant sits on David's throne ruling over David's kingdom. It extends from the destruction of Jerusalem and the emptying of the throne of David by Nebuchadnezzar until the ultimate repentance. The Bible indicates that this ultimate repentance of Israel will not take place until the second coming of Jesus Christ, the Son of David, to this earth. Through a vision revealed to Nebuchadnezzar, which was interpreted to him by Daniel, the course of history during these significant times of the Gentiles was unveiled.

Through the great image made up of four different metals (Dan. 2), it was revealed that the land given to Abraham's descendants, and the descendants themselves, would be subjected to the authority of four distinct world empires.

The Babylonian empire was represented by a head of gold; the Medo-Persian empire, by arms and a chest of silver; the Grecian empire, by the belly and thighs of bronze; and the Roman empire, by legs of iron that gave way to feet that were a mixture of iron and clay. Further, the vision revealed that these ruling empires would eventually be brought to destruction by "a rock . . . cut out, but not by human hands. It struck the statue on its feet of iron and clay and smashed them. Then the iron, the clay, the bronze, the silver and the gold were broken to pieces at the same time and became like chaff on a threshing floor in the summer. The wind swept them away without leaving a trace. But the rock that struck the statue became a huge mountain and filled the whole earth" (vv. 34-35).

Thus it was revealed that the Messiah, the rock in Nebuchadnezzar's dream, will destroy the nations that subordinated Israel to their authority during the times of the Gentiles, and He will establish a kingdom that will fill the whole earth. Therefore Israel must be redeemed from Gentile bondage in order to become the theocracy through which God ultimately will demonstrate His right to rule.

Years later a parallel to this revelation was given to Daniel himself through the imagery of four beasts that emerged from the sea (Dan. 7:3), which in prophetic Scripture often refers to Gentile nations. According to this vision, four world empires were to rule over Daniel's people. The first was the winged lion which represented the Babylonian empire. The second was the lopsided bear which represented the Medo-Persian empire. (In the coalition of the Medes and the Persians to destroy Babylon, Persia soon overshadowed the Medes, hence the symbol of lopsidedness.)

The third beast was the leopard with four wings which represented the Grecian empire. The leopard was already one of the fastest of the beasts but it was able to move with unusual speed because of the addition of the four wings. This symbolized the speed with which Alexander conquered Persia and extended his rule over the areas previously occupied by Medo-Persia and Babylon.

The fourth beast was described not by its external appearance but rather its internal characteristics. It was "terrifying and frightening and very powerful. It had large iron teeth; it crushed and devoured its victims and trampled underfoot whatever was left" (Dan. 7:7). John in Revelation gave us the external appearance of this fourth beast: Parts of it were like a leopard and parts like a bear and parts like a lion (Rev. 13:2). This mongrel beast represented the Roman empire which in its conquest swallowed up the territories, the peoples, the customs, the laws of the previous three empires and incorporated them into itself.

The unique thing about this fourth beast Daniel saw was that it had ten horns (Daniel 7:7). The significance of these horns is explained in Daniel 7:24: "The ten horns are ten kings who will come from this kingdom." At its inception Rome was characterized by its irresistible power and its devastating destructiveness. But as the empire progressed over the years it was marked by progressive weakness, deterioration, and ultimate division.

When Rome fell before the invading forces from central and northern Europe, the political power of Rome did not pass to the conquerors, as the power of Babylon had passed to Medo-Persia, the power of Medo-Persia had passed to Greece, and the power of Greece had passed to Rome. Instead, the political power at the fall of Rome was divided among many separate individual nations. According to Daniel's vision, the Roman empire would continue in this divided state until the ultimate reunion of these nations under one head.

This reunion is to be brought about by the one whom Daniel refers to as the little horn (7:8). He is referred to again as the king of "fierce countenance" (8:23, KJV), or as the ruler who will come (9:26), the king who will do as he pleases (11:36), or the abomination that causes desolation (12:11). In Revelation 17:12, John refers to these same ten horns, or the ten nations that merged out of the Roman empire, and tells us that these ten "have one purpose and will give their power and authority to the beast" (Rev. 17:13). Thus the times of the Gentiles will culminate in a reunion of ten nations that emerge out of the old Roman empire to form a false kingdom in opposition to the kingdom of God.

The head of this confederation of nations is the final Gentile ruler. He is Satan's masterpiece of deception and will deceive the world (13:14) by miracles performed in establishing his rule. Often nicknamed Antichrist, he will be established by Satan as a world ruler (13:7) and as the world's god (2 Thes. 2:3-4).

The times of the Gentiles, then, is a period marked by the world's rejection of God, its rejection of Christ, and its organized opposition to and rebellion against God under the leadership of Satan himself. The prophecies in Daniel 2 and 7 reveal the course of that period during which Israel is dispersed from its land, is subject to the authority of Gentile rulers and in which time no Davidic descendant rules on a throne over the covenant people.

God working through Gentiles

It is clear from Isaiah 44:28–45:4 that God is working through Gentiles. God said of Cyrus, "He is my shepherd and will accomplish all that I please; he will say of Jerusalem, 'Let it be rebuilt,' and of the temple, 'Let its foundations be laid.' This is what the Lord says to his anointed, to Cyrus, whose right hand I take hold of to subdue nations before him and to strip kings of their armor, to open doors before him so that gates will not be shut: I will go before you and will level the mountains; I will break down gates of bronze and cut through bars of iron. I will give you the treasures of darkness, riches stored in secret places, so that you may know that I am the Lord, the God of Israel, who summons you by name. For the sake of Jacob My servant, of Israel My chosen, I summon you by name and bestow on you a title of honor, though you do not acknowledge Me.'"

This pagan king, Cyrus, in a Gentile nation was called God's anointed! (Isa. 45:1) He was set apart by God to be the instrument that would bring about the end of the Babylonian captivity. God called attention to the fact that what He permitted Cyrus to do and the blessings conferred on him were not because of what God found in Cyrus. Rather God did what He did "for the sake of Jacob My servant, of Israel My chosen" (v. 4). God's purposes for His people were unchanged in spite of their disobedience—because God's covenant was unchangeable.

The same principle was illustrated in the experience of Nehemiah. The report came to him, "Those who survived the exile and are back in the province are in great trouble and disgrace. The wall of Jerusalem is broken down, and its gates have been burned with fire" (Neh. 1:3). Nehemiah turned to the Lord in prayer because he recognized that God is a God who "keeps His covenant of love with those who love Him and obey His commands" (v. 5). His prayer was a prayer of repentance on behalf of his people. He acknowledged their sin (vv. 6-7), recognizing that the dispersion of the people and the condition of Jerusalem was the fulfillment of what God had promised in Deuteronomy 28.

What's more, he referred to God's word to Moses, "If you are unfaithful, I will scatter you among the nations, but if you return to Me and obey My commands, then even if your exiled people are at the farthest horizon, I will gather them from there and bring them to the place I have chosen as a dwelling for My name" (vv. 8-9). This was a direct reference to that part of the Palestinian Covenant found in Deuteronomy 30:1-3.

In short, Artaxerxes, ruler in Persia, granted Nehemiah the right to return to Jerusalem to build the walls of the city. Thus the principle was clearly confirmed that though disobedience must bring discipline and even disaster, repentance will bring restoration to the privileges and blessings of the covenant, for the covenants are eternal, unchangeable, and must ultimately be fulfilled.

The time of Christ

When the New Testament opens we find the nation Israel subjected to the authority of the fourth, or Roman, empire as outlined in Daniel's prophecy. It is also at this time that God sent the last and greatest of His prophets to the people of Israel (Matt. 11:11). His first recorded word as God's messenger was, "Repent, for the kingdom of heaven is near" (3:2). He viewed the nation as being sinful (vv. 7-11) and called on them to prove the genuineness of their repentance by submitting to his baptism.

Christ, who is God's ultimate "messenger of the covenant" (Mal.

3:1), in His first recorded public proclamation echoed John's message: "Repent, for the kingdom of heaven is near" (Matt. 4:17). The emphasis in both cases was to move the people to repentance by announcing that the promised, covenanted kingdom was at hand.

Christ, during the course of His ministry, "began to denounce the cities in which most of His miracles had been performed, because they did not repent. 'Woe to you, Korazin! Woe to you, Bethsaida! If the miracles that were performed in you had been performed in Tyre and Sidon, they would have repented long ago in sackcloth and ashes. But I tell you, it will be more bearable for Tyre and Sidon on the day of judgment than for you'" (11:20-22). Christ's message to a disobedient people continued to be a call to repentance.

In response to a challenge by the leaders to prove conclusively that He was Messiah, Christ said, "A wicked and adulterous generation asks for a miraculous sign! But none will be given it except the sign of the Prophet Jonah. For as Jonah was three days and three nights in the belly of a huge fish, so the Son of Man will be three days and three nights in the heart of the earth. The men of Nineveh will stand up at the judgment with this generation and condemn it; for they repented at the preaching of Jonah, and now one greater than Jonah is here" (12:39-41).

When Christ sent the Twelve out to preach (Mark 6:7-11), "they went out and preached that people should repent" (v. 12). There was only one message delivered to a disobedient people, and that was that they should repent. Jewish theology taught that every calamity was the direct result of sin. When Pilate slaughtered some Galileans, the question in the minds of those who heard of the tragedy was, "What did these people do to deserve such a judgment?" Christ rejected that teaching and said, "Unless you repent, you too will all perish" (Luke 13:3, 5).

The Pharisees taught that God hated sinners and rejoiced in their deaths so He could separate them from Himself. Since Christ welcomed sinners and ate with them, the religious leaders concluded that Christ could not be God or He would have had God's same attitude. To reveal God's real attitude toward sinners, Christ told of the man who lost one of his sheep and then eagerly sought it until he found it. Making application, He said that likewise there will be more joy in heaven over one sinner who repents than over ninety-nine just persons who need no repentance (Luke 15:1-7).

Christ supplemented this illustration with the story of the woman who had lost the dowry coin and searched diligently until she found it. Again Christ made the application "there is rejoicing in the presence of the angels of God over one sinner who repents" (v. 10). And He went on in the Parable of the Searching Father to show that repentance will bring showers of God's love to the penitent (v. 20), as well as restoration of lost privileges and forfeited authority.

Thus Christ emphasized that the Father loves the sinful nation, seeks its restoration, and in response to its repentance will restore all of the covenanted privileges and blessings that have been forfeited by disobedience. Most important, throughout the gospels we see that the message brought by those who were sent to Israel was a direct outgrowth of the Palestinian Covenant (Deut. 28–30). Because of disobedience Israel was suffering at the hands of the Romans—but repentance could bring them full enjoyment of covenanted blessings.

Same message in Acts

This same message of repentance based on the Palestinian Covenant was proclaimed to the nation Israel in the opening chapters of the Book of Acts. Peter, divinely appointed as God's messenger, addressed the Jews as a generation accused and under judgment (see Acts 2:23). He then exhorted them, "Save yourselves from this corrupt generation" (v. 40). The judgment Peter envisioned was that physical, temporal judgment of which Christ warned. Jesus had repeatedly told that generation that if they persisted in believing the Pharisees who said, "It is only by Beelzebub, the prince of demons, that this fellow drives out demons" (Matt. 12:24), they would experience judgment. The Pharisees rejected Christ as the Son of God, claiming that He was the son of Satan and that He got His power not from heaven but from hell. Christ warned that if they persisted in this belief that generation would be guilty of a sin for which there could be no forgiveness, and judgment would be inescapable.

The form of that judgment was revealed in Luke 21:24 where Christ said, "Jerusalem will be trampled on by the Gentiles until the times of the Gentiles are fulfilled." Again in Matthew 23:38 Christ said, "Your house is left to you desolate." And in Matthew 24:2 Christ predicted, "Not one stone here will be left on another; every one will be thrown down." True to Scripture, judgment fell on that generation through the invasion of Titus, who destroyed

Jerusalem in A.D. 70. Because that generation—through their leaders—finally rejected Jesus Christ as the Messiah, judgment was certain.

As members of that generation, those who listened to Peter on the Day of Pentecost were already under judgment. Peter offered them individually a way of escaping the judgment which would fall on the nation, saying, "Repent and be baptized, every one of you, in the name of Jesus Christ so that your sins may be forgiven" (Acts 2:38). Peter exhorted individuals in the guilty nation to repent—meaning they would acknowledge the sin of the nation in rejecting Jesus Christ. They would evidence the genuineness of their repentance by baptism in the name of Jesus Christ, thus indicating their faith in Him.

This message was perfectly in keeping with the promise of God in the covenant in Deuteronomy 30:1-5. Again, Peter addressed a message to the "men of Israel" (Acts 3:12). Vindicated as God's messenger with God's message through the miracle of healing the man who had been born lame, Peter called on the people to "Repent, then, and turn to God, so that your sins may be wiped out, that times of refreshing may come from the Lord, and that He may send the Christ, who has been appointed for you—even Jesus. He must remain in heaven until the time comes for God to restore everything, as He promised long ago through His holy prophets" (vv. 19-21). The only way the nation could inherit the covenanted blessings was to repent, that is, to acknowledge their sin in rejecting Jesus Christ as Saviour and Sovereign. Based on that repentance, God would fulfill His covenant promises and bring the covenanted blessings to His covenant people. These covenanted blessings or the "times of refreshing" would come through Jesus Christ, whom that generation had rejected.

The great tribulation

Thus the message, as recorded in the Book of Acts, centers around the call to repentance that was a precondition to blessing under the Palestinian Covenant. Christ in Matthew 24:14 predicted that "this Gospel of the kingdom will be preached in the whole world."

The Gospel of the kingdom is the message that John the Baptist proclaimed to Israel. It involved first a call to repentance, then an invitation to behold or to look by faith to the Lamb of God that takes away the sin of the world (John 1:29). This is the same message that will be proclaimed in the world during that period Christ called, literally, "the tribulation, the great one" (Matt. 24:21). This future period is the unfulfilled seven years of Daniel's prophecy of the seventy weeks (Dan. 9:24-27).

During this period the Gospel of the kingdom will be preached to Gentiles by 144,000 who will be sovereignly redeemed and commissioned to be God's servants (Rev. 7:1-8). They will proclaim salvation by grace through faith based on blood so that men can have "washed their robes and made them white in the blood of the Lamb" (v. 14).

The same message will be proclaimed by the two witnesses (11:3), prophets God will raise up to bring a message to the nation Israel. Indeed, their message is no different than the one the prophets have always brought to a disobedient covenant people down through the ages.

The general response to both the witness of the 144,000 and that of the two witnesses is found in Revelation 9:20-21: "The rest of mankind that were not killed by these plagues still did not repent of the work of their hands; they did not stop worshiping demons, and idols of gold, silver, bronze, stone and wood—idols that cannot see or hear or walk. Nor did they repent of their murders, their magic arts, their sexual immorality or their thefts." In Revelation 16:9-11 we find the same response. In fact, again and again in these passages we can see that in spite of all the wrath God poured out on unbelievers, men refused to repent.

The Tribulation is a period in which God will significantly deal with the nation Israel to bring it to repentance, thus setting the stage for the fulfillment of the covenanted blessings believers will experience and the establishment of the kingdom after Christ's second advent. This emphasis on repentance stresses the significance of the covenant God made in Deuteronomy 28–30, where repentance was seen as a precondition to the enjoyment of the covenanted blessings.

Repentance and the Epistles

Very little mention is made of repentance in the Epistles. Why? Because the covenants were not made with the church; they were made with Israel. The call to repentance is emphasized always in connection with God's program for that covenant people.

From the original statement of the provisions of the Palestinian Covenant, it is easy to see that, on the basis of a literal fulfillment, Israel must be converted as a nation, regathered from her worldwide dispersion, installed in her land, witness the judgment of her enemies, and receive the material blessings vouchsafed to her. This covenant, then, obviously has a wide influence on our future expectations. Since these things have never been fulfilled, and since an eternal and unconditional covenant demands a fulfillment, we must include just such a program in our outline of future events. This is the same expectation of the prophets who write to Israel in such passages as Isaiah 11:11-12; 14:1-3; 27:12-13; 49:8-16; 66:20-22; Jeremiah 16:14-16; 23:3-8; 30:10-11; 31:8, 31-37; Ezekiel 11:17-21; 20:33-38; 34:11-16; 39:25-29; Hosea 1:10-11; Joel 3:17-21; Amos 9:11-15; Micah 4:6-7; Zephaniah 3:14-20; and Zechariah 8:4-8.

Such was the promise offered to Israel. Whether they should live to see the Messiah confirm these promises, or whether they reached the land through resurrection, peace was theirs as they awaited that which God promised.

Summary

It is impossible to understand the recorded history of the covenant nation as found in the Scriptures apart from an understanding of the principle laid down in the Palestinian Covenant, nor to understand the emphasis on repentance in the message of the Old Testament prophets or in the messages of John the Baptist and Christ Himself, apart from that covenant. That covenant is a key that unlocks the mystery of God's dealing with His people.

11

The Kingdom under Joshua and the Judges

As we might expect from our study of the Palestinian Covenant, Deuteronomy 28 forms an important background for understanding the Book of Judges. In Deuteronomy 28 God promised blessing for obedience and discipline for disobedience, and subsequently Judges records the outworking of that principle.

Joshua as theocratic administrator

Viewed in this light, we can recognize that the books of Joshua and Judges fall into the same time period and situation. Empowered by the Spirit of God, Moses had operated by divine appointment. Now, as Moses laid down the mantle of leadership, Deuteronomy 34:9 records, "Now Joshua son of Nun was filled with the spirit of wisdom because Moses had laid his hands on him. So the Israelites listened to him and did what the Lord had commanded Moses." This verse identifies Joshua as Moses' successor in the line of theocratic leadership. In other words, the authority that had belonged to Moses was now transferred to Joshua.

That the Israelites immediately fell into line behind Joshua demonstrated their recognition of this transfer of authority, his right to rule as God's representative. God's appointment is further emphasized in Joshua 1:5, which reads, "No one will be able to stand up against you all the days of your life. As I was with Moses, so I will be with you; I will never leave you or forsake you." This did not mean there would be no opposition to Joshua; it did mean, however, that no one in the nation could legitimately question his right to rule. As God had led Moses, so he would lead Joshua.

Joshua's marching orders

As Joshua assumed his responsibility as the divinely appointed administrator over God's people, God had some important instructions for him.

First, because it was his responsibility to divide the land, Joshua was exhorted to be strong and courageous (Josh. 1:6). Dividing the land among the conquering tribes was a sign of his theocratic leadership, and he was to execute that task courageously and authoritatively.

Joshua received a *second* exhortation from God to operate according to the Law of Moses. God said, "Be strong and very courageous. Be careful to obey all the Law My servant Moses gave you; do not turn from it to the right or to the left, that you may be successful wherever you go. Do not let this Book of the Law depart from your mouth; meditate on it day and night, so that you may be careful to do everything written in it. Then you will be prosperous and successful" (vv. 7-8). Here again is the obvious principle that obedience is the prerequisite to blessing, but there was more.

Joshua, while exercising his authority, was to be guided and bound by the Law that God had revealed through Moses. God told him, "Be careful to obey all the Law My servant Moses gave you" (v. 7). Joshua was viewed as an administrator of the Law. As such, the Law was not only to guide him in his personal exercise of responsibility, but—even more—as the Law's administrator, he was to guide the nation in keeping with the Law.

It was clearly demonstrated in the Book of Genesis that God's answer to man's lawlessness was to impose law. Following the catastrophe in the Garden of Eden, the law of human conscience was instituted (Gen. 4). Following the cataclysm of the Flood, the law was administered through human government (Gen. 9). And following the redemption from Egypt, the law was administered through the Mosaic Law (Ex. 19–20). In each case, law was designed to do the same thing: to curb lawlessness and to provide an atmosphere in which righteousness could flourish and righteous men could live without fear.

If Joshua was to capably function as an administrator, he was compelled to administer the Law that was designed to produce a perfect theocracy—an environment in which man would be obedient to God and conform to the Law of God. So when God told Joshua, "Do not let this Book of the Law depart from your mouth" (Josh. 1:8), He did not mean that Joshua should keep it for himself; He meant that the Law should never depart from Joshua as the dominant influence in everything that came from his mouth. God was not just instructing him to live by it, but to administer it so that the entire nation would be brought under its control, that the Law might do its intended work. This was a large part of Joshua's work as the theocratic administrator.

Joshua received a *third* exhortation: "Have I not commanded you? Be strong and courageous. Do not be terrified; do not be discouraged" (v. 9). This was followed by the promise "for the Lord your God will be with you wherever you go." This same promise was given to Moses in Exodus 33:14.

At the close of the Book of Joshua, then, we find that Joshua used the same method of theocratic administration Moses had used. The text says, "Israel served the Lord throughout the lifetime of Joshua and of the elders who outlived him and who had experienced everything the Lord had done for Israel" (Josh. 24:31). While Joshua was the theocratic administrator, elders served under him. Possibly these were a continuation of the seventy which Moses had appointed. While there is no indication of their number in the Book of Joshua, it is apparent that there were men who assisted Joshua in the administration of the theocracy and were under his oversight.

Later the transition between the death of Joshua and the appointment of the judges was in the hands of these overseers, or elders, who continued the work they had been doing under Joshua.

The judges as theocratic administrators

Judges 2:7 takes up where the Book of Joshua had closed. This verse is, in fact, identical to the statement made in the Book of Joshua (24:31). But verse 11 includes the tragic statement, "Then the Israelites did evil in the eyes of the Lord and served the Baals." This departure from serving the Lord God of their fathers can be attributed to their natural rebelliousness, but more than that, there was no authoritative figure to keep them in line. We can naturally conclude from this that the seeds of rebellion and apostasy were in the hearts of God's people all the time. It did not suddenly appear at Joshua's funeral—it had always been there but had not broken out under Joshua's leadership because he exercised the authority given to him by God.

The tragic result of apostasy after Joshua's death was that God in His anger against Israel handed the nation over to raiders who plundered them. He sold them to their enemies on all sides, whom they were no longer able to resist. And whenever Israel went out to fight, the hand of the Lord was against them to defeat them, just as He had sworn would happen to them (Jud. 2:14-15). This, then, is the first clear-cut illustration of the outworking of the principle laid down in Deuteronomy 28.

Rebellion against God because of the absence of a theocratic administrator brought about divine discipline. Even though the nation turned to other gods, God nevertheless raised up judges to restore them. Like the giving of the Law, this was both an extension of God's grace and an expression of His righteousness.

It is important to recognize that the responsibility of the judges was not to punish the nation for their apostasy; the nation was already under discipline when the judges were raised up. But God did not desire that the nation continue in apostasy. It was His purpose to bring the nation into subjection to Himself so that He could bless them. To that end, therefore, He raised up judges.

In short, the judges were to be *deliverers*. This in itself was an indication that disobedience by the nation could not nullify or abrogate the Abrahamic Covenant. If the Abrahamic Covenant could be canceled because of disobedience, God would never have raised up a judge. He would, instead, have let Israel be destroyed and accomplished His purpose through other means. But God was determined to bless Abraham's descendants, for He had covenanted to bless them. Therefore, blessing must come, and God raised up judges to bring about the conditions which would make blessing possible.

The role of a judge

Genesis 18 reveals some helpful background concerning this concept of a judge. Here God Himself is said to be "the Judge of all the earth" (Gen. 18:25). From the context, we can see that the role of the judge is to administer justice, to discern between the righteous and the wicked, to punish the wicked, and to deliver the righteous.

Thus, the judge was an administrator who had authority to enforce or impose judgment on man in his lawlessness. For example, in Genesis 19 the enforced penalty was destruction of the men of Sodom and the deliverance of righteous Lot.

Our concept of a judge today is determined by our contemporary use of the term. In modern jurisprudence the judge is one who provides or acts as an arbitrator in court. He is the referee between two opposing lawyers. Most people think of the judge in reference only to pronouncing judgment on the guilty. The term *judge*, however, as it was used in Genesis 18, was a far broader concept that granted authority to administer the affairs of man. This is why God is called the Judge of all the earth.

The Book of Judges, then, concerns not just civil administrators—as we would think of judges—but leaders who were charged with the responsibility of keeping men under control and in submission to the laws, punishing offenders and rewarding those who did good. This is the same concept mentioned in Romans 13 and 1 Peter 3 in the New Testament.

It should also be noted that the judges were directly chosen by God. According to the Scriptures, "Then the Lord raised up judges" (Jud. 2:16). Part of a judge's work that God raised him up to do was to drive back those nations that had come into the land in order to discipline Israel because of its apostasy. So, the Old Testament concept of judge includes the idea of deliverance as well as administration. In this sense the judges were a bridge between the Moses-Joshua administration of the theocracy and the theocratic administration that came through the kings. Under Moses and Joshua the emphasis was on deliverance. Moses delivered God's people from Egypt, while Joshua delivered them from the wilderness and into the land. Under the kings, however, the emphasis was on rulership. During the transition between the two, the judges were both deliverers like Moses and Joshua, and rulers like the kings who would follow.

Judges 2 also informs us that "the Lord had compassion on them [the Israelites] as they groaned under those who oppressed and afflicted them" (v. 18).

It was out of compassion that God raised up judges, but His actual deliverance was based on the response of the people of Israel. Deuteronomy 30 stated the principle that God would remove the discipline whenever the people came to repentance. Repentance is usually considered to be a change of mind, but, as John preached it in the Old Testament context, it was more than a change of mind or attitude. It was also an acknowledgment of sin, followed by an offering to God which would restore the offenders to fellowship. Until sin was acknowledged and an offering provided, the sinning Israelite was not viewed as repentant.

The point here is that discipline was not viewed as *punishment*, which is payment in kind. Rather, the invasions against the land of Israel were disciplines which were designed to *teach, correct, and conform.* The disciplines were imposed to bring the people to confession, repentance, and restoration. And according to Deuteronomy, the discipline could not be lifted apart from repentance. That's why the discipline had to be heavy enough not only to make the people groan, but beyond that to bring them to repentance. As long as they could bear the discipline, they would keep going their own way. When the load got too heavy to bear, however, they would cry to God, and it is this cry or "groaning" that Judges 2:18 indicates is really an expression of repentance.

Through the cycle

To summarize, disobedience brought discipline. Discipline brought confession and restoration, and the discipline was lifted. In this process, the judges were instruments God used to bring the people to confession and repentance so there could be restoration and deliverance from oppression. The judges would impose the Law on the people and make them conform to it. Then God would be ready to let the judge lead them out in battle, where He would give them victory, drive out their enemies, and restore to them land (part of the Abrahamic promise) they had previously lost.

Judgeship was not an hereditary office. The divine seal of approval for a judge was his victory in battle; conversely, failure in battle would be good evidence God had not sent him·

The Book of Judges reiterates over and over again the cycle of apostasy, discipline, confession, and deliverance. It does not, however, provide a picture of the nation as a unified nation. Rather, there were areas within the nation over which particular judges ruled. The judges were not sovereign over the whole nation, but rather were local leaders who delivered the portion of God's people who had come under discipline.

The chronological problems inherent in the Book of Judges cannot be solved without recognizing that overlapping judges ruled in different areas. We are not told who every ruler was, but there seems to have been some form of administration, whether patriarchal or an appointed government. For some reason we do not know, the whole story is not told. Only a summary sketch is given in order to draw our attention to the fact that from Joshua to Saul and David, there was a theocratic administration and a channel through which the theocracy operated.

God's kingdom rule

It is pointed out many times in the Book of Judges that all these judges were controlled by the Spirit of God. For example, Judges 3:10 says of Othniel, "The Spirit of the Lord came upon him, so that he became Israel's judge and went to war." The same thing is said of Gideon (6:34), of Jephthah (11:29), and of Samson (13:25; 14:6, 19; 15:14). These men did not operate by natural power but by supernatural power. They were not necessarily men of high moral character, and often their role was in the physical realm, providing physical deliverance from captors. They functioned simply as appointed mediators in connection with God's administration of Israel.

It should also be pointed out that these judges possessed no dynastic rights. During the period of the judges, in fact, there was only one attempt to establish such a dynastic succession. This was initiated by Abimelech, a son of Gideon, whose three-year reign was ended by a woman who dropped a millstone on his head (Jud. 9).

Judges could not be elected, because the right to appoint administrators was in the hands of God, not in the hands of the people. This was also why Samuel's sons could not be legitimate judges. So far in the development of the theocracy we have seen no such thing as a democracy. And in 1 Samuel 12 we find a significant statement by Samuel who, in reviewing the history of the judges who had delivered Israel from all their enemies, said that the people had done wrong in asking for a king, because "the Lord your God was your king" (v. 12). Of course, God did not rule directly; but He did rule indirectly through the judges.

Gideon also made this point when he said, "I will not rule over you, nor will my son rule over you. The Lord will rule over you" (Jud. 8:23). Any authority he had came from God and was an extension of God's right to rule. Therefore the people in Judges 8 wrongly offered Gideon the right to establish a royal dynasty (though God had affirmed it would be established through the tribe of Judah). Gideon rightly refused to become a king, but he did not refuse to be a judge. Gideon obviously knew that the right to rule did not come from the people, but rather from his appointment by God.

The well-known conclusion to the Book of Judges reads, "In those days Israel had no king; everyone did as he saw fit" (21:25). It might appear as though the kingdom of darkness had triumphed over the kingdom of the God of heaven. Regardless of appearances, however, the Bible shows us that God was ruling over Israel, though not through anyone who was recognized as a king. In fact, later we see that Israel's concept of a king was determined entirely by their perception of kings in surrounding nations. God was Israel's king, but the judges who ruled for Him were not recognized by the title "king" or given the honor that was associated with a king. Nevertheless they carried out their divinely mandated duties of restoration and administration.

Summary

A survey of the entire Book of Judges leads us to the conclusion that God is presented as Israel's King, and that He ruled indirectly through judges. The judges had a twofold responsibility. First, they were to administer the Law and keep the people in subjection to God. Secondly, they were to deliver a repentant people from the discipline that their unbelief had incurred.

During this extended time in Israel's history, God exercised His rule through the judges. This preserved the nation and eventually ushered in a new form of theocracy—the monarchy, or theocracy administered through kings.

12

Transition through Samuel

The ministry of Samuel

First Samuel 3 records the call of Samuel during his childhood, and because of the significant episode there, many have spent so much time with Samuel's childhood that they've missed the conclusion of the chapter and his adulthood.

The point of this chapter is that from the time of his earliest youth, under the tutelage of Eli, Samuel was being prepared to fill a role in the transition of the theocracy. By the chapter's end we read, "The Lord was with Samuel as he grew up, and He let none of his words fall to the ground. And all Israel from Dan to Beersheba recognized that Samuel was attested as a prophet of the Lord" (1 Sam. 3:19-20).

The event that confirmed Samuel as a prophet was the judgment he prophesied against Eli's sons (3:12-14). In Deuteronomy 18:18, God had predicted that a prophet very much like Moses would arise. As far as the biblical and historical records are concerned, Samuel was the first prophet Israel recognized as a prophet from God since Moses. Therefore it would have been quite natural for the people to question whether or not Samuel was the prophet spoken of by Moses. Once he was confirmed, however, a prophet was recognized as one who had authority from God. As one appointed from God, Samuel was God's messenger with God's message.

Passing over the intervening years of Samuel's ministry, we discover in 1 Samuel 8:1 that when he grew old, "he appointed his sons as judges for Israel." The problem was that Samuel's sons did not walk in his ways, but turned aside after "dishonest gain and accepted bribes and perverted justice" (v. 3). As a result, a general rebellion stirred among the people against the authority of these sons. Former generations of judges had all been appointed by God; yet there's no record that God told Samuel to appoint his own sons. This raises the question of whether or not they were valid theocratic administrators.

The second problem with their reign was that not only had they not been appointed by God, but they were not fulfilling the function for which theocratic administrators had been appointed. Instead of maintaining law and order and providing an atmosphere in which righteousness could flourish, instead of upholding God's Law and curbing lawlessness, they did exactly the opposite. This seems to indicate that the people of God did not need to submit to a government which was not fulfilling the God-appointed role of government. In other words, the power of government is not absolute. It does not apply to every sphere.

The New Testament demonstrates that there are various spheres of God-appointed authority in which certain authorities can operate. If government steps out of its assigned sphere and moves into a sphere in which it has not been given authority, then it does not need to be obeyed. The Book of Acts records an illustration of this principle when Peter refused to submit to the authority of government because it transgressed its God-ordained sphere (Acts 4:17-20).

Applying this principle, then, to the case of Samuel's sons, it was because God had not appointed them as judges, and because they were not fulfilling the function for which God appointed administrators, that the elders of the people asked for someone who would. Therefore, they were not in rebellion against God. Instead, they were in rebellion against that which was an imitation of what God had designed. Consequently they asked for a king (1 Sam. 8:5).

What basis for a king?

The basis for their request, however, was that they wanted a king to lead them "such as all the other nations have" (1 Sam. 8:5). God had promised Abraham, "I will make nations of you, and kings will come from you" (Gen. 17:6). During the period of the judges there was outright lawlessness, and as a result, division and disunity. So the

the people decided that if they could have a king, they would have unity. They had been one people under Moses and Joshua, but that was hundreds of years before. The tradition had been passed down and they remembered that time.

Appealing for a king in and of itself was not necessarily bad. Two other passages predicted the possibility of Israel having a king. One is Deuteronomy 17:14-20, where God had made provision for Israel to have a king. Another passage is Genesis 49:10, which promises that the "scepter will not depart from Judah." There was a line of teaching in the Mosaic tradition, then, that anticipated a king.

Certainly the people of Israel, by looking at the surrounding nations, could see the benefits of having a king. The judges had produced division and the last judges, appointed by Samuel, not only perpetuated division, but also introduced corruption.

Regardless, Samuel was displeased by this request. So he prayed to the Lord—but the Lord answered, saying, "Listen to all that the people are saying to you; it is not you they have rejected as their king, but Me" (1 Sam. 8:7). This is an interesting statement because it affirms that through the past periods of the theocratic administration God was indeed ruling His people. God *was* King. Even during the period of corruption and strife under the judges, God was still King. How, then, can we explain all the division that existed?

The answer is found in Deuteronomy 28, where we learned that Israel's disobedience would bring discipline, and only after confession would discipline be removed and the people restored. Thus, division and disunity under the judges was the result of disobedience. God was still the King and in fact exercised His kingship by bringing the discipline He had predicted. If the discipline had not come, it would have shown that He was not in authority.

Therefore, in crying for a change of administration, the people were in effect rebelling against God's authority, because God was the one who had raised up the judges. As 1 Samuel 8:8 indicates, the need for a king arose because of the defection of the people "as they have done from the day I brought them up out of Egypt until this day, forsaking Me and serving other gods."

Counting the cost

Before Samuel told the Israelites they could have a king, he asked them to consider carefully what a king would cost them. He outlined the absolute authority that belongs to a king and showed how it would affect their lives in a number of different areas. The chariots and horses of 1 Samuel 8:11 indicate there would be a military draft. Israel had never had a military draft, and we can well imagine the difficulty the judges had raising armies. While it was true a king would provide an army, daughters would become slaves and perfumers, cooks and bakers (v. 13). In addition, the king would have absolute power over the land and distribute it according to his will. He would take the best of the fields and begin a system of taxation (v. 15) in order to support a centralized bureaucracy. Until this time, the only taxation Israel had ever had was the five shekels they paid to the tabernacle.

In spite of Samuel's warning, however, the people refused to listen. They said they were willing to pay the price for a king (vv. 19-20). Note carefully that the Lord's answer was not that *He* would *give* them a king, but rather that *they* should *appoint* a king. Most important, notice that 1 Samuel 9:1 states that this king came from the tribe of Benjamin, which meant that he could not be the one of whom Genesis 49 spoke, since he was not from the tribe of Judah.

The means of deliverance

God's promise to provide a deliverer for His people from the Philistines was because "I have looked upon My people, for their cry has reached Me" (1 Sam. 9:16). Back in the nation of Egypt, Israel had cried for a deliverer. Under the judges they had cried for a deliverer. Now again, under Samuel the people cried for a deliverer.

This time the oppressor was the Philistines. This provides a clue concerning why the people had asked for a king—they had decided that a divided front was not able to resist the Philistines and throw off their yoke. They wanted a king who could conscript an army and unite the people so they could successfully go out to battle.

God seems to have heard that as a legitimate cry—a legitimate cry for deliverance. Thus, He said He would give them Saul, and called Samuel to anoint Saul as deliverer. So in 1 Samuel 10:1, Samuel took a flask of oil, poured it on Saul's head, and kissed him, saying, "Has not the Lord anointed you leader over His inheritance?" Again, from this standpoint it seems to have been a legitimate request.

In chapter 12, however, Samuel said he would "call upon the

Lord to send thunder and rain. And you will realize what an evil thing you did in the eyes of the Lord when you asked for a king" (v. 17). On one hand, God seems to have approved of their request for a king—but on the other hand, He seems to have disapproved. How can we account for this seeming contradiction?

The answer is found in the fact that Israel was oppressed by the Philistines because of their disobedience. Because of that, the divinely prescribed method of lifting the discipline was repentance and confession. The people, however, were saying that if they had a king, they wouldn't have to operate by God's principles. Instead, their king could go out and take care of their enemies and they would not have to go through the pain of confession and the humiliation of repentance. Their wickedness, then, was not in wanting deliverance, but rather in rejecting God's prescribed method of deliverance.

Time and again during the period of the judges, when the people confessed, God had raised up a deliverer for them. Now, however, the people were saying that they did not want to wait for God to send a deliverer. Instead of having to trust God and meet His conditions, they wanted a king who would ride to war and deliver them.

Summary

Samuel played an important part in the development of the theocracy. As God's prophet he was the instrument God used to set Saul apart as king. Later Samuel would pronounce judgment on Saul because of his failure to fulfill the functions of the delegated administrator in God's kingdom, and anoint David, through whom God's covenanted program would come to its fulfillment.

13

The Davidic Covenant

As early as the days of Abraham it was anticipated that eventually the theocracy in Israel would be administered through kings. God had said to Abraham, "Kings will come from you" (Gen. 17:6). This concept was reinforced by Jacob's prophecy concerning Judah: "The scepter [the symbol of royal authority] will not depart from Judah, nor the ruler's staff from between his feet, until he comes to whom it [that is, the right to rule] belongs" (49:10).

From Saul to David

It was not until after the extended theocratic administration of the judges that Israel came under the authority of kings. Israel, however, became impatient for that which had been revealed as God's ultimate purpose for them. So the elders united and demanded that Samuel give them a king (1 Sam. 8:4-5).

For His own reasons, God granted their wish (1 Sam. 8:22). But Saul had not been on the throne more than two years before God announced His rejection of Saul (13:13-14) who had taken to himself the privileges that belonged to the priests alone (13:8-10). Let us look at several episodes that precipitated God's rejection.

Because of the cowardness of Saul's army, Saul recognized his need of divine help. This help was to be sought through Samuel's intercession. But when Samuel delayed to come to the battle scene (1 Sam. 13:8), Saul sought divine aid by offering sacrifice. In the absence of a priest Saul officiated at the sacrifice as a priest. This was an act of deliberate disobedience to the requirements of the Law. Disobedience, even for noble purposes, cannot be acceptable to God. Therefore God announced the rejection of Saul as a theocratic administrator. If the administrator himself is disobedient how could the people be expected to obey the Law?

Saul's reign was marked by continued disobedience. After Samuel had anointed David to be king, Saul showed his rejection of the designated theocratic administrator by his continued opposition, even as far as attempts on David's life. This indicates Saul's refusal to accept God's rejection of him.

The final act of disobedience by Saul is recorded in 1 Samuel 15. God had given specific instructions that the Amalekites were to be annihilated because of their treatment of the nation following the exodus from Egypt (15:2). The instructions were very specific and clearly understood by Saul. It was Saul's responsibility as administrator of the theocracy to see that the instructions were executed exactly as God had said. But Saul failed to exercise his authority and permitted the soldiers to take spoils from the conquest, and even spared the king of Amalek. While Saul attempted to excuse himself by blaming the men, God rejected the explanation and held Saul personally responsible for the disobedience. As a result God said, "To obey is better than sacrifice, and to heed is better than the fat of rams. For rebellion is like the sin of divination, and arrogance like the evil of idolatry. Because you have rejected the word of the Lord He has rejected you as king" (vv. 22-23).

It was pride on Saul's part that convinced him that he was above the Law and that he could disobey with impunity. But disobedience brought discipline. Although he acknowledged his sin (v. 24), the results of his disobedience removed him from leadership.

The history of Saul is a graphic illustration of the responsibility resting on the theocratic administrator to enforce the Law and to bring the people into obedience to it. Failure to discharge this responsibility would bring discipline on the administrator, thus stressing the importance of an administrator who would be perfectly obedient to the Law and would maintain righteousness in his kingdom. This principle demands a kingdom under the rulership of *the* Obedient One.

Because of Saul's disobedience Samuel announced, "The Lord has torn the kingdom of Israel from you today and has given it to one of your neighbors—to one better than you" (15:28). And Samuel was sent to anoint David as king (16:12-13).

David's victory over Goliath, who was the strong man of the Philistines (1 Sam. 17), was an indication that God would enable David to establish a kingdom of peace and righteousness that would triumph over the kingdom of darkness. After the death of Saul (1 Sam. 31) David was acknowledged as king in Judah (2 Sam. 2:1-4) and then over Israel (5:1-5), and Jerusalem became the capital of David's kingdom (5:6-12). God enabled David to expand the borders of his kingdom (8:1-18). And, quite significantly, David recognized that consolidation of his rule and the expansion of the borders of his kingdom were because of God's faithfulness to him and God's people based on His covenants with them. In response, David's desire was to honor the Lord and recognize His goodnesses by building a temple as an earthly dwelling place for the presence of God.

Reviewing the reign of Saul

As a result of Saul's reign, conditions were radically different in the nation of Israel. It is a mistake to say that God gave Israel a king and he made a mess of the country. By any standard of judgment, Saul was good for Israel—but he was not God's king.

Saul's reign was really only a transition from the judges to the monarchy. God had already decreed that the ultimate fulfillment of His covenant program would come through the tribe of Judah (Gen. 49:10). Yet God said of Saul through Samuel, "You have not kept the command the Lord your God gave you; if you had, He would have established your kingdom over Israel for all time. But now your kingdom will not endure; the Lord has sought out a man after His own heart and appointed him leader of His people, because you have not kept the Lord's command" (1 Sam. 13:13-14). This statement does not mean that God had abandoned His original plan, but had this Benjaminite obeyed he would have reigned in a parallel kingdom with the king from Judah.

In asking for a king, men were trying by human effort to accomplish what God had purposed to do by a divinely appointed king. Still, there were some benefits from those human efforts. Prosperity, peace, and expanded boundaries were all a result of Saul's reign. But it can be said that Saul's reign was the reign of a false king in a false kingdom preceding the reign of a God-appointed king in the kingdom of the God of heaven on earth.

Back to the Abrahamic Covenant

We need to recall at this point that the great future implications of the Abrahamic Covenant were found in the words *land* and *seed*. The *land* promises of the Abrahamic Covenant were further enlarged and confirmed through the Palestinian Covenant. In the next of Israel's great covenants—the one we will see God made with David—God enlarged and confirmed the *seed* promises.

We will see this as we take a closer look at the passages that establish the foundation for the Davidic Covenant:

> When your days are over and you rest with your fathers, I will raise up your offspring to succeed you, who will come from your body, and I will establish his kingdom (2 Sam. 7:12).

> I have made a covenant with My chosen one, I have sworn to David My servant, I will establish your line forever and make your throne firm through all generations (Ps. 89:3-4).

> "I will make the descendants of David My servant and the Levites who minister before Me as countless as the stars of the sky and as measureless as the sand on the seashore. . . ." This is what the Lord says: "If I have not established My covenant with day and night and the fixed laws of heaven and earth, then I will reject the descendants of Jacob and David My servant and will not choose one of his sons to rule over the descendants of Abraham, Isaac and Jacob" (Jer. 33:22, 25-26)

In short, the seed promise contained in the Abrahamic Covenant was made the center or nucleus of the Davidic promise. And it is through the Davidic Covenant that the seed promises in general and the seed line of David in particular—including his kingdom, his descendants, and his throne—are amplified.

The importance of the Davidic Covenant

Within our study of the Davidic Covenant we encounter many of the crucial issues of biblical prophecy, future things, and what theologians call "eschatology." Some of these important questions include: Will there be a literal millennium (one-thousand year reign of Messiah on earth)? Is the church the kingdom? What is God's kingdom? What is Christ's kingdom? Will the nation Israel be regathered and restored under her Messiah? Are the kingdom of God and the kingdom of heaven the same or different? Is the kingdom present or future?

These and many more crucial issues can be clarified only through an accurate understanding of God's covenant with David.

The provisions of the Davidic Covenant

God's covenant promise to David is found in 2 Samuel 7:12-16, where we read:

> When your days are over and you rest with your fathers, I will raise up your offspring to succeed you, who will come from your own body, and I will establish his kingdom. He is the one who will build a house for My Name, and I will establish the throne of his kingdom forever. I will be his father, and he will be My son. When he does wrong, I will punish him with the rod of men, with floggings inflicted by men. But My love will never be taken away from him, as I took it away from Saul, whom I removed from before you. Your house and your kingdom will endure forever before Me; your throne will be established forever.

The historical background of the Davidic Covenant is very familiar. Once David had come to power and authority in the kingdom and dwelt in a house of cedar, it seemed unthinkable to him that the One from whom he received his authority and government should still dwell in a house of skins (the tabernacle). David resolved in his heart to build a suitable dwelling place for God—but because he had been a man of warfare and bloodshed, David was not permitted to build that house. That responsibility was left to Solomon, the prince of peace. However, God made certain promises to David concerning the perpetuity of his house.

The provisions of the Davidic Covenant include the following items:

(1) David is to have a child, yet to be born, who will succeed him and establish his kingdom.

(2) This son (Solomon), instead of David, will build the temple.

(3) The throne of his kingdom will be established forever.

(4) The throne will not be taken away from him (Solomon) even though his sins justify God's discipline.

(5) David's house, throne, and kingdom will be established forever.

House, kingdom, throne

The essential features of the Davidic Covenant are found in these three words in 2 Samuel 7:16: *house, kingdom,* and *throne.*

The term *house* must refer to David's *physical descendants.* This meant that a line stemming from David would continue indefinitely and would be the divinely recognized royal line. The term *throne* refers not so much to the material throne on which David sat as to the *right to rule,* the *authority as king* vested in him. The term *kingdom* must refer to the *political body* David would rule and over which David's descendants would successively reign.

Just as important as these three terms, the word *forever* must refer to any time during which the descendants of Abraham exist. Even though there might be temporary interruptions in the exercise of royal authority because of divine discipline, the authority would never transfer to another line.

As we have seen concerning other covenants of God with Israel, this covenant with David is restated and reconfirmed elsewhere in Scripture. In Psalm 89, for example, the psalmist wrote, "I will not violate My covenant or alter what My lips have uttered. Once for all, I have sworn by My holiness—and I will not lie to David—that his line will continue forever and his throne endure before Me like the sun; it will be established forever like the moon, the faithful witness in the sky" (vv. 34-37).

The Davidic Covenant is also confirmed in such passages as Isaiah 9:6-7; Jeremiah 23:5-6; 30:8-9; 33:14-17, 20-21; Ezekiel 37:24-25; Daniel 7:13-14; Hosea 3:4-5; Amos 9:11; and Zechariah 14:4, 9. God's promise to David was established as a formal covenant and throughout Scripture thereafter is referred to as the basis on which God operates in regard to the kingdom, the house, and the throne.

The character of the Davidic Covenant

As in the preceding covenants, the character of the Davidic Covenant itself is what determines its certainty and validity. Is it conditional and temporary, or is it unconditional and eternal?

Some theologians today argue for a conditional covenant and a spiritualized fulfillment, so that the throne on which Christ is now seated at the right hand of the Father becomes the "throne" of the covenant, the household of faith becomes the "house" of the covenant, and the church becomes the "kingdom" of the covenant. These theologians contend that all the temporal aspects and material provisions of the covenant were fulfilled by Solomon, and that the eternal provisions are fulfilled by the present reign of Christ over the church. This makes the church the "seed" and the "kingdom" promised in the covenant. The kingdom becomes heavenly, not earthly. The Davidic rule becomes merely a "type" or "allegory" of the reign of Christ.

Such conclusions can be reached only by extensive allegorization. This runs contrary to all the principles of sound Bible interpretation, and leaves us with no way of determining which portions of Scripture should be understood normally and which should be taken as allegorical or mystically symbolic. The serious student of Scripture, on the other hand, will approach these important issues by letting the plain language of the Bible speak for itself. Unless there is a good reason in the sacred text to understand it other than normally and literally, the words of the Bible should logically be understood according to their real and intended meaning.

Operating this way, then, let us further discover the character of the Davidic Covenant.

The Davidic Covenant is unconditional in its character
The only conditional element in this covenant was whether or not the descendants of David would *continually* occupy the throne or exercise the right to rule. It is apparent that within the stipulations of this covenant, disobedience might bring about chastening, but it would never abrogate or nullify the covenant. In reality, David never anticipated an unbroken succession of kings in his line; nevertheless he affirmed the eternal character of the covenant. In Psalm 89 David foretold the overthrow of his kingdom (vv. 38-45) before that which had been promised would be realized (vv. 20-29). Still, he anticipated the fulfillment of the promise (vv. 46-52) and blessed the Lord because of it. Such was the faith of David!

There are several reasons for recognizing that this covenant is unconditional:

(1) Like the other of Israel's covenants, it is called eternal in 2 Samuel 7:13, 16; 23:5; Isaiah 55:3; and Ezekiel 37:25. The only way it could be called eternal is that it is unconditional and rests entirely on the faithfulness of God for its execution.

(2) Again, this covenant only amplified the "seed" promises of the original Abrahamic Covenant—which we have already seen is unconditional—and therefore retains the character of the original covenant.

(3) Further, this covenant was reaffirmed after repeated acts of disobedience on the part of the nation. In fact, Christ, the Son of David, came to offer the Davidic kingdom after generations of apostasy! If the covenant was conditional based on the obedience or faithfulness of the nation Israel, these reaffirmations could never have been made.

The Davidic Covenant is to be interpreted literally
There are several reasons for this:

(1) Portions of the covenant that already have been fulfilled have been fulfilled literally. As we've seen before, it is entirely logical and consistent that we determine our method of understanding unfulfilled portions by observing the nature of those portions that have been partially fulfilled. Since all the partial fulfillments have been literal and historical, we can safely assume that the unfulfilled portions will be the same.

(2) It is apparent that David understood the covenant as literal, and its future fulfillments as literal. Throughout Scripture we can readily see that he never considered it as anything but a literal covenant, to be fulfilled literally (2 Sam. 23:5; 1 Kings 1:30-37). And David was so led by God to interpret it.

(3) We also find support for the literal interpretation of the covenant in the way it was interpreted by the nation of Israel. We have already mentioned the way the literal aspects of the covenant were emphasized in all the Old Testament prophetic books. This same literal emphasis continued throughout Jewish history, as we will see in more detail later.

(4) There is evidence for the literal interpretation from the New Testament references to the covenant made with David. Consider, for example, that the New Testament contains no fewer than 59 references to David. It also has many references to the present ministry of Jesus the Messiah. Comparing these with one another, a

search of the New Testament reveals that there is *not one reference connecting the present session of Christ with the Davidic throne.* It is almost incredible that in so many references to David and in so frequent reference to the present session of Christ at the Father's throne, there should be no references connecting the two in any authoritative way. The New Testament is totally lacking in positive teaching that the throne of the Father in heaven is to be identified with the Davidic throne. The inference is plain that Christ is seated on the Father's throne, but that this is not at all the same as being seated on the throne of David.

It can also be shown that in all the preaching concerning the kingdom by John (Matt. 3:2), by Christ (4:17), by the Twelve (10:5-7), and by the seventy (Luke 10:1-12), *not once is the kingdom offered to Israel as anything but an earthly, literal kingdom.* Even after the rejection of that offer by Israel and the announcement of the mystery of the kingdom (Matt. 13), Christ anticipated such a literal, earthly kingdom (25:1-13, 31-46).

It is likewise interesting to observe that the angel, who did not originate his own message, but announced that which was delivered to him by God, said to Mary: "You will be with child and give birth to a son, and you are to give him the name Jesus. He will be great and will be called the Son of the Most High. The Lord God will give Him the *throne* of his father David, and He will reign over the *house* of Jacob forever; His *kingdom* will never end" (Luke 1:31-33, italics mine). This angelic message centered around the three key words of the original Davidic Covenant—the *throne*, the *house*, and the *kingdom*—all of which were here promised a fulfillment.

Another important observation we can make from the New Testament is that *the Davidic Covenant held an important place in the discussion at the first church council* (Acts 15:14-17). A close examination of this passage reveals that there is a progression of thought leading to James' conclusion. *First,* God visits the Gentiles, taking from them a people for His name. In other words, God has promised to bless the Gentiles as well as Israel, but each in his own order. The Gentile blessing is first. *Second,* Christ will return—*after* the outcalling of the people for His name. *Third,* as a result of the coming of the Lord, the tabernacle of David will be built again; that is, the kingdom will be established exactly as promised in the Davidic Covenant. Amos clearly declared that this rebuilding will be done "as it used to be" (Amos 9:11); that is, the blessings will be

145

earthly and national and will have nothing to do with the church. *Fourth*, the residue of men will seek the Lord; that is, all the Gentiles will be brought to a knowledge of the Lord after the kingdom is established. This same truth is taught in passages like Isaiah 2:2; 11:10; 40:5; and 66:23.

So we see, then, that throughout the New Testament, as well as in the Old, the Davidic Covenant is everywhere treated as literal in its provisions as well as its fulfillment.

The problems of literal fulfillment

The position that the Davidic Covenant is to be interpreted literally is not without its problems. Let's consider these one at a time.

(1) There is a problem of the relation of Christ to the covenant. Concerning this problem, two contradictory answers emerge.

The problem of fulfillment does not arise in the question of whether Christ is the One who fulfills the promises, but rather in the issue of *how* Christ fulfills the covenant and *when* He fulfills it. Concerning this question, there have been two principal answers: (a) Christ fulfills the promise by His present session at the right hand of the Father in heaven; or (b) Christ will fulfill the promise of His return and righteous reign on earth during the Millennium, His yet future thousand-year reign on David's throne.

As we have seen, according to the established principles of interpretation, the Davidic Covenant demands a literal fulfillment. This means that Christ must reign on David's throne on the earth over David's people forever. And since this has not yet happened, it is a literal fulfillment that is yet future.

(2) The second problem is in relation to the history of Israel since David's and Solomon's day. Problems arise because there has been no continuous political development in which a Davidic descendant has ruled on David's throne. Instead, Israel has experienced deportation and captivity, and in the centuries since Christ has been without a Davidic king to rule over them. Some theologians use these facts to try and prove that a literal interpretation of the original covenant is impossible.

Here it is extremely important to recognize that only a partial historic fulfillment, or an interruption, in God's program for Israel in no way contradicts its future fulfillment. There are four reasons for this. *First*, the Old Testament prophets expected a literal fulfillment even during Israel's periods of great apostasy and obvious deviation from God's plan. *Second,* the covenant demands a literal interpretation which automatically assumes a future fulfillment. *Third,* the New Testament teaches that the present mystery form of the kingdom in no way abrogates or nullifies its future literal fulfillment in keeping with God's unilateral, unconditional covenants. *Fourth,* the very words of the covenant teach that—although Solomon would be disobedient—the covenant would nevertheless remain in force. Moreover, Solomon's seed was not promised perpetuity. *The only necessary feature is that the lineage cannot be lost, not that the throne be occupied continuously.*

Interruption of the kingdom did not mean the whole program was set aside. As long as the prerogatives of the throne were intact the kingdom might be reestablished. We have already referred to many New Testament passages that show expectation of a literal fulfillment. Why does this expectation still exist? Because as far as the New Testament writers are concerned, interruption of the Davidic kingdom does not militate against the expectancy of a literal restoration of that same kingdom.

Has this covenant been fulfilled historically?
Periodically the argument is raised that all the provisions of the Davidic Covenant were fulfilled during Solomon's reign. Those who hold this view contend that the land ruled over by Solomon according to 1 Kings 4:21 fulfilled the covenant, and no future fulfillment should be expected.

In answer to this, it should be observed first and foremost that those who present this argument are admitting upfront that the terms of the Davidic Covenant require a literal fulfillment. Isn't it interesting, then, that most frequently these same people also argue for a "spiritual" fulfillment of the Davidic Covenant in the church? The two are mutually exclusive and make for an illogical and inconsistent theology all the way around.

Regardless, in reference to the argument itself we can readily observe several details of the Davidic Covenant that were not fulfilled by Solomon. For example, there was no permanent possession of the land as promised to Abraham. Moreover, all the land was not possessed. "From the river of Egypt" (Gen. 15:18) and "from the border of Egypt" (1 Kings 4:21) are not equivalent terms geographically. Solomon did not occupy all this land; he merely collected tribute. Obviously, temporary overlordship is not everlasting possession. Finally, hundreds of years after Solomon's time the Scriptures still abound in promises concerning future possession of the land. This proves that God and His prophets realized—whether or not some modern theologians do—that Solomon did not fulfill the Abrahamic Covenant.

Since the Davidic Covenant has not been fulfilled literally in Israel's history, because of its unconditional character there must be a future literal fulfillment of the covenant.

The prophetic implications of the Davidic Covenant

Because the Bible anticipates a future literal fulfillment of the Davidic Covenant, certain facts present themselves concerning Israel's future. These include:

(1) Israel must be preserved as a nation.

(2) Israel must have a national existence, and be brought back into the land of her inheritance. Since David's kingdom had definite geographical boundaries and those boundaries were included in the promise to David concerning his descendant's reign, the nation must possess that land as their national homeland.

(3) David's Son, the Lord Jesus Christ, must return to the earth, bodily and literally, in order to reign over David's covenanted kingdom. The claim that Christ is seated on the Father's throne reigning over a spiritual kingdom, the church, simply does not fulfill the promises of the covenant.

(4) A literal earthly kingdom must exist over which the returned Messiah will reign.

(5) This kingdom must become an eternal kingdom. Since the "throne," "house," and "kingdom" were all promised to David in perpetuity, there must be no end to Messiah's reign over David's kingdom from David's throne.

We see, then, that the Davidic Covenant is of vital importance for understanding future events, as well as the future form of the God's kingdom. The covenant God made with David became the foundation of Israel's hope. It was the basis for Israel's expectation that a king would arise from the house of David who would be Israel's deliverer from bondage to the Gentiles, and who would bring them into the blessings of the covenants God made with their fathers.

The Prophet *Isaiah* in chapters 9 and 10 predicted a dissemination of the people from the land of Israel because "the people have not returned to Him who struck them, nor have they sought the Lord Almighty" (Isa. 9:13). This was in keeping with the warnings of Deuteronomy 28. But Isaiah also anticipated deliverance from Israel's enemies:

> A shoot will come up from the stump of Jesse; from his roots a Branch will bear fruit. The Spirit of the Lord will rest on Him—the Spirit of wisdom and of understanding, the Spirit of counsel and of power, the Spirit of knowledge and of the fear of the Lord—and He will delight in the fear of the Lord. He will not judge by what He sees with His eyes, or decide by what He hears with His ears; but with righteousness He will judge the needy, with justice He will give decisions for the poor of the earth. He will strike the earth with the rod of His mouth; with the breath of His lips He will slay the wicked. Righteousness will be His belt and faithfulness the sash around His waist (11:1-5).

The deliverer was to come from the family of Jesse, who was the father of David. And David's descendant—Messiah the Branch—would establish a kingdom characterized by righteousness and peace, the fulfillment of the covenant that God gave to Abraham. Isaiah gave further hope to those in the northern kingdom who had already experienced the discipline of captivity when he said:

> Come, all you who are thirsty, come to the waters; and you who have no money, come, buy and eat! Come, buy wine and milk without money and without cost. Why spend money on what is not bread, and your labor on what does not satisfy? Listen, listen to me, and eat what is good, and your soul will delight in the richest of fare. Give ear and come to me; hear me, that your soul may live. I will make an everlasting covenant with you, my unfailing kindness promised to David. See, I have made him witness to the peoples, a leader and commander of the peoples (55:1-4)

Isaiah anticipated the coming of one whom God would send and through whom the desire of the nation would be fully met. This one was to be "a leader and commander of the peoples" (55:4). And this one would be none other than the Davidic descendant through

149

whom the covenant God made with David would be fulfilled.

This hope was also why *Jeremiah* could comfort the people of Judah who had gone into captivity to Babylon. The prophet declared:

> "The days are coming," declares the Lord, "when I will fulfill the gracious promise I made to the house of Israel and to the house of Judah. In those days and at that time I will make a righteous Branch sprout from David's line; He will do what is just and right in the land. In those days Judah will be saved and Jerusalem will live in safety. This is the name by which it will be called: The Lord Our Righteousness." For this is what the Lord says: "David will never fail to have a man to sit on the throne of the house of Israel. . . . If you can break My covenant with the day and My covenant with the night, so that day and night no longer come at their appointed time, then My covenant with David My servant . . . can be broken and David will no longer have a descendant to reign on his throne. I will make the descendants of David My servant and the Levites who minister before Me as countless as the stars of the sky and as measureless as the sand on the seashore" (Jer. 33:14-22).

Although the nation had entered the times of the Gentiles and David's throne was no longer occupied by one of David's sons, Jeremiah could give the exiled nation hope because God's covenant with David is an eternal, unchangeable covenant and must come to a final fulfillment!

The Prophet *Ezekiel*, writing to give consolation and hope to those who were enduring the Babylonian captivity, delivered a similar message from God: "I will place over them one shepherd, My servant David, and he will tend them; he will tend them and be their shepherd. I the Lord will be their God, and My servant David will be prince among them. I the Lord have spoken. I will make a covenant of peace with them . . . there will be showers of blessing" (Ezek. 34:23-26).

The message is repeated:

> My servant David will be king over them, and they will all have one shepherd. They will follow My laws and be careful to keep My decrees. They will live in the land I gave to My

servant Jacob, the land where your fathers lived. They and their children and their children's children will live there forever, and David My servant will be their prince forever. I will make a covenant of peace with them; it will be an everlasting covenant I will establish them and increase their numbers, and I will put My sanctuary among them forever. My dwelling place will be with them; I will be their God, and they will be My people (37:24-27).

Even in exile Israel had the comfort of knowing that a faithful God would carry out the covenant promises He had given to David, and that the nation eventually would experience the blessings of the covenant God had given to their forefathers.

Hosea, along with his message of judgment on a disobedient nation, brought a word of hope when he said, "The Israelites will return and seek the Lord their God and David their king. They will come trembling to the Lord and to His blessings in the last days" (Hos. 3:5).

The empty throne was an indication that God had brought the judgments of Deuteronomy 28 on a guilty people; but there was also the future certainty—according to God's prophets—that the people will one day return and seek the Lord their God to meet the requirements of Deuteronomy 30:1-5. At that time a descendant of David will rule on David's throne, and Israel will inherit the blessings of the kingdom.

The Prophet *Amos*—after giving a message warning of coming dispersion because of disobedience (Amos 9:1-10), a fulfillment of the disciplines of Deuteronomy 28—concludes with a message of hope: "'In that day I will restore David's fallen tent. I will repair its broken places, restore its ruins, and build it as it used to be, so that they may possess the remnant of Edom and all the nations that bear My name,' declares the Lord, who will do these things" (vv. 11-12). "David's tent" refers to a descendant of David who will restore the theocracy and bring the people who have been dispersed back into their land where they will receive the covenanted blessings. Through this Davidic descendant a kingdom will be established, centered in the land that God had given to Abraham, from which they will never be exiled again (v. 15).

Micah, in his prophecy in Micah 5:2, identified Bethlehem, a small village in the inheritance of Judah, as the birthplace of one who was to "be ruler over Israel." This ruler would be the one who would fulfill the prophecy of Genesis 49:10, a Davidic descendant through whom the Davidic Covenant would be brought to fruition.

Zechariah anticipated the coming of this descendant of David when he said, "Rejoice greatly, O Daughter of Zion! Shout, Daughter of Jerusalem! See, your king comes to you, righteous and having salvation, gentle and riding on a donkey, on a colt, the foal of a donkey" (Zech. 9:9).

Old Testament imagery tells us that someone riding on a donkey is in the role of a servant, thus Israel's king would be the servant of Jehovah. Because of His essential character, only He could institute a kingdom of peace and righteousness. And because He is just and humble, justice and righteousness could characterize His kingdom. Moreover, those who come under the authority of this king will themselves partake of the characteristics of the king. Zechariah went on to deliver the words of God who said, "I will pour out on the house of David and the inhabitants of Jerusalem a spirit of grace and supplication. They will look on Me, the one they have pierced, and they will mourn for Him as one mourns for an only child, and grieve bitterly for Him as one grieves for a firstborn son" (12:10).

Those who would enter the kingdom ruled over by David's Son will themselves meet the requirements of Deuteronomy 30:1-5 and will have offered true repentance to the Lord. That repentance was described in 2 Chronicles 7:14, and is demonstrated in Zechariah 12:10. The humility and righteousness that characterize the Davidic king will likewise characterize those who are in His kingdom. And as a result of that repentance Zechariah foretells, "On that day a fountain will be opened to the house of David and the inhabitants of Jerusalem, to cleanse them from sin and impurity" (13:1).

The cleansing fountain was opened by the death of Christ, but the nation—because it refused to repent—has never availed itself as a nation of that which was made available by the death of Christ. However, through the coming of David's Son the nation will be brought to repentance and will receive the benefits available through the death of Christ. The King will establish a universal kingdom (14:9) and He will be the object of worship (v. 16) so that the Jews and Gentiles alike, as the subjects of His reign, will come to offer worship to this One who is none other than the Lord of Hosts. It is in His reign of righteousness and peace that the Davidic Covenant comes to its ultimate fulfillment.

Thus prophet after prophet gave comfort to the nation by reaffirming the hope of the Davidic Covenant—that one of David's sons would sit on David's throne and rule over David's kingdom, and that under that reign Israel would experience the blessings of the Abrahamic Covenant.

Jesus the "Son of David"

When the New Testament opens, we find that Matthew introduced Jesus Christ first of all as "the son of David" (Matt. 1:1). In the geneology in Matthew 1:1-17 Matthew traced Jesus' legal descent from David through Joseph, His foster father, by whom (according to the Levitical laws of inheritance) Jesus could claim legal descent from David and thus be counted eligible to occupy the throne.

In his geneology (Luke 3:23-38), Luke traced Jesus' physical descent from David through Mary His mother, likewise establishing His right to sit on David's throne. Thus both Gospel writers deliberately affirmed that what was promised to David will have its fulfillment through Jesus. Jesus legally and physically possesses all rights to David's throne.

In preparation for the advent of the one through whom the biblical covenants would find their fulfillment, an angel sent from God brought a significant message to Mary: "You will be with child and give birth to a son, and you are to give Him the name Jesus. He will be great and will be called the Son of the Most High. The Lord God will give Him the throne of His father David, and He will reign over the house of Jacob forever; His kingdom will never end" (Luke 1:31-33).

The angel's announcement first of all concerned the person who was to be born to Mary. He would be "the Son of the Most High," affirming His absolute deity. The second portion of the announcement concerned His role. Three significant words found in the covenant God made with David (2 Sam. 7:14)—*house, kingdom,* and *throne*—here were reiterated by the angel, signifying that the child born to Mary was the one who would ultimately fulfill God's covenant with David. He was to occupy David's throne, rule as king over the house of Jacob (thus fulfilling the prophecy of Jacob in Genesis 49:10), and institute an eternal kingdom here on this earth.

God made it clear at the time of John the Baptist's birth that his significant role was to introduce the Davidic king to Israel. His father Zechariah "was filled with the Holy Spirit and prophesied: 'Praise be to the Lord, the God of Israel, because He has come and has redeemed His people. He has raised up a horn of salvation for us in the house of His servant David'" (Luke 1:67-69). Zechariah announced the coming of the king who would fulfill the promises in the David Covenant.

Christ's relationship to David is established even by the fact that when the Romans decreed a census to assess taxes, it was necessary for both Joseph and Mary to go into Judea to the city of David— which is called Bethlehem—because they both were of the house and lineage of David (Luke 2:4). By way of explanation, the Roman method of taxation was to assess personal property. Therefore each individual had to go to the place of his inheritance, establish his rights to property, then wait while that property was evaluated and taxed. Since both Joseph and Mary were of Davidic descent, it was necessary for them to go to David's city where their inheritance lay.

In short, there can be no question about Jesus' relationship to David or about His eligibility to fulfill the Davidic Covenant. In fact, by the time of Christ, the idea of a coming Davidic descendant who would occupy David's throne and reestablish his kingdom was so well established that the term *son of David* had come to be synonymous with the title Messiah (Matt. 12:23).

Further proof can be found in the fact that as anxious as religious leaders were to disprove Christ's claim to be the Messiah (one who had the right to occupy the Davidic throne) they never questioned Jesus' legal or physical rights to that throne. Genealogical records were preserved in the temple, and without doubt the religious leaders had examined those records to see if they could disprove Jesus' claim to be the Davidic king. No such objection, however, was ever raised.

Thus we see that throughout the time of Christ's earthly life anticipation of the fulfillment of the Davidic Covenant was uppermost in the people's minds. They were waiting for the coming of David's son to sit on David's throne and rule over David's house.

The expectation continues

Christ reaffirmed this expectation to the Twelve when He said to them, "I tell you the truth, at the renewal of all things, when the Son of Man sits on His glorious throne, you who have followed Me will also sit on twelve thrones, judging the twelve tribes of Israel" (Matt. 19:28). The Twelve certainly understood this as an affirmation that the Davidic Covenant would be fulfilled and they would be associated with the king in the administration of His kingdom.

This concept never left the apostles. Even after Christ's death and resurrection they asked him, "Lord, are You at this time going to restore the kingdom to Israel?" (Acts 1:6) To "restore" could only mean reestablish the throne upon which a Davidic descendant would rule over the kingdom God had promised to David, but which had been interrupted by the times of the Gentiles. Nothing that had taken place during the lifetime of Christ on earth, nor had anything He taught, altered their concept of a literal fulfillment of the David Covenant.

In the final book of the New Testament, John portrays the consummation of God's kingdom program here on the earth. And, as we might now expect, that program finds its fulfillment in "the Lion of the tribe of Judah, the Root of David" (Rev. 5:5). The "Lion of the tribe of Judah" looks back to Genesis 49:10, while the "Root of David" refers back to Isaiah 11:1.

When Christ is referred to as Lord of lords and King of kings (Rev. 17:14) or as King of kings and Lord of lords (19:16), He is seen as the One who has come triumphantly to fulfill nothing less than the Davidic Covenant. These are not arbitrary titles. In order to have any meaning at all, they must refer to the covenant God made with David.

The One through whom the revelation contained in this book is given identifies Himself: "I am the Root and the Offspring of David, and the bright Morning Star" (22:16). As David's Son, Christ has triumphed over every adversary and every manifestation of the false kingdom, and He alone has the right to sit on David's throne and to rule as King of kings and Lord of lords in the kingdom of the God of heaven on earth.

Summary

After the failure of Saul to fulfill the responsibilities of theocratic administrator, God appointed David from the tribe of Judah to that significant role. God later entered into an eternal, unconditional covenant with David, establishing the Davidic dynasty as the sole rightful occupant of His earthly throne. Through David a kingdom of peace and righteousness would be established over the covenant people in the land that God had previously promised to them. This covenant will have its eventual literal fulfillment here on earth at the second advent of Christ as King of kings and Lord of lords. This covenant was made through David with the nation Israel, and must be fulfilled by Israel. Thus the present session of Christ at the right hand of His Father in heaven and His rule over the church cannot be a fulfillment of the Davidic Covenant.

14

The Decline
of the Monarchy

As we study the Old Testament, we can readily recognize that under Saul, David, and Solomon, the kingdom reached its zenith. Saul began the process with military might. David, as a man of war, was given remakable victories by God. Under Solomon, the man of peace, the nation was extended to the greatest limits it had ever known and achieved great material prosperity.

The spoils of war had particularly enriched the Davidic kingdom. Therefore costly projects were undertaken, the chief of which was the building of the temple. The city of Jerusalem became magnificent—even many common residences had wood paneling instead of rough stone or whitewashed plaster. And all of the building successfully united the nation for it provided common projects to which each could contribute.

However, during the reign of Solomon in particular, seeds were sown that eventually brought about a division of the united monarchy and ultimately dissolved this form of the theocracy.

The division of the monarcy

Many years before, Moses prophetically had given the nation the guidelines God had intended its kings to follow. He wrote, "When you enter the land the Lord your God is giving you and have taken possession of it and settled in it, and you say, 'Let us set a king over us like all the nations around us,' be sure to appoint over you the king the Lord your God chooses" (Deut. 17:14-15).

It seems that God had long ago anticipated the people's desire for a king, and He did not rebuke them for wanting one. It was commendable that they desired to be united instead of divided. God had promised them a king and they saw the benefits that would come to them from a king. God did not rebuke them for that. There were, however, certain limitations as to what the king should and should not do.

First, the text in Deuteronomy went on to stipulate that he should be from among his own brothers. In other words, he was not to be a foreigner. Though Saul was not from the appropriate tribe of Judah, nevertheless he was from the Israelite tribe of Benjamin. It seems Israel did obey this injunction.

Second, "the king, moreover, must not acquire great numbers of horses for himself or make the people return to Egypt to get more of them" (v. 16). When we think of horses, we think of the strength of Egypt's army that was based on her horses and chariots. Multiplying horses meant to build an army. So the king of Israel was instructed by God not to institute a military state. Why not?

Israel, from the time of redemption out of Egypt, had been a special object of God's preserving grace. They had no army when they left Egypt, but God protected them. They had no army when they went into the lands of Moab and Edom, but God protected them there from people who did have armies. For forty years in the wilderness God protected them without an army. Then when under Joshua they came to the Promised Land, God gave them the land in spite of the fact that the people had never had military experience. He did not do it by military might—remember, Joshua equipped his men with trumpets—but by supernatural means. God gave them victory after victory.

The men of Israel, of course, fought some battles, but Joshua's soldiers never became a professional army. Israel never needed an army, for God had instructed them in Deuteronomy that when they got into the land, they were to continue to trust God, and He would preserve and protect them. In short, their security was to be in God, not in the king. But as we well know, Solomon multiplied military forces and fortified cities so that Israel's confidence was in their horses and military establishment, not in God. This was disobedience.

Third, the king of Israel was instructed not to take "many wives" (v. 17). However, history records that Solomon loved many foreign women and had married "seven hundred wives of royal birth and three hundred concubines, and his wives led him astray. As Solomon grew old, his wives turned his heart after other gods, and his heart was not fully devoted to the Lord his God, as the heart of David his father had been. He followed Ashtoreth the goddess of the Sidonians, and Molech the detestable god of the Ammonites. So Solomon did evil in the eyes of the Lord; he did not follow the Lord completely, as David his father had done" (1 Kings 11:3-6).

Fourth, the coming king of Israel was told "he must not accumulate large amounts of silver and gold" (Deut. 17:17). In 1 Kings 10:11-22, we have the record of how Solomon disobeyed this mandate also. In fact he accumulated so much silver and gold that all the vessels in his house were made of solid gold!

Cause and effect

Previously we looked at Deuteronomy 28 and the principle that obedience would bring blessing while disobedience would bring discipline. Solomon was disobedient, and the division of the kingdom that followed Solomon's death was a divine judgment for his disobedience. Solomon's disobedience created insurmountable social and economic problems. Solomon wanted to glorify his city, so he built a temple. This took a great deal of manpower which in turn meant that he had to conscript labor. Instead of volunteer or paid labor, Solomon used as slaves all the non-Israelites living in the land. In addition, he instituted a levy under which 30,000 men had to cut down trees and bring wood for one month out of three (1 Kings 5:13). This disruption to the home and social life of the community undoubtedly was very unpopular with the people.

David's kingdom was supported by the spoils of war. After David's conquests the kingdom enjoyed peace. But since Solomon did not have the spoils of war, the people of Israel themselves had to support the luxuries and extravagances of Solomon's kingdom. This inevitably led to heavy taxation, as unpopular then as it is now. Even that was not enough, however, so Solomon gave twenty cities in Galilee to Hiram, king of Tyre (9:11). This conversion of Israelite land into Gentile territory would have been even more unpopular with the people.

Thus it was that the Lord said to Solomon, "Since this is your attitude and you have not kept My covenant and My decrees, which

159

I commanded you, I will most certainly tear the kingdom away from you and give it to one of your subordinates" (11:11).

Nevertheless, because of His covenant with David, God said He would not bring this calamity during Solomon's lifetime. Instead He would tear the kingdom out of the hand of his son and leave him but one tribe for the sake of Jerusalem and His servant David (vv. 12-13). This passage is extremely important for understanding God's division of the kingdom. It was divine discipline. God had promised David that as long as the land was ruled by one of Abraham's offspring, it would be ruled by a Davidic descendant. God could not set aside the Davidic dynasty and introduce a new one—but He could allow the other tribes to depart and give the tribe of Judah plus the small tribe of Benjamin to a descendant of David. This would carry out God's program of discipline without violating His promise to David.

The downward spiral

In 1 Kings 12 we find the story of Rehoboam, Solomon's son, who went to Shechem where all the Israelites had come to make him king. Jeroboam, who was exiled by Solomon to Egypt, and all the congregation of Israel came and spoke to Rehoboam. Jeroboam demonstrated no rebellion or threat to become king over part of the nation, nor did he aspire to rule over the whole nation. He showed submission to Rehoboam and came with the rest of the assembly to crown Rehoboam king. The assembly's only request was that the taxes be reduced. They said, "Your father put a heavy yoke on us, but now lighten the harsh labor and the heavy yoke he put on us, and we will serve you" (v. 4).

Rehoboam promised to think about it for three days. He first went to his advisors and older men, who rightly counseled him to listen to the voice of the people. However the young men, with whom Rehoboam had been brought up in luxury, could not accept a lower standard of living and counseled him to increase the taxes so that the people would stay busy and not have time to complain. Their argument was very similar to that of Pharaoh at the time of the Exodus—the assumption was that by making the work or taxes heavier, rebellion would cease. Unfortunately Rehoboam followed the unwise advice of his young friends and promised to make the people's yoke even heavier than his father had.

The immediate response of the Israelites was to go home (v. 16). Subsequently Rehoboam was crowned king over the southern part of the nation, while Jeroboam was acknowledged as king over the ten tribes in the north. Thereafter there was continual warfare between Jeroboam and Rehoboam. This constant attempt at reuniting the nation (15:6) was doomed to failure because the division was a divine judgment.

Jeroboam became king in a false kingdom, established as an enemy of the true kingdom of the God of heaven. The southern kingdom of Judah had a succession of Davidic kings until the final discipline predicted by God in Deuteronomy 28. The northern kingdom went into captivity under Assyria in 722–721 B.C., followed by the southern kingdom that went into captivity in 606–605 B.C. under Nebuchadnezzar, when Daniel and the princes of Israel were taken. In 597 B.C. Ezekiel and many of the inhabitants of Jerusalem were taken captive. Finally in 586 B.C. the city was destroyed and those previously left behind were taken.

Termination and restoration of the monarchy

As a captive in Babylon, Ezekiel was given a vision from God to explain why the Captivity had taken place. God also outlined His program to restore the theocracy to Israel. In his writings Ezekiel further explained why the theocratic administration had terminated and described the program leading up to its reinstitution. For example, chapter 36 of Ezekiel foretells the regeneration of the nation, chapter 37 the cleansing of Israel, chapters 38 and 39 the regathering of Israel, and chapters 40–48 the return of Christ and the setting up of the millennial kingdom and temple.

Ezekiel was even given a revelation of the corruption taking place in the temple. Whether he was transported to Jerusalem physically or saw a vision is unclear, but it is clear that by the power of God he accurately saw the degeneration of Israel's worship. God commanded him to dig through the wall and open a door (Ezek. 8:8). What Ezekiel found was a secret entrance to the holy of holies. There was to have been only one entrance and that was through the veil, but the Israelites had opened up a secret passage into the holy of holies through which Ezekiel was told to enter.

Because he was a priest and would have been eligible to minister in the temple, what he saw must have shocked him greatly. All over the walls were painted pictures of unclean, detestable animals and the idols Israel was worshiping. In addition to Jaazaniah acting as a heathen priest, there were also the seventy elders of the house of Israel, each worshiping "at the shrine of his own idol" (v. 12).

Verse 13 and following describe even more detestable things Ezekiel saw. He saw women mourning for Tammuz, which is another name of Marduk, the god of the Babylonians. This mother-child cult had come out of Babylon after its beginning in Genesis 10–11. *Babel,* meaning "the gate of God," was the root form of the word *Babylon* and very similar to the Hebrew word translated *confusion.* Forty days of fasting for Tammuz commemorated his reputed death and restoration to life by his mother Semiramis. It was the most detestable of false religions, one that even today attempts in various forms to counterfeit the Gospel of grace.

Continuing to worsen, the scene in verse 16 records that there were twenty-five men with their backs toward the temple of the Lord, "bowing down to the sun in the east." This Canaanite practice demonstrated the merging of Babylonian and Canaanite religious ritual into a syncretistic paganism that required nothing less than divine judgment.

Afterward, chapter 10 records that Ezekiel's attention was drawn toward the cherubim in the holy of holies where he saw the radiance of the glory of God move out from that sacred place to the court, and then to the threshold of the temple (v. 18), then to the east gate of the Lord's house (v. 19), and finally to the Mount of Olives on the east side of the city (11:23). This departure of the glory of God from its dwelling place between the cherubim marked the temporary end of this form of theocratic administration.

There were two things that made Israel a theocratic people. The first was Israel's redemption out of Egypt, and the second was a voluntary submission to the Law given at Sinai. God had revealed His presence among His people, first by the shining of the pillar of fire by night and the pillar of cloud visible above the tabernacle by day as they left Egypt; then by the shining of light in the tabernacle itself. Because of God's presence the people could say "Immanuel"—God with us.

That glory was evident to Israel throughout her history. From the time of the giving of the Law and the founding of the tabernacle, God was with His people. But with the departure of that glory, God no longer dwelt among His people. This signified the end of an administration, after which God would use a new vehicle through which He would accomplish His work.

It is critical that we recognize that this does *not* mean Israel will not be restored and again become a people of the kingdom. Even the conclusion of the Book of Ezekiel describes the glory of the God of Israel coming again (Ezek. 43) in direct contrast to its departure in the early chapters of the book.

But just as Ezekiel described the termination of the program through the kings, so Daniel—as a contemporary of Ezekiel—introduced the new administrative program through the Gentile nations. In chapters 2 and 7, Daniel revealed that four future nations or empires would rule over Israel. They—not a Davidic monarch— would be the temporary channels through which God would work. In effect, this was a return to a previous form of theocratic adminis- tration, that of human government. Thus began the "times of the Gentiles," which continue through the present day.

The time of the Gentiles, then, is that extended period in which Jerusalem is occupied by Gentiles and the seed of Abraham is ruled over by Gentiles. Today Israel has no Davidic king and God is working through Gentile nations rather than through Israel. And while Israel will some day be the theocratic kingdom again, during the present "times of the Gentiles," it is under Gentile domination.

Summary

Thus it is observed that because of the excesses of Solomon the kingdom was divided. Ten tribes followed a Benjaminite king to form the northern kingdom of Israel and two tribes remained under the administration of a Davidic descendant to form the southern kingdom of Judah. This division generated continued conflict be- tween the two kingdoms, disrupting the peace brought about through David and Solomon. This conflict continued until the north- ern kingdom fell to Assyria and the southern kingdom fell to Baby- lon as divine discipline in keeping with Deuteronomy 28. The cove- nant people came under the rule of Gentiles, which would continue until there was national repentance, at which time a Davidic king would assume the throne again.

15

The New Covenant

By way of review, to the unconditional Abrahamic Covenant were added conditional blessings. Before the covenant nation could enjoy the covenanted blessings it must walk in obedience to the laws of God. The obedience required was outlined for the nation in the Mosaic Law, which was given alongside the Abrahamic Covenant (Gen. 17:19) to define what God expected as a prerequisite for blessing.

As we have seen, the nation was unable to fulfill the obedience the Law required. For one, the Law was weak because it depended solely on the energy of the flesh (Rom. 8:3). Further, the nation of Israel was characterized by God as being stiff-necked (Jer. 17:23) and hardened and obstinate (Ezek. 3:7). If the nation was to experience the blessings of the covenant they would need forgiveness for sins, a new heart characterized by obedience, and empowerment from outside themselves.

A covenant that guarantees Israel these divine provisions is given in Jeremiah 31:31-34:

> "The time is coming," declares the Lord, "when I will make a new covenant with the house of Israel and with the house of Judah. It will not be like the covenant I made with their forefathers when I took them by the hand to lead them out of Egypt, because they broke My covenant, though I was a husband to them," declares the Lord. "This is the covenant I will make with the house of Israel after that time," declares the

Lord. "I will put My law in their minds and write it on their hearts. I will be their God, and they will be My people. No longer will a man teach his neighbor, or a man his brother, saying, 'Know the Lord,' because they will all know Me, from the least of them to the greatest," declares the Lord.

Again in Jeremiah 32:37-42 we read: "I will surely gather them from all the lands where I banish them in My furious anger and great wrath; I will bring them back to this place and let them live in safety. They will be My people, and I will be their God. I will give them singleness of heart and action, so that they will always fear Me for their own good and the good of their children after them. I will make an everlasting covenant with them: I will never stop doing good to them, and I will inspire them to fear Me, so that they will never turn away from Me. I will rejoice in doing them good and will assuredly plant them in this land with all My heart and soul."

Further in Ezekiel 16:60-62 we read: "Yet I will remember the covenant I made with you in the days of your youth, and I will establish an everlasting covenant with you. Then you will remember your ways and be ashamed when you receive your sisters, both those who are older than you and those who are younger. I will give them to you as daughters, but not on the basis of My covenant with you. So I will establish My covenant with you, and you will know that I am the Lord."

And in Ezekiel 36:24-32 we find:

For I will take you out of the nations; I will gather you from all the countries and bring you back into your own land. I will sprinkle clean water on you, and you will be clean; I will cleanse you from all your impurities and from all your idols. I will give you a new heart and put a new spirit in you; I will remove from you your heart of stone and give you a heart of flesh. And I will put My Spirit in you and move you to follow My decrees and be careful to keep My laws. You will live in the land I gave your forefathers; you will be My people, and I will be your God. I will save you from all your uncleanness. I will call for the grain and make it plentiful and will not bring famine upon you. I will increase the fruit of the trees and the crops of the field, so that you will no longer suffer disgrace among the nations because of famine. Then you will remember

165

your evil ways and wicked deeds, and you will loath yourselves for your sins and detestable practices. I want you to know that I am not doing this for your sake, declares the Sovereign Lord. Be ashamed and disgraced for your conduct, O house of Israel.

Discipline . . . and hope

The Prophet Jeremiah spoke a great message contained in chapters 30–33 of his prophecy, delivered at the time of Nebuchadnezzar's first invasion of Judah (606–605 B.C.). In it he described an awesome judgment that would fall on the land: "This is what the Lord says: 'Cries of fear are heard—terror, not peace. Ask and see: Can a man bear children? Then why do I see every strong man with his hands on his stomach like a woman in labor, every face turned deathly pale? How awful that day will be! None will be like it. It will be a time of trouble for Jacob, but he will be saved out of it' " (Jer. 30:5-7). Again, "This is what the Lord says, 'A voice is heard in Ramah, mourning and great weeping, Rachel weeping for her children and refusing to be comforted, because her children are no more' " (31:15).

The judgment of which Jeremiah spoke would come on the nation because of their sin. God said, "I have struck you as an enemy would and punished you as would the cruel, because your guilt is so great and your sins so many. . . . Because of your great guilt and many sins I have done these things to you" (30:14-15). This judgment was the one God had warned the nation about in Deuteronomy 28:15-68. Israel was about to experience the ultimate discipline resulting from disobedience.

But Jeremiah was sent not only to announce and explain the forthcoming judgment, but also to give comfort and hope to God's people under discipline. Because the covenants God had made with Israel were unconditional, it was impossible for them to be canceled even because of disobedience. Along with the announcement of discipline was the promise of restoration: " 'I will surely save you out of a distant place, your descendants from the land of exile. Jacob will again have peace and security and no one will make them afraid. I am with you and will save you,' declares the Lord. 'Though I completely destroy all the nations among which I scatter you, I will not completely destroy you. I will discipline you but only with justice; I will not let you go entirely unpunished' " (Jer. 30:10-11).

Or again, "This is what the Lord says: 'I will restore the fortunes of Jacob's tents and have compassion on his dwellings; the city will be rebuilt on her ruins, and the palace will stand in its proper place. From them will come songs of thanksgiving and the sound of rejoicing. I will add to their numbers, and they will not be decreased; I will bring them honor, and they will not be disdained. Their children will be as in days of old, and their community will be established before Me; I will punish all who oppress them. Their leader will be one of their own; their ruler will arise from among them. I will bring him near and he will come close to Me, for who is he who will devote himself to be close to Me?' declares the Lord. 'So you will be My people, and I will be your God' " (vv. 18-22).

In Jeremiah 31:1-9 we read:

"At that time," declares the Lord, "I will be the God of all the clans of Israel, and they will be My people. . . . The people who survive the sword will find favor in the desert; I will come to give rest to Israel." The Lord appeared to us in the past, saying: "I have loved you with an everlasting love; I have drawn you with loving-kindness. I will build you up again and you will be rebuilt, O Virgin Israel. Again you will take up your tambourines and go out to dance with the joyful. Again you will plant vineyards on the hills of Samaria; the farmers will plant them and enjoy their fruit. There will be a day when watchmen cry out on the hills of Ephraim, 'Come, let us go to Zion, to the Lord our God.' " This is what the Lord says: "Sing with joy for Jacob; shout for the foremost of the nations. Make your praises heard, and say, 'O Lord, save Your people, the remnant of Israel.' See, I will bring them from the land of the north and gather them from the ends of the earth. Among them will be the blind and the lame, expectant mothers and women in labor, a great throng will return. They will come with weeping; they will pray as I bring them back. I will lead them beside streams of water on a level path where they will not stumble, because I am Israel's father, and Ephraim is my firstborn son."

Again, " 'So there is hope for your future,' declares the Lord. 'Your children will return to their own land' " (31:17). And, "This is what the Lord Almighty, the God of Israel, says: 'When I bring them back from captivity, the people in the land of Judah and in its towns will once again use these words: "The Lord bless you, O righteous dwelling, O sacred mountain." People will live together in Judah and all its towns—farmers and those who move about with their flocks. I will refresh the weary and satisfy the faint' " (vv. 23-25).

Divine enablement

This future restoration of Israel, which was offered as hope even though Israel's discipline must first come, will be possible because of the nation's repentance.

"So I poured out My wrath on them because they had shed blood in the land and because they had defiled it with their idols. I dispersed them among the nations, and they were scattered through the countries; I judged them according to their conduct and their actions" (Ezek. 36:18-19). This dispersion was the outworking of the unconditional Palestinian Covenant, which also stated in Deuteronomy 30 that if the nation would turn in faith to God and show the genuineness of their faith by obedience, they would again experience the full blessings of the covenants.

Therefore the basis of the hope Jeremiah held out to a nation about to undergo discipline was not that they would become strong in themselves and would be able to obey the Lord, but rather that God would give them a New Covenant that will provide the divine enablement necessary for them to walk in obedience and experience the blessings of the covenant (Jer. 31:31-34).

This covenant—which the prophet says is a new covenant—stands in sharp contrast to the covenant God gave to the nation at Sinai. That covenant (the Law) defined the obedience God required as a prerequisite to blessing, but it provided no enablement (Rom. 8:3).` It was a conditional covenant.

The New Covenant, on the other hand, is an unconditional covenant, as proven by the number of times God affirms "I will" as He outlines all the things He will perform through this covenant. It is wholly unconditional because it rests solely on the affirmation of what God Himself will do.

Moreover, this New Covenant is an eternal covenant. God said, "In My faithfulness I will reward them and make an everlasting covenant with them" (Isa. 61:8). In Ezekiel 37:26 God said, "I will make a covenant of peace with them; it will be an everlasting covenant." It is viewed as everlasting as the sun and the moon and the stars (Jer. 31:35-36).

Further, this covenant is based on blood. The New Covenant guarantees Israel a converted heart as the foundation of all her blessings. According to the Old Testament principle, this type of conversion cannot be permanently effected without the shedding of blood. This covenant makes necessary as its foundation a sacrifice acceptable to God.

And concerning the coming of the king who will bring this covenant of blessings to Israel, Zechariah the prophet said, "He will proclaim peace to the nations. His rule will stem from sea to sea, and from the River to the ends of the earth. As for you, because of the blood of My covenant with you, I will free your prisoners from the waterless pit" (Zech. 9:10).

Results of the New Covenant

Within the original Abrahamic Covenant were promises concerning *land, seed,* and *blessings.* The Palestinian Covenant developed the *land* promises; the Davidic covenant furthers the *seed* promises. Now it is the New Covenant that develops and guarantees the *blessing* promises of the original Abrahamic Covenant.

The prophets Jeremiah and Ezekiel, who devote so much consideration to the New Covenant, have a great deal to say about the blessings that will flow from this covenant. In spite of the disobedience of the nation, this covenant necessitates the *continuation* of the nation. Even continued disobedience cannot remove Israel from her covenanted position (Jer. 31:34-35). Further, the nation is promised a *restoration* to the land (Jer. 32:37; 33:11; Ezek. 11:17; 36:28-35; 37:21-22, 25). Since this return to the land is viewed as a permanent restoration, these prophecies could not have been exhausted in the return from Babylon.

In addition, the prophets speak of the *rebuilding* of the city of Jerusalem (Jer. 31:38-40) and in that rebuilt city a *temple* which becomes the center of worship is to be rebuilt (Ezek. 37:27-28). The blessings the nation is to receive are based on this covenant (Isa. 61:8-9; Hos. 2:18-20). Specifically, among those blessings the nation will be brought into a close *relationship with God* so that they become the people of God and God Himself becomes their God

(Jer. 30:22; 31:33; 32:38-41; Ezek. 11:20; 34:25-27; 37:27). The nation which had been redeemed to be God's possession (Ex. 19; Isa. 43:1) will be brought into that intimate relationship to which they had originally been appointed.

Also as a result of the blood of the New Covenant, the nation's *sins will be forgiven.* God declared through Jeremiah, "I will forgive their wickedness and will remember their sins no more" (Jer. 31:34; see also 33:8; Ezek. 36:25; Micah 7:18-20). This forgivness will be the final fulfillment of what was anticipated by Israel's observance of the Day of Atonement. On the Day of Atonement the nation as a nation assembled at the tabernacle to acknowledge their sin before God (Heb. 10:3). The sacrifices on the Day of Atonement, however, could provide only a temporary covering for sin. In His forbearance, God left those sins unpunished (Rom. 3:25) until One would come who—through the offering of a better sacrifice based on better blood—would put away sin permanently. One of the major blessings of the New Covenant, then, would be the provision of a way for God to put away sin and receive sinners to Himself.

Men throughout the Old Testament were characterized by their ignorance of God, but the New Covenant promises that *ignorance will be removed* and there will be *universal knowledge of God* and of God's requirements (Jer. 31:34). The New Covenant therefore will provide for a *new mind.*

It also will provide for a *new heart,* as the prophets clearly state (Isa. 59:21; Jer. 31:33; 32:39, 41; Ezek. 36:26). With a new mind men will know God, and with a new heart they will love God.

However, knowing God and loving God do not in themselves provide enablement to walk in the obedience required to receive the blessings of the covenant. Therefore God promised that *the Holy Spirit would be given* as His gift to those who enter into the New Covenant. This gift was announced by Joel who said, "I will pour out My spirit on all people . . . I will pour out My spirit in those days" (Joel 2:28-29).

Ezekiel expanded on Joel's prophecy by saying, "I will give them an undivided heart and put a new spirit in them. I will remove from them their heart of stone and give them a heart of flesh" (Ezek. 11:19). He said again, "I will give you a new heart and put a new spirit in you; I will remove from you your heart of stone, and give you a heart of flesh, and I will put My Spirit in you" (36:26-27). As a result of the indwelling of the Spirit, "They will follow My decrees and be careful to keep My laws. They will be My people and I will be their God" (11:20). The Spirit in them will "move you to follow My decrees and be careful to keep My laws. You will live in the land I gave your forefathers. You will be My people and I will be your God. I will save you from all your uncleanness" (36:27-29).

Thus the people who had failed to give God the prerequisite obedience under the Law to make them eligible for covenanted blessings—because they were weak—will be empowered to implicit obedience by the Spirit of God. This obedience in turn will bring them the blessings of the covenants.

Blessings in full

In addition to these blessings of the New Covenant, the material blessings promised to Israel in the land will be the blessing of the Palestinian Covenant. Further, they will enter into the blessings of the Davidic Covenant because they will be ruled over by David their king (Jer. 30:9; Ezek. 37:24-25). They will no longer be subjected to discipline at the hands of the Gentiles but "their leader will be one of their own. Their ruler will arise from among them" (Jer. 30:21). This ruler will be none other than the Davidic descendant through whom the Davidic Covenant will be fulfilled.

This New Covenant, then—which is an unconditional, eternal covenant based on the shedding of blood—guarantees the preservation of Israel as a nation and her ultimate restoration to the land originally given by God to Abraham and Abraham's descendants. It provides for forgiveness of sin and the removal of all uncleanness from the nation. It provides for a new mind so that the nation as a nation may know God, and for a new heart so that those in the nation may love God. It promises the indwelling of the Holy Spirit who will enable them to walk in obedience to the demands of God. And as a result of this covenant, the blessings Israel never found through the Law will at last be experienced.

Important distinctions

Several important observations need to be made. *First,* this New Covenant was made "with the house of Israel and with the house of Judah" (Jer. 31:31). It is undeniable that the Mosaic Covenant was made with Israel—and since this covenant supplants the Mosaic

171

Covenant, *it must of necessity be made with the same people with whom the original Mosaic Covenant had been made.* This is further affirmed in such passages as Isaiah 59:20-21; 61:8-9; Jeremiah 32:37-40; 50:4-5; and Ezekiel 16:60-63; 34:25-26; 37:21-28.

The *second* observation is that from the time of the first announcement of the New Covenant onward throughout the Old Testament, that covenant was viewed as future (Isa. 55:3; Jer. 31:31; Ezek. 16:60, 62; 20:37; 34:25-26; Hos. 2:18-20). This means that Israel did not enter into the benefits of the New Covenant at any time in its Old Testament experience, and since Israel has not yet entered into the blessings that flow from the New Covenant, its *ultimate fulfillment must still be viewed as yet future.* In other words, it can only be experienced after Israel's conversion at the second advent of Christ (Rom. 11:26) and in His thousand-year reign that will follow.

In its historical setting, the disciples who heard the Lord refer to the New Covenant in the upper room the night before His death would certainly have understood Him to be referring to the New Covenant of Jeremiah 31. Based on that, we can observe several things concerning Christ's words on that occasion.

In Matthew 26:28 and Mark 14:24 the statement is recorded: "This is *My* blood of the New Covenant" [italics mine]. In this statement emphasis is placed upon the soteriological (salvation) aspects of that covenant. The blood being offered was that required by the promised New Covenant and was for the purpose of providing a basis for the remission of sins.

In Luke 22:20 and 1 Corinthians 11:25 the statement is recorded: "This cup is the *New Covenant* in My blood" [italics mine]. This statement emphasizes the eschatological (prophetic) aspects of the New Covenant, stating that the New Covenant would be instituted with His death. This would be according to the principle of Hebrews 9:16-17: "In the case of a will [testament], it is necessary to prove the death of the one who made it, because a will is in force only when somebody has died; it never takes effect while the one who made it is living."

Since the disciples would certainly have understood any reference to the New Covenant as referring to Israel's anticipated covenant recorded in Jeremiah, it seems certain that the Lord was stating that that very covenant was being instituted with His death, and that they (the disciples) were ministers of the blood (the soteriological aspects) of that covenant (2 Cor. 3:6). But those to whom it was primarily and originally made (Israel as a nation) will not receive its fulfillment or its blessings until the second advent of Christ, when "all Israel shall be saved . . . and this is My covenant with them when I take away their sins" (Rom. 11:26-27).

In other words, *there is a marked and critical difference between the institution of the covenant and the realization of its benefits.* By His death, Christ laid the foundation for Israel's New Covenant— but its benefits will not be received by Israel until the second advent of Messiah.

Is the church Israel?

Though the teaching that the church has taken Israel's place in God's kingdom program has been popular at different times and in different places throughout church history, several considerations support the view that the church is *not* now fulfilling Israel's New Covenant:

(1) The term *Israel* is not used in the Scriptures to describe anyone but the physical descendants of Abraham. Since the church today is composed of both Jews and Gentiles without national distinction, it would be impossible for the church to fulfill God's promises made exclusively to the nation of Israel.

(2) Within the New Covenant—as its provisions have previously been outlined—there were promises of spiritual blessings and promises of earthly blessing. While the church—like Israel—is promised salvation, the forgiveness of sin, and the ministry of the Holy Spirit, the church is *never* promised inheritance in a land, material blessings on the earth, or rest from oppression, all of which are parts of the promise to Israel. The New Covenant not only promised Israel salvation, it also promised a new life as all her covenants are realized under the kingship of her Messiah on earth for a thousand years. The church certainly is not fulfilling the material portions of this covenant!

(3) Since the church receives blessings of the Abrahamic Covenant (Gal. 3:14; 4:22-31) by faith without being under or fulfilling that covenant, so the church may receive blessings from the New Covenant without being under or fulfilling it, simply by God's grace. As Paul reminded the Ephesians, "Remember that at that time you were separate from Christ [Messiah], excluded from citi-

zenship in Israel and foreigners to the covenants of the promise, without hope and without God in the world. But now in Christ Jesus you who once were far away have brought near through the blood of Christ" (Eph. 2:12-13).

(4) The time element contained within the covenant itself—both in its original statement and in its restatement in Hebrews 8— precludes the church from being the agent in which it is fulfilled. The covenant simply cannot be fulfilled and realized by Israel until *after* the period of Israel's tribulation and her deliverance by the advent of Messiah. While the church has had periods of persecution and tribulation, it never has passed through the Great Tribulation preannounced by biblical prophecy. And certainly the church is not now in the millennial age.

Romans 11:26-27 clearly indicates that this covenant can only be realized after the Second Advent of the Messiah. Since the tribulation, Second Advent, and millennial age are yet future, the fulfillment of this promise must be yet future, and the church cannot now be fulfilling this covenant, though it is obviously partaking of some of its blessings.

The church and the New Covenant

The question then arises: What is the relationship of the church to the New Covenant?

There are those who insist since Jeremiah 31:31-34 is quoted in the Book of Hebrews—which is addressed to believers—this means that the church has supplanted Israel in the program of God and is today fulfilling the New Covenant and experiencing its blessings. However, we are forced to recognize that this simply is not the intent of the writer to the Hebrews.

To the contrary, the author of Hebrews was quoting Jeremiah 31 to show that when Jeremiah promised a New Covenant to Israel, he was indicating that the Old Covenant under which they had been operating was to be viewed as temporary. While it is true that by the blood of the New Covenant believers in the church today receive benefits from that blood (such as the forgiveness of sins, the impartation of the Holy Spirit as God's gift), it certainly does *not* mean that the church is fulfilling the New Covenant.

On the other end of the argument are those who take a very narrow view and say that the New Covenant was made with the house of Israel and Judah, and that the church has no relationship to the New Covenant whatsoever. These point out that apart from forgiveness of sins and the indwelling ministry of the Spirit, none of the promised blessings come to the church; thus the church must be entirely unrelated to the New Covenant.

However, because of our Lord's statement to the Eleven in the upper room on the eve of the Crucifixion, it seems impossible to say that the church has no relationship to the New Covenant! A more acceptable understanding is that while the New Covenant was made with the house of Israel and Judah, there are benefits from the enactment of that covenant of which the church (comprising both Jews and Gentiles) partake.

Let's not forget that the original Abrahamic Covenant promised, "All peoples on earth will be blessed through you" (Gen. 12:3). In that original covenant was the promise of universal blessing. While these universal blessings are not found in the Palestinian Covenant, the expectation of universal blessing is found in the Davidic Covenant through the rule of David's Son on David's throne over all the earth. The nations who are a part of that Davidic kingdom will enter into righteousness and peace through the reigning king.

Thus while the New Covenant was made with the covenant nation at the time of the death of Christ, benefits from that covenant may be applied to those outside the nation. As Matthew noted Christ's words, "This is My blood of the covenant, which is poured out for many for the forgiveness of sins" (Matt. 26:28). We can logically and consistently conclude, then, that this covenant is Israel's covenant; but on the basis of the blood of the covenant, those outside that nation likewise may experience the removal of guilt and the forgiveness of sins.

The New Covenant in the prophetic future

The prophetic implications of the New Covenant are very significant, and show just how extensive a prophetic program awaits fulfillment. According to this covenant, Israel must be restored to the land of Palestine, which they will possess as their own. This also entails the preservation of the nation. Israel must experience a national conversion, be regenerated, and receive the forgiveness of sins and the implantation of a new heart—which will take place following the return of Messiah to the earth.

Israel must experience the outpouring of the Holy Spirit so that He may produce righteousness and full knowledge in the individual. Israel must receive material blessings from the hand of the King into whose kingdom they have come. Palestine must be reclaimed, rebuilt, and made the glorious center of a new glorious earth. And the Messiah who came and shed His blood as the foundation of this covenant must personally come back to the earth to effect the salvation, restoration, and blessing of the nation Israel.

Again, all of these important areas of eschatological [end times] study are made necessary by this covenant. In short, when Israel enters into the full experience of the blessings promised in the New Covenant, the kingdom necessitated by God's program will be made possible.

Meanwhile, the New Covenant becomes the basis of the message proclaimed throughout the New Testament. Paul in Romans 11:27 referred to "My covenant with them when I take away their sins," envisioning Israel's entrance into the benefits of the New Covenant established by the death of Christ. Paul also declared that he was a minister of the New Covenant (2 Cor. 3:6). The writer of Hebrews declared that Jesus Christ is the mediator of the New Covenant (Heb. 9:15; 12:24). "The blood of the eternal covenant" (13:20) is the foundation of all the believer's blessings.

In fact, one of the major arguments presented by the author of Hebrews is that the New Covenant is a *better* covenant than the Mosaic Covenant. He thus referred indirectly to Jeremiah 31:31, where the prophet promised the coming of a New Covenant that would supersede the old Mosaic Covenant. Thus the New Covenant has been established through the death of Christ, but Israel's reception of its benefits awaits that nation's future repentance. Meanwhile benefits accrue to believers today—by grace through faith—based on the blood of Israel's covenant.

Summary

To this point in our study, we have surveyed four covenants God initiated with the nation Israel to show that they are unconditional and eternal covenants, made with a covenant people, and to be fulfilled because of the faithfulness of the One making the covenants to those to whom they were given.

These covenants not only had a relation to the nation at the time of their inception and built a foundation on which God dealt with Israel, but they bind God to a course of action in relation to future events, as illustrated in Bible prophecy.

Moreover, when these covenants are studied analytically we find seven great features which are distinct and determinative:

(1) a nation forever;

(2) a land forever;

(3) a King forever;

(4) a throne forever;

(5) a kingdom forever;

(6) a New Covenant; and

(7) abiding blessings.

16

The Kingdom and the Prophets

The authority of the prophet

Israel had been prepared for the advent of a prophet. In Deuteronomy 18:18-19 God said He would raise up a prophet like Moses. And the nation of Israel was to listen to him, for he would come with God's authority and, like Moses, deliver God's message. As the people had submitted to Moses, so in the same way they were to submit to the prophet.

Ultimately, of course, this prophecy looked forward to Messiah. However, it was inherent in the office of the prophet that he came by divine authority with God's message, and that he demanded obedience and submission. There were, therefore, two lines of authority under the monarchy: the authority of the king and the authority of the prophet. The king was not a prophet and the prophet was not a king. However, both had authority, and their respective realms of authority did not overlap. Neither was there a conflict between them. Rather, each was to operate in his own realm.

The king was charged with the responsibility of administering social or governmental authority. Whenever the king moved out of that realm and began to operate as a priest, he came under divine judgment because he transgressed his assigned authority. Authority in one realm did not give him authority in another.

The authority of the prophet, on the other hand, was in the things of God. He was God's representative with God's message, and that realm was distinct from the civil realm in which the king operated.

Two classes of prophets

The two classes of prophets were (1) the speaking prophets and (2) the writing prophets. The speaking prophets had the essential role of calling the people to repentance. Thus, the speaking prophets condemned sin and demanded that the people conform to the Law as proof of their repentance. John the Baptist was very typical of a speaking prophet.

In the Old Testament, speaking prophets surveyed the historical situation, pointed out sin, condemned it, and called the people to repentance. That's why so much of the prophetic message related to social injustices, such as oppression of the poor, that were symptomatic of disobeying God's Law. No one was exempt from the condemnation of these speaking prophets. The prophets even stood in judgment over kings, for though the king had absolute authority in his realm, the prophet could exercise his divinely given authority and call the king to repentance. Along with the message of condemnation, the prophets also exposed private, public, and social sin and announced judgment by predicting what would happen. This pronouncement of impending judgment, of course, was in keeping with the message of Deuteronomy 28, that disobedience would bring discipline.

The writing prophets likewise condemned the sin of the nation and called the people to repentance, but they also began to outline God's prophetic program for Israel and the nations of the world. The writing prophets also seemed more concerned with vindicating the character of God.

God had entered into a covenant with His people, and whatever God had covenanted must be fulfilled. Yet the Assyrian and Babylonian captivities might have seemed to indicate that God had not been faithful to His covenants. Thus, while the writing prophets repeatedly predicted judgment, they just as consistently wrote about how God would fulfill the blessings promised in His covenants.

The prophetic message

The prophetic message in its essence is *an unfolding of the divine plan concerning the times of the Gentiles, the coming Messiah, the restoration of Israel, the millennial blessings, and all details that are part of these themes.* This is why our understanding of biblical prophecy and the events of the end times comes largely out of the writing prophets who wanted to confirm God's faithfulness to His covenants and reveal the prophetic program. In fact, we must recognize the role and message of God's prophets in relation to His covenant program. It is our only option for understanding biblical prophecy at all.

There is a perfect continuity among the prophets from the time of Saul, through the Exile, and down to Malachi. After this final "Old Testament prophet," there was a time lapse until John the Baptist— but in reality John the Baptist picked up exactly where the post-exilic prophets left off. Again, there is a perfect, logical, literal, historical continuity among all of God's prophets.

Conditional element in the prophetic message

The judgments foretold by the prophets were always to be understood as conditional, even when no conditions were stated. Jonah's ministry to Nineveh was an excellent example of this. He preached that in forty days Nineveh would be destroyed—yet it was not destroyed. How can this be explained? Jeremiah (3:22; 18:8; 26:2-6) and Ezekiel (18:21-22, 30-32; 33:10-15) both contain passages that reveal if there comes a message of judgment, but the cause of that judgment is removed, then the judgment also may be removed.

In other words, repentance may remove judgment. In this sense, the message of judgment was usually conditional, though Jeremiah (27:1-10) and Ezekiel (5:7-12) each came to a point where they said in relation to Judah it was too late—the judgment was inevitable and nothing could avert it, so the people should accept the judgment from the hand of God. It is safe to say that context nearly always will determine whether or not there was a conditional element to an announced judgment.

Prophetic influence on the southern kingdom

In 2 Chronicles 29 we read about a revival in the southern kingdom under Hezekiah. (It's interesting to note that there was no revival in the northern kingdom because its unbroken succession of godless kings demonstrated a continuous and progressive apostasy, without confession or restoration. The northern kingdom also had its prophets—but their message always went unheeded.)

Hezekiah, in the first year of his reign "opened the doors of the temple of the Lord and repaired them. He brought in the priests and Levites, assembled them in the square on the east side and said: 'Listen to me, Levites! Consecrate yourselves now and consecrate the temple of the Lord, the God of your fathers. Remove all defilement from the sanctuary. Our fathers were unfaithful; they did evil in the eyes of the Lord our God and forsook Him'" (2 Chron. 29:3-6).

The previous generations had forgotten God and had defiled His temple. Hezekiah restored the worship, reinstituted the priesthood, and sanctified the sanctuary. All of this was necessary because the temple worship had been totally neglected, with the result that Judah and Jerusalem were under God's wrath.

Therefore Hezekiah said, "Now I intend to make a covenant with the Lord, the God of Israel, so that His fierce anger will turn away from us. My sons, do not be negligent now, for the Lord has chosen you to stand before Him and serve Him, to minister before Him and to burn incense" (vv. 10-11).

So the Levites assembled themselves, were consecrated, and purified the temple of the Lord, as the king had ordered according to the word of the Lord (v. 15). Hezekiah had promised to make a covenant with the Lord God of Israel acknowledging that the only way discipline could be lifted was for the people to turn back to the Lord in accordance with the principles stated in Deuteronomy 30. And the first step in turning the people back to the Lord was to reinstitute the temple worship services.

Second Chronicles gives no indication of what prompted Hezekiah to do this. Jeremiah 26, however, provides a clue. The context records that some of the elders of the land stepped forward in defense of Jeremiah and said, "Micah of Moresheth prophesied in the days of Hezekiah king of Judah. He told all the people of Judah, 'This is what the Lord Almighty says: "Zion will be plowed like the field, Jerusalem will become a heap of rubble, the temple hill a mound overgrown with thickets." Did Hezekiah king of Judah or anyone else in Judah put him to death? Did not Hezekiah fear the Lord and seek His favor? And did not the Lord relent, so that He did not bring the disaster He pronounced against them?'" (Jer. 26:18-19)

Micah had announced judgment as divine discipline, but Hezekiah feared the Lord—and the Lord relented and did not bring the disaster He had pronounced. Hezekiah's repentance was demonstrated by cleansing the temple, an act of confession or acknowledgment of sin. This act of repentance rectified the wrong and, on that basis, Hezekiah could plead with the Lord to lift the discipline and spare Judah the same kind of judgment that had come on the northern kingdom.

In Hezekiah's case the king submitted to the prophet as his superior and did what he was told to do. He met the conditions of Deuteronomy 30 and, as a result, judgment was averted. This vividly illustrates the effect a prophet could have on the king and consequently on the nation. The point is that the prophet did much more than predict the future. The prophet was an instrument God used in the administration of His kingdom, an agent of God to preserve the people of the kingdom.

We find another illustration in 2 Kings 22, which is a record of the reign of Josiah. It was written of Josiah that he did what was right in the sight of the Lord, walked in the way of David his father, and did not turn aside to the right or to the left (v. 2). This summary statement doesn't tell us what caused Josiah to walk in the way of the Lord and do what was right, but we read on to find out about Josiah's discovery of the Law. The Law revealed what was right, and it was the Law by which God governed His theocratic people.

Josiah's reign began only two years after the death of King Manasseh, whose long and wicked reign certainly made Judah ripe for judgment. What made the difference with Josiah? It was certainly not his father, Amon, or his grandfather Manasseh. But as verses 8 and following of chapter 22 record, Hilkiah, the high priest, had found the Book of the Law in the temple. As Shapan, the king's secretary, read the book before the king, Josiah tore his clothes as a sign of mourning and confession. He then gave orders that the Lord be consulted as to how to avoid judgment. He said, "Go and inquire of the Lord for me and for the people and for all Judah about what is written in this book that has been found. Great is the Lord's anger that burns against us because our fathers have not obeyed the words of this book; they have not acted in accordance with all that is written there concerning us" (v. 13).

In obedience to the king, the prophetess Huldah was consulted. Her message was that God had intended to bring judgment, but "because your heart was responsive and you humbled yourself before the Lord when you heard what I have spoken against this place and its people" (v. 19), the Lord heard Josiah's cry of repentance and his eyes were not forced to witness the disaster in Judah that had come upon Israel.

Again, we see the effect of the Law on the king. The prophet was an advocate of the Law, and whether judgment fell or blessing was bestowed depended on the response of the people to the Law and the prophet's message. We often develop our concept of the theocracy from the standpoint of the king—but it is a mistake to eliminate the prophet. Each was authoritative in his own sphere. Thus, the prophet was God's messenger with God's message, appealing to God's Law to control the actions of the people. Obedience would bring blessing and disobedience would bring discipline. This was the prophetic office and the prophetic message.

Summary

Much of the message of the prophets was devoted to contemporary issues and contained messages to their own people. However, much was also devoted to the prophetic program. And it is in the prophetic aspect of the writing prophets that we find God's outline for the program concerning His kingdom.

In the pages of the prophets, we can readily find the message of the prophets concerning the King, the kingdom, the nature of the kingdom, and the program leading up to its initiation. Because this is true, our understanding of biblical prophecy and end time events should be basically built not on the New Testament, but rather on the Old Testament. Except for the church—which is revealed in the New Testament—everything else in God's prophetic program is revealed in the Old Testament.

Many people have problems with eschatology (the doctrine of "last things," or biblical prophecy) because they've never examined the teaching of the prophets as a systematic, unified whole, particularly in light of God's kingdom program. For that reason, we have provided in the appendix an outline of the eschatology of the Old Testament prophets. Although this book is not intended to be a primer on biblical prophecy alone, we strongly encourage the reader to take the time to examine the logical, systematic consistency of God's message through His prophets, and the way that message is continually moving toward literal, historical fulfillment.

17

The Kingdom in the Gospels: Introduction of the Promised Seed

Chronologically speaking, there is a 400-year gap between Malachi and Matthew. Logically and thematically, however, there is no gap at all.

The New Testament immediately takes up where the Old Testament prophets left off. In fact, technically the "New" Testament does not begin with Matthew, but with the Book of Acts. The Gospels demonstrate that God's program still continued with the nation Israel. Israel was still under the Law, and everything continued as it had during the prophetic period. The message was directed to the lost sheep of the house of Israel (Matt. 10:6) and excluded the Gentiles. The Law, in fact, was not abolished at the birth of Christ, but rather at His death; and the message of the Gospels concerns the fulfillment of all that the prophets predicted. Thus there is an unbroken continuity between the prophets and the Gospels.

Not a biography

A careful examination of the Gospel records demonstrates that we do not find in them a biography of Christ. Rather, we find three thematic interpretations of the facts, with each author presenting aspects concerning Christ which are in keeping with his theme.

It is commonly accepted that we can find three portraits of Christ in the "synoptic" Gospels (those written from the "same viewpoint"), each examining different aspects of His messianic office. In the

Book of Matthew, Christ is presented as the King. As Israel's King, the Messiah is related to the covenants and the promises of God.

Mark, on the other hand, presents Christ as the Servant—which should be understood in the Old Testament concept as the Servant of Jehovah. Thus we see Christ in His relationship to His Father as a Servant related to His Master.

In the Book of Luke, meanwhile, we see Christ presented in His humanity as the Son of Man. The Old Testament demonstrates that the Son of Man is a messianic title or concept (Dan. 7:13) by which Messiah will fulfill God's purpose for man as a man (Gen. 1:26-27).

Each Gospel author took historical incidents as they actually happened and interpreted them to emphasize one aspect of Messiah. In a study of a harmony of the life of Christ these different aspects are arranged historically and chronologically in order to see their progressive development. By combining these three and adding the Gospel of John, the historical events can be reconstructed.

And from these historical events we can trace the development of the kingdom.

The birth narratives

When we turn to the birth narratives of the New Testament we find frequent reference to four biblical covenants we have thus far discussed: the Abrahamic Covenant, the Palestinian Covenant, the Davidic Covenant; and the New Covenant. We will study each narrative further to see the importance they place on the covenant, as well as the relationship between the coming of Christ and the fulfillment of those covenants.

Matthew's account
Matthew opened his Gospel with the words, "The book of the genealogy of Jesus Christ, the son of David, the son of Abraham" (Matt. 1:1). It is particularly significant that although Matthew gave an extended geneology of Jesus Christ, he singled out David and Abraham for special mention in his introduction. The apparent reason for this is that two of the crucial covenants that determine God's program for the nation of Israel were made with David and Abraham. Matthew's special notation clearly indicates that Jesus Christ had come as the Son of David to rule over Abraham's descendants in the land that God promised them.

185

Another reference to the covenant program is found in Matthew 1:18-25, where an angel told Joseph about the coming birth of Christ. The angel said to Joseph concerning Mary, "She will give birth to a son; and you are to give Him the name Jesus, because He will save His people from their sins" (v. 21). The salvation promised through Mary's Son was a reference to Jeremiah 31:34, where God promised to provide a basis for total forgiveness of sin.

The chief priests and scribes who identified the birthplace of Christ for Herod (2:1-8) also made reference to the fulfillment of God's covenant program by quoting Micah's prophecy. "But you, Bethlehem, in the land of Judah, are by no means least among the rulers of Judah; for out of you will come a ruler, who will be the shepherd of My people Israel" (v. 6). Bethlehem was David's city, and from David's line would come the promised Davidic descendant who would rule over the nation Israel. Thus the chief priests inadvertently gave testimony to the fulfillment of the Davidic Covenant—which promised a king—and to the Abrahamic Covenant, which promised the perpetuity of Abraham's descendants until they are gathered into Messiah's kingdom.

Luke's account

The first reference to the covenants in Luke's account of the birth narrative is found in Luke 1:13-17. There we find that joyous news was brought to Zechariah: he and Elizabeth would have a son who would be given the name John. The angel who made the announcement then said, "He will be a joy and delight to you, and many will rejoice because of his birth, for he will be great in the sight of the Lord. He is never to take wine or other fermented drink, and he will be filled with the Holy Spirit even from birth. Many of the people of Israel will he bring back to the Lord their God. And he will go on before the Lord in the spirit and power of Elijah, to turn᾽ the hearts of the fathers to their children and the disobedient to the wisdom of the righteous—to make ready a people prepared for the Lord" (vv. 14-17).

The angel announced that John would be set apart to the Lord's service from infancy in a manner similar to one in the Old Testament who had taken a Nazarite vow. John's ministry was unique in that while he fulfilled the prophetic office, he would be filled with the Holy Spirit so that everything he said and did would be under the Spirit's control. The angel emphasized that John's ministry was to be a ministry of turning a disobedient people back to the Lord. His ministry was limited to the nation Israel, and he was to do in his generation what Elijah had done before.

Elijah had appeared in a time of national apostasy to warn the nation of imminent judgment unless the people confessed their sin and repented. Elijah's ministry was in keeping with Deuteronomy 30, which emphasized that such repentance, confession, and restoration was a prerequisite to blessing.

The angel announced that John was to have a ministry of turning a disobedient people back to the Lord their God in order to "make ready a people prepared for the Lord" (v. 17). In light of this, we can see that John's ministry was directly related to the promised blessings Israel would enjoy under the Abrahamic Covenant. As we have established, enjoyment of those blessings was conditioned on obedience. And since the nation was disobedient, John would call the people to confession and restoration so that the blessings of the Abrahamic Covenant might be theirs.

Another clear reference to God's covenants is found in the angel's announcement to Mary in Luke 1:26-38—"You will be with child and give birth to a son, and you are to give Him the name Jesus. He will be great and will be called the Son of the Most High. The Lord God will give Him the throne of His father David, and He will reign over the house of Jacob forever; His kingdom will never end" (vv. 31-33). As a result of the Holy Spirit's ministry, Mary would conceive a Son who, when born, would be given the name Jesus. The Greek word *Jesous* (Jesus) is the counterpart of the Hebrew word *Yhoshua* (Joshua). Joshua was the one who delivered Israel out of their wilderness experience and brought the nation into the land and life of blessing as had been promised through God's covenant with Abraham. Thus when the name Jesus was given to Mary's Son, it suggested the future fulfillment of the Abrahamic Covenant, through which Israel will enjoy blessings in the land God gave to Abraham's descendants.

Further, the angel's message contained a specific reference to the Davidic Covenant: "The Lord God will give Him the *throne* of His father David, and He will reign over the *house* of Jacob forever; His *kingdom* will never end" (vv. 32-33, italics added). The angel employed the three most significant words of the Davidic Covenant as it is found in 2 Samuel 7:16—*throne, house,* and *kingdom.* God could not have made it clearer that Mary's Son had come to

187

fulfill the covenants God had made with Abraham and with David.

Elizabeth's response to Mary's visit to their house (Luke 1:39-45) contains yet another reference to the covenants. "When Elizabeth heard Mary's greeting, the baby leaped in her womb, and Elizabeth was filled with the Holy Spirit. In a loud voice she exclaimed: 'Blessed are you among women, and blessed is the child you will bear! But why am I so favored, that the mother of my Lord should come to me?' " (vv. 41-43) The phrase *my Lord* is a Messianic phrase found in Psalm 110:1-2, where we read, "The Lord says to my Lord: 'Sit at My right hand until I make Your enemies a footstool for Your feet.' The Lord will extend Your mighty scepter from Zion; You will rule in the midst of Your enemies." In this passage the Father addressed the Son, whom He has appointed to rule, by the title "my Lord." When Elizabeth addressed Mary as "the mother of my Lord," she was referring to her as the mother of the one who, in keeping with the Davidic Covenant, has the God-given right to rule.

Mary's response to Elizabeth's salutation contained numerous references to God's covenant program (Luke 1:46-55). Mary acknowledged that God was her Saviour (v. 47) and that "the Mighty One has done great things for me" (v. 49). Among the "great things" God had done was to set in motion His plan to bring a king to rule over her people. Thus, "He has brought down rulers from their thrones" (v. 52).

Mary also equated the advent of her Son with God's promises to Abraham. "He has helped His servant Israel, remembering to be merciful to Abraham and His descendants forever" (vv. 54-55). The Abrahamic Covenant promised blessings not only to Israel but also to all the earth through Abraham's descendants. In keeping with that covenant, God was now sending one in Abraham's line to bring blessings to Israel.

Moreover, it had been promised that one of David's sons would triumph over Israel's enemies and rule in peace and righteousness (cf. Isa. 9:6-7; Micah 5:2-5). Based on this, Mary anticipated the rule of her Son in fulfillment of the Davidic Covenant, and she eagerly awaited the blessings God had promised to her ancestors.

The prophecy of Zechariah, given under inspiration of the Holy Spirit (Luke 1:67-79), likewise was filled with references to the biblical covenants. Zechariah prophesied that God had "redeemed His people" (v. 68). That redemption specifically refers to Israel being rescued "from the hand of our enemies" (v. 74). Notice, then, that the promised redemption will occur because God has remembered His covenant with David. According to Luke 1:69-70, He "has raised up a horn of salvation for us in the house of His servant David (as He said through His holy prophets of long ago)." God's deliverance is also in keeping with "the oath He swore to our father Abraham" (v. 73). Zechariah obviously was anticipating the fulfillment of both the Abrahamic and the Davidic Covenant promises.

But further, Zechariah was anticipating deliverance from sin. He said that this child would "give to His people the knowledge of salvation through the forgiveness of their sins, because of the tender mercy of our God, by which the rising sun will come to us from heaven" (vv. 77-78). This looks back to the New Covenant of Jeremiah 31:31-34, where God has promised that He would make provision for forgiveness of sins. That forgiveness would be offered to the nation by the one John would introduce. Thus Zechariah was fully conscious of God's covenant promises when he spoke of the blessings that would be introduced through the coming Messiah.

Christ's birth, of course, did not go unannounced, and once again there was a clear reference to the New Covenant. An angel was dispatched to meet shepherds near Bethlehem with a glorious message: "I bring you good news of great joy that will be for all the people. Today in the town of David a Saviour has been born to you; He is Christ the Lord" (Luke 2:10-11). The One who was born in Bethlehem was a Saviour, none other than Christ the Lord. According to the Old Testament, the Messiah was to have two principal responsibilities: to redeem and to reign. He was to be both Saviour and Sovereign. In his announcement to the shepherds, the angel referred to the first of those two great works when he presented Christ as "a Saviour" (v. 11), and then immediately referred to the second of those works when he described Christ as "the Lord" (v. 11). His work as both Saviour and Sovereign was based on the covenants made in 2 Samuel 7:16 and Jeremiah 31:34; therefore the angel bore testimony to the importance of those covenants in his announcement of the coming of Christ.

We read later that on the eighth day Jesus was circumcised (Luke 2:21) in obedience to the Abrahamic Covenant. The significance of this act simply cannot be understood apart from the Old Testament and God's covenant program (Gen. 17:9-14). Through circumcision, Jesus was identified with the Abrahamic Covenant people.

The words of Simeon at the presentation of Christ in the temple forty days after His birth also contain reference to the covenants (Luke 2:22-35). Simeon, controlled by the Holy Spirit, said, "Sovereign Lord, as You have promised, You now dismiss Your servant in peace. For my eyes have seen Your salvation, which You have prepared in the sight of all people, a light for revelation to the Gentiles and for glory to Your people Israel" (vv. 29-32). In praising God for "Your salvation," Simeon was referring to Isaiah 52:6-10 where the reign of the appointed king was announced (v. 7) and salvation or redemption was provided for Jerusalem (v. 9). In giving this messianic prediction, Isaiah anticipated the fulfillment of the Davidic Covenant in the reign of Christ. He also looked forward to the redemption of Israel, which was further amplified a century later in the New Covenant of Jeremiah 31.

So then when Simeon spoke of Jesus as "a light of revelation to the Gentiles," he was probably referring to Isaiah 42:6 where Isaiah said of Christ, "I will keep You and will make You to be a covenant for the people and a light for the Gentiles." Simeon's reference to the "glory to Your people Israel" could well look back to Isaiah 49:6-7 where we read, " 'It is too small a thing for You to be My servant to restore the tribes of Jacob and bring back those of Israel I have kept. I will also make You a light for the Gentiles, that You may bring My salvation to the ends of the earth.' This is what the Lord says—the Redeemer and Holy One of Israel—to Him who was despised and abhorred by the nation, to the servant of rulers: 'Kings will see You and rise up, princes will see and bow down, because of the Lord, who is faithful, the Holy One of Israel, who has chosen You.' "

In this passage God speaks to His Son, the Messiah, and promises Him a throne from which He will rule and before which the nations will bow. By quoting Isaiah's messianic prophecies, Simeon made direct reference to both Davidic Covenant and New Covenant promises, inferring that Jesus would redeem as well as reign.

It is not said of Anna that she spoke under the control of the Spirit, but she did make a prophetic statement when she spoke "about the child to all who were looking forward to the redemption of Jerusalem" (Luke 2:38). This verse shows us that there was in Jerusalem a small remnant who possessed the messianic hope. This remnant did not include the Pharisees or Sadducees as a whole, though certainly some in those groups were looking for the redemption of Jerusalem. This redemption would not be limited to a soteriological redemption, but would include all of Messiah's work for the people of Israel. He would not only provide salvation as the Lamb of God, but would also be the smiting stone (Dan. 2:44-45), subdue the nations to Himself, and bring peace to Israel.

Even the wise men came (Matt. 2:1-12) looking for a king. When they saw Jesus, first they fell down and worshiped Him. This was not only in recognition of His person, but more in recognition of His royal prerogatives and as a sign of submission to His royal authority. Second, they offered gifts. The gifts they gave were the same kinds of gifts Jacob sent with his sons to Egypt to give Pharaoh when they sought his favor (Gen. 43:11-12). Just as Jacob's gifts were a sign of submission to Pharaoh's authority so the wise men's gifts were intended for and befitting royalty. This shows a recognition of Messiah by men from Gentile nations, submission to Him as a king, and dependence on Him for favors. Ironically, the nation to whom Christ came would reject Him, as indicated by John 1:11 and Matthew 2:23 (in which the label "Nazarene" suggests rejection by the religious establishment).

Israel not disqualified

In summary, a careful examination of the birth narratives shows that they freely alluded to the four eternal, unconditional covenants God gave to His covenant people Israel: the Abrahamic Covenant, the Palestinian Covenant, the Davidic Covenant, and the New Covenant. Under the inspiration of the Holy Spirit, Matthew and Luke clearly saw Christ's coming as an essential part of God's program to establish the kingdom of the God of heaven here on earth through Israel, in fulfillment of His covenants and promises to that nation. The very fact that Messiah came to fulfill those covenants proves that Israel's disobedience had not disqualified them or nullified their place in the plan of God. As we read Israel's history in the Old Testament we are faced with a continual record of disobedience, lawlessness, and apostasy. Yet, the prophets who appeared in those generations of despair anticipated the fulfillment of the covenants and called the covenant people to confession and restoration so that the promised blessings could be theirs. If disobedience could have abrogated the covenants in any sense, Christ would never have come to fulfill them.

The role of John the Baptist

Before introducing us to the ministry of Jesus Christ, the synoptists (Matthew, Mark, Luke) introduced us to His forerunner, John the Baptist, and identified the place of his ministry. Matthew said John the Baptist came preaching in the "Desert of Judea" (Matt. 3:1). Luke told us that he went into "all the country around the Jordan" (Luke 3:3). As the son of a priest, John might have succeeded his father in a priestly ministry in the temple. However, God called John to a unique ministry that began outside Jerusalem—which was the religious center of the land—and outside the established religious system.

All three synoptists were careful to identify John with the prophetic program revealed in the Old Testament. All quoted Isaiah 40:3-5 in explaining the ministry of John. The reason for this is that in Isaiah 40 the prophet brought a comforting message to a distressed, oppressed people. The northern kingdom had already gone into captivity. The southern kingdom was threatened with a similar exile. No visible hope for the nation loomed on the horizon. Yet God sent His prophet with a promise that the Gentile rule would be terminated and the nation's warfare would cease. God would pardon all the nation's sins. Isaiah promised the coming of a Messiah who would bring redemption from sin and deliverance from Gentile aggressors.

Isaiah went on to prophesy that Messiah would be preceded by a forerunner who would make an announcement concerning His coming. The voice, the prophet said, would not be heard in the temple or in Jersualem, but outside the city in the desert. This is extremely significant, for when the temple was originally built God occupied the temple as His dwelling place (2 Chron. 5:13-14). Because of Israel's iniquity, however, God departed from the temple, a sign graphically portrayed in Ezekiel 10–11. Having removed Himself due to His people's sins, God judged the nation. This judgment included Nebuchadnezzar's invasion, the destruction of Jerusalem, and the deportation of the people. Therefore when God returned to His people, said Isaiah, He would speak to them outside Jerusalem and the temple.

God's plan unfolded exactly as foretold when John appeared as the messenger of Messiah. John did not come in priestly robes (which he by birth was eligible to wear), but rather in the attire of a prophet. Matthew recorded, "John's clothes were made of camel's hair, and he had a leather belt around his waist" (Matt. 3:4). John's camelhair garment was the equivalent of the sackcloth Old Testament prophets wore when they appeared in mourning with a message of judgment. John did not come with the splendid waistband of a priest (Ex. 28:8), but rather with a simple leather belt around his waist.

Neither was John's food that of a priest. The priests ate the flesh of temple sacrifices. But John lived by what the desert provided—locusts and wild honey. And even though John appeared in the role of a prophet, he was not introduced as such, but simply as John the Baptist.

We need to recognize at this point that the nation to which John came with his message was extremely familiar with the ritualistic use of water in baptism. The Greek word *baptizo* came from the root *bapto*, which literally means "to dip" or "to dye." It was a common word among those in the fuller's trade, where undressed cloth was prepared for use by first dipping it into bleach and then into dye. The emphasis of the word, however, was not on the procedure of dipping but rather on the *result* of the procedure. The word metaphorically meant *to change identity*, to change appearance, or even *to change relationships*.

To the Jewish mind, *baptizo* included the idea of *cleansing* as well as *consecration* to a new identity or relationship. As we know, water was used extensively in the Old Testament in connection with ceremonial cleansing. We find sprinkling referred to in Leviticus 14:7. It is stipulated in Leviticus 15:8 that an unclean person had to wash himself with water to remove his uncleanness before he could be restored to fellowship. In Leviticus 16:4 we learn that before the high priest could perform the functions of the Day of Atonement, he had to wash himself with water. This washing not only signified that the high priest had been cleansed from ceremonial defilement, but also that he was set apart to God to perform a specific office, or function, on behalf of the nation Israel.

The concept of setting apart, or taking on a new identity, is illustrated in the requirement that a proselyte to Judaism had to undergo a washing, called a baptism. By his baptism a proselyte signified that he was terminating his relationship to his old society, including his allegiance to his old gods, and was joining himself with the community of Israel and submitting himself to Israel's God.

In the Old Testament, water could be applied, according to Leviticus 14:7-8 and Numbers 19:18-19, by sprinkling it on what was unclean. According to Leviticus 11:32 and 2 Kings 5:14, what was unclean could be dipped in water. And according to 2 Kings 3:11, water could be poured over what was unclean. In the Old Testament, then, the most important thing was not the mode of the water's application, but rather what the water signified. Moving into New Testament times the Jews continued to place much emphasis on ceremonial cleansing (cf. Mark 7:4-8).

Although the Jews were familiar with baptism and John did baptize, there are several important reasons for concluding that he was not merely performing the Old Testament ritual of cleansing. Most obvious, the text does not tell us he was functioning as a priest, using water for cleansing as provided by the Law. Rather, it is specifically stated that John preached "a baptism of repentance" (Luke 3:3). Thus Scripture plainly distinguishes his baptism from a baptism for ceremonial cleansing. Further, four specific facts about John's baptism are recorded: (1) John's baptism was in view of the coming Messiah (Matt. 3:2-3). (2) It was in view of the people's spiritual uncleanness (Mark 1:5). (3) It was based on confession and repentance (1:4). And (4) it was with a view to receiving forgiveness of sins (1:4).

John's message was twofold. First he pointed to Jesus as "the Lamb of God, who takes away the sin of the world!" (John 1:29) Jesus, as a new Moses, would do what Moses did for a people in bondage: He would provide a basis for redemption through sacrifices as well as protection from judgment. This part of John's message was soteriological, or salvation-related.

The second part of John's message was eschatological, or prophecy-related. He said "The kingdom of heaven is near" (Matt. 3:2). These two parts of John's message *together* constituted "the Gospel of the kingdom," since that concept was firmly implanted in the minds of the people through the message of the prophets.

The Old Testament recognizes that God is sovereign in an eternal and universal kingdom (1 Chron. 29:12; Ps. 103:19; 145:13). Yet because of God's covenant with Abraham—and more particularly His covenant with David (2 Sam. 7:16)—the Jews expected God to send a Messiah into this world who would subdue all things to God's authority. The Jews looked for a literal kingdom here on earth over which the Messiah would rule from David's throne, with the result that the world would experience righteousness and peace. Certainly the prophets taught that God's eternal rule would be manifested on earth through the reign of Messiah (Isa. 9:6; Amos 9:11; Micah 5:2; Zech. 14:9). And while some Jews may have anticipated a political Messiah to deliver them from Roman bondage, John as an Old Testament prophet proclaimed the same kingdom as the prophets.

John announced a literal kingdom on the earth under the personal rule of God's covenanted Messiah. The establishment of this kingdom would fulfill the covenant God made with David, which promised that one of David's sons would sit on David's throne and rule over David's house. John said this kingdom was near. Such a glorious promise was an impetus to bring the nation to repentance, and John's announcement generated widespread interest. Mark recorded, "The whole Judean countryside and all the people of Jerusalem went out to him" (Mark 1:5). And many of those who went willingly submitted to John's baptism.

Same old message: "Repent"

Not surprisingly, the Bible informs us that John's preaching began with the word *repent* (Matt. 3:1), which brings an important Old Testament truth to us. In Deuteronomy 28 God had clearly revealed the principle with which He would deal with His covenant people. Obedience would bring blessing; disobedience would bring discipline. The culminating discipline for continued disobedience would be bondage to the Gentiles. In Deuteronomy 30 God revealed that the discipline could not and would not be lifted until the nation turned back to God from their sin and obeyed His commands (v. 2).

Repentance, then, was just such a return to God. Israel's obedience to God's Word would serve as the catalyst for His faithfulness. Their obedience would cause God to turn back to them in blessing, regather them from the nations where they had been scattered, and restore them to their land. And God would circumcise their hearts (i.e, remove impurity from them).

This principle appeared throughout the Old Testament. Prophet after prophet ministered to the nation, forewarning it of judgment and exhorting the people to turn back to God to prevent the coming judgment. Even so, judgment fell, with the result that both the northern and southern kingdoms were carried off into captivity.

Nevertheless, God promised that if the people subsequently returned to Him He would send the Messiah to bless them.

In calling the nation to repentance, then, John was functioning as an Old Testament prophet. His ministry was in keeping with the principle of Deuteronomy 28 and 30. Before Messiah's blessings could come, the people would have to turn from their sin to God. They would have to seek His forgiveness. God had said to Solomon, "If My people, who are called by My name, will humble themselves and pray and seek My face and turn from their wicked ways, then will I hear from heaven and will forgive their sin and will heal their land" (2 Chron. 7:14). As God's spokesman, John likewise required changed lives when he called on the people to repent. He asked them to do more than confess their sins—He asked them to forsake their sin and turn in faith to God and walk before Him in obedience.

We see, therefore, that John was not the one who would forgive sin. Rather, he was identifying with and introducing the One who would forgive sin. And there was a genuine note of urgency in John's preaching as well as an explanation why they should repent. He announced, "The kingdom of heaven is near" (Matt. 3:2). "Near" meant that the only thing preventing the institution of the kingdom announced by John was the repentance of the nation.

Thus John gathered together around his message a company who believed his word and who anticipated the coming of the Messiah. The Messiah would provide them with the forgiveness of sin and institute a kingdom of peace and righteousness in which they would enjoy the benefits of His reign.

Two responses

In response to John's preaching, the crowd seemed to be divided into two parts. On the one hand were the religious leaders of the day. The Pharisees and Sadducees arrived where John was baptizing (Matt. 3:7), though these religious leaders in their self-righteousness considered themselves already acceptable to God. They denied having sin that needed to be confessed or unrighteousness that needed to be forgiven. By virtue of their physical birth, they saw themselves as Abraham's children, acceptable to God, and already members of His kingdom.

John easily recognized their rejection of his message and called them a "brood of vipers" (v.7). According to the Law, a viper (poisonous snake) was unclean and unacceptable to God and would defile anything it touched. By calling them snakes, John said they were unclean and that they spread defilement to everyone they came in contact with. He repudiated their teaching that one's physical relationship to Abraham was a basis for entrance into the kingdom, reminding them that God could give life to stones to make them the children of Abraham if He so desired. In this way John stressed the need for repentance as a precondition to the reception of the covenanted blessings.

John demanded repentance of the religious leaders. Asking them to demonstrate the genuineness of their repentance, he exhorted them to "produce fruit in keeping with repentance" (v. 8). Again we see a note of urgency in John's message: When he called for repentance, he told them that judgment was at hand. "The ax is already at the root of the trees, and every tree that does not produce good fruit will be cut down and thrown into the fire" (v. 10). This was entirely consistent with the Old Testament revelation that the Messiah would come as a Judge and remove sinners from His kingdom. In Psalm 24:3 David asked rhetorically, "Who may ascend the hill of the Lord? Who may stand in His holy place?" David meant, "Who will be accepted in the Messiah's kingdom when He comes?" The answer given is: "He who has clean hands and a pure heart, who does not lift up his soul to an idol or swear by what is false" (v. 4).

Based, then, on the judgment that would be meted out to the nation at the advent of Messiah, John exhorted the religious leaders to escape this judgment by exhibiting lives that resulted from a true repentance.

Now we note a second group that was affected by John's ministry. These were the outcasts. They were as acceptable to John as the religious leaders who considered themselves to be sons of the kingdom. Unlike the religious leaders, however, this group did not resist God's message. Rather, they asked, "What should we do then?" (Luke 3:10) John required the same from these as he had from the religious leaders; that is, the fruit or evidences of a genuine repentance. Using Isaiah 58:6-7 as an example of true repentance that could bring one into a right relationship with God, John made demands of these individuals in the crowd.

According to Luke 3:11, a concern for the needy was an evidence of genuine repentance. In verses 12-13 John indicated that the tax collectors could prove the genuineness of their repentance by not collecting more in taxes than the Romans required. Soldiers could exhibit genuine repentance by not misusing their authority (v. 14). They should not be violent or accuse anyone wrongfully. They should be content with their pay. In short, repentance was the requirement for acceptance into Messiah's kingdom, whether one was a self-righteous religious leader or an outcast within the Jewish community.

Hope, promise, and a sign

John's message not only included a scathing denunciation of sin and urgent exhortations to repentance, but it also offered hope and promise. The synoptists record for us a summary of the promise John gave to his hearers: "the people were waiting expectantly" (Luke 3:15). They knew John's message was messianic. Therefore a question arose in their minds concerning whether or not John himself could be the Messiah. From the biblical record, however, we know that John pointed men from himself to the Lord Jesus Christ. In fact, John presented himself as Messiah's servant. More accurately, he considered himself to be unworthy even to be a servant! He said he was unworthy even to stoop down and untie the straps of the sandals belonging to the One he came to introduce (Mark 1:7).

John himself was widely recognized because of his baptism. Baptism was so associated with John's ministry that it became his identifying sign, ultimately causing him to be known as John the Baptist. This sign was purely external.

Israel in the course of her history had several peculiar identifying signs given to her by God. Circumcision was the external sign signifying that a person was rightly related to Abraham and to his covenant. Sabbath observance was the sign that one was rightly related to Moses and his Law. Now the sign that one was rightly related to John and his message was submission to the external rite of water baptism.

John next made it clear that when Messiah came, He would have a new sign by which to identify God's people. It had, in fact, been promised in Joel 2:28 and Ezekiel 36:25-27 that God would give His Holy Spirit as a gift to all those in Messiah's kingdom. Therefore John promised that when Messiah came, He would "baptize you with the Holy Spirit" (Luke 3:16). The One who would give the

Spirit as an identifying sign of relationship would be the true Messiah—not the one who gave the external preparatory sign. Messiah's baptism would not be external, but internal. Any external sign could be duplicated by men, but the work which Messiah would do in giving the Holy Spirit to believers could not. Such a baptism would identify the true Messiah and also be a true identification of those who belong to Him.

John gave a second part of the baptizing work of the Messiah when he said, "He will baptize you . . . with fire" (v. 16). Fire was associated with judgment, just as was the winnowing fork of Matthew 3:12. When Messiah comes to rule, John was saying, He will remove all that is worthless, useless, and lifeless; He will accept into His kingdom only that which has life—the life men have received from Him. It is significant that in denying that he was the Messiah and in introducing the true Messiah, John appealed to the Old Testament Scriptures. The concept of Messiah was so well established in the Judaism of John's day that it was scarcely necessary for John to describe Him.

The baptism of Jesus

When Jesus Himself came to John for baptism, John immediately tried to deter Him. Remember that John from his birth had been filled, or controlled, by the Holy Spirit (Luke 1:15). Because of the Spirit's ministry, John recognized the Person who was presenting Himself for baptism. Baptism by John was a sign of confession and repentance with a view to forgiveness of sin, but Jesus Christ was sinless; He had no need for repentance or confession. The nature of John's baptism eliminated Jesus as an eligible candidate.

At John's baptism of Jesus, the one baptizing was the same, but the baptism was not the same. The use of water was the same, but the significance was not identical. The baptism of Jesus by John was a special, unique, one-of-a-kind baptism. It was distinct both from John's baptism and from Christian baptism, just as John's baptism was distinct from a believer's baptism today (cf. Acts 19:3-5).

John knew that Jesus did not need his baptism. John also recognized that he was unworthy to do the baptizing. Indeed, John saw that he himself needed the baptism the prophets had promised Messiah would give when He came. John had spoken of this baptism in Luke 3:16, and confessed that he was awaiting the baptism by the Holy Spirit that Messiah will provide in fulfillment of the prophecies of Joel and Ezekiel.

Notice that Jesus did not deny John's statement that He was sinless and did not need John's baptism. But in response to John's reluctant attitude, Jesus said, "Let it be so now; it is proper for us to do this" (Matt. 3:15). If Jesus was the Messiah, then John who was anticipating Messiah's coming was obligated to submit to His authority. It was this submission in recognition of His identity as Messiah that Jesus required of John. In obedience to the entreaty of Jesus, John baptized Him. But why, then, was Jesus baptized by John?

We have already noted that it was not because Jesus had sin to confess for which He needed forgiveness. If Jesus had needed John's baptism, this would have signified He was awaiting the coming of the Saviour who would forgive sin instead of being the Saviour Himself. Some have thought Jesus was baptized by John to be inducted into His priestly office. They have pointed out that Jesus was approximately thirty years of age at this time, the age when Old Testament priests were inducted into office in a ritual that included a ceremonial washing with water. But while it is true Jesus was set apart by His Father to be a Priest, He was not to be a priest after the order of Aaron—instead, He was to be a Priest after the order of Melchizedek (Ps. 110:4). From the time the Levitical law was instituted, God limited the priesthood to members of the tribe of Levi and the family of Aaron. Since Jesus Christ was not of the right tribe or family, He was ineligible to serve as a Levitical priest. Therefore there would have been no point in trying to induct Him into an office for which He was not eligible. Jesus Christ's appointment to be a priest after the order of Melchizedek awaited His resurrection. Only then could He be inducted into the priestly office by His Father.

Scripture offers several reasons for the baptism of Christ. The *first* reason, according to Matthew's Gospel, was "to fulfill all righteousness" (Matt. 3:15). The Law said a priest was consecrated to office with the washing of water (Lev. 16:4); thus the Law demanded that one entering into an office should go through a ritual of cleansing. Jesus Christ was inducted into the office of Messiah, not that of priest. But in order to fulfill the demands of the Law, Christ was baptized, signifying that He was consecrated to God and acceptable to Him for service.

A *second* reason for Christ's baptism is given in John 1:33-34: "I would not have known Him, except that the One who sent me to baptize with water told me, 'The Man on whom you see the Spirit come down and remain is He who will baptize with the Holy Spirit.' " John recognized Jesus as the Messiah when He presented Himself for baptism, but John was not permitted to reveal to Israel what he by the Spirit understood. It was only after the Spirit descended that John could make a public announcement that the One whom he had promised had now arrived and had begun His ministry. Christ's baptism, then, released John to make a public announcement concerning the coming of Messiah.

Third, the baptism of Jesus was performed that He might identify Himself with the believing remnant in Israel. John's ministry had brought men to faith in his word and in the promise of God. This believing remnant was bound together by the sign of John's baptism. When Jesus Christ came, He came not to identify Himself with the Pharisees, the Sadducees, the Herodians, or the Zealots, but rather to identify Himself with that believing remnant who were expecting the fulfillment of God's promises.

Fourth, Jesus was baptized to identify Himself with sinners. Sinners were coming to John to confess their sin, to confess their need of a Saviour, and to give an outward sign of their faith that the Saviour would come and redeem them from sin. Jesus Christ came to identify Himself with sinners so that through that identification He might become their substitute. This was Paul's point in 2 Corinthians 5:21: "God made Him who had no sin to be sin for us, so that in Him we might become the righteousness of God." Just as it was necessary for Israel to be identified with the scapegoat and the scapegoat to be identified with Israel through the laying on of hands, so Jesus Christ identified Himself with sinners so that they might be identified with Him when He gave Himself as a substitute for their sins.

Fifth, at His baptism Jesus Christ was anointed by the Holy Spirit of God to fulfill the functions of the messianic office. Luke stated, "God anointed Jesus of Nazareth with the Holy Spirit and power" (Acts 10:38). This anointing for His messianic work took place at Jesus' baptism. Jesus was praying at the time of His baptism. And while the substance of this prayer is not given, it quite probably was a prayer in which Jesus separated Himself to the Father's will and work which He—as Messiah—was to accomplish.

The voice of the Father

At this time God confirmed to John and others who witnessed this baptism that Jesus was precisely who John had introduced Him to be—the Messiah, the Saviour, the King. "The Holy Spirit descended on Him in bodily form like a dove" (Luke 3:22). All present could see this visible sign, and in addition there was an audible sign—a voice from heaven said, "You are My Son, whom I love; with You I am well pleased" (v. 22; cf. Matt. 3:17).

Summary

At His baptism Jesus the Son was officially recognized by God the Father as Israel's King. Jesus was anointed by the Spirit for the work that He had come to perform. The Father bore witness of the relationship between the Son and Himself, saying, "You are My Son, whom I love." There was a witness of the Father as to the life of the Son: "With You I am well pleased."

In the prayer we see a relationship of Christ to the Father: Christ was dedicating Himself to the Father's will and work. We see a relationship of Christ to the Holy Spirit: The Spirit descended on Him to empower Him in the work He was to do. John had prepared the people for this momentous event. The Father had confirmed the appointment of the Son to the messianic work. Now the Son was officially presented by the designated forerunner to the nation Israel with God's full approval of His person and work.

18

The Kingdom Offered—
and Rejected

Kingdoms in conflict

Following His baptism, Jesus was led by the Spirit into the wilderness to be tested by Satan (Matt. 4:1-11). This marked only the beginning of the conflict between the prince of the kingdom of darkness and the One appointed as King in the kingdom of the God of heaven here on earth. Throughout Christ's earthly life, Satan would repeatedly attempt to harm the Messiah, beginning in Nazareth (Luke 4:29). Very frequently, following visible proof of the authority of Jesus, an attempt was made on His life (John 5:18; 7:1, 25; 8:37; 11:47-51). By stone and by storm, Satan carried on his relentless warfare in order to prevent Christ from coming to His appointed throne in the kingdom He had come to establish.

The entire life and ministry of Christ must be understood in the light of the conflict between the kingdom of Satan and the kingdom of the God of heaven on earth. It is quite significant that many of Christ's miracles were performed in the demonic realm, proving His authority over Satan. It was necessary for Christ to demonstrate that His power as King exceeded that of Satan's whose rule over the earthly realm began at the Fall.

The question of the multitudes

It was after the temptation—by which His moral right to rule and His authority over Satan were demonstrated—and after the end of

John's ministry (Matt. 4:12) that Jesus began His public ministry. His first recorded words duplicated John's message: "Repent for the kingdom of heaven is near" (v. 17). Jesus was officially presenting Himself as the covenanted Davidic king and was offering the covenanted kingdom to the covenanted people. The only condition was their repentance in keeping with 2 Chronicles 7:14. Because all the prophesied prerequisites had been fulfilled, this was a *genuine* offer of the kingdom to the covenant people.

To authenticate His identity as well as His offer of the covenanted kingdom to Israel, "Jesus went throughout Galilee, teaching in their synagogues, preaching the good news of the kingdom, and healing every disease and sickness among the people" (Matt. 4:23). As a result, great multitudes of people from Galilee, from Decapolis, from Jerusalem, from Judea, and from beyond the Jordan followed Him (v. 25). Those who followed were those who heard John's message, were convinced of the need of righteousness, were awaiting the establishment of Messiah's kingdom, and were willing to be taught by Jesus. By responding in this way, these would initially have been called Jesus' "disciples."

This multitude came to Jesus to learn from the King Himself the conditions upon which they would be admitted to His kingdom. The Old Testament had made it very clear that only the righteous would be accepted into Messiah's kingdom. The Prophet Zechariah had shown that apart from confession of sin and the reception of cleansing for sin there could be no entrance into Messiah's kingdom (Zech. 12–13). So too had the psalmist (Ps. 24:3-4). In Ezekiel 36:26-27, God had promised that He would provide a new heart and a new spirit and would cause the people to walk in His statutes. Unless they were saved from their uncleanness, they could not share the glory of Messiah's kingdom.

Righteousness, then, was a prerequisite to entrance into the kingdom. Unfortunately, the multitudes knew nothing of righteousness except as it was defined by the Pharisees. According to the teaching of the Pharisees, observing the traditions of men (as they had established them) would make all of Abraham's physical descendants eligible for entrance into Messiah's kingdom. So the question on the collective mind of the multitude was whether the righteousness of the Pharisees was sufficient for entrance into the kingdom. Christ addressed this important question as He gathered the multitudes to Him and opened His mouth to teach them.

The required righteousness

The Lord on this occasion did what He so frequently did when discussing the question of righteousness. He turned to the Law. In the Sermon on the Mount, Jesus used the Law *lawfully* to reveal the holiness of God as well as the demands the holiness of God makes on those who desire to walk in fellowship with Him. Christ discussed first the subjects of the kingdom (Matt. 5:1-16), describing their character (vv. 1-12) and their influence (vv. 13-16).

The major portion of the Sermon on the Mount showed the King's relationship to the Mosaic Law (5:17–7:6). In this portion Christ revealed Himself as the One who perfectly fulfills the Law (5:17-20), then proceeded (5:21-48) to reject the Pharisees' traditional interpretation of the Law concerning murder (vv. 21-26), adultery (vv. 27-30), divorce (vv. 31-32), oaths (vv. 33-37), retaliation (vv. 38-42), and love (vv. 43-48). He rejected their tradition—not because they didn't know the Law, which was accurately quoted—but because it was based on their misinterpretation of the Law. They taught that God was concerned only with external actions, not with internal attitudes.

Christ next rejected the Pharisees' practice of the Law (6:1–7:6). He rejected their practice of alms giving (6:1-4), of prayer (vv. 5-15), and of fasting (vv. 16-18). He rejected their attitude toward wealth (vv. 19-24), their practice of faith (vv. 25-34), and their practice of judging (7:1-6). Jesus then concluded the sermon by giving instruction to those who desired entrance into the kingdom (7:7-27). He taught them concerning prayer (vv. 7-11) and true righteousness (v. 12). He showed them the way of access into the kingdom through faith in His words (vv. 13-14). He warned them against the false teachers who sought to lead them astray (vv. 15-23) and offered them a true foundation upon which to build (vv. 24-27).

Thus the Lord, in rejecting both the Pharisaic interpretation of the Law and the Pharisaic practice of the Law, brought the multitude to the conclusion "that unless your righteousness surpasses that of the Pharisees and the teachers of the Law, you will certainly not enter the kingdom of heaven" (5:20). He closed by offering Himself as the narrow way and as the solid foundation through whom they could come into the kingdom and upon which they could stand. The sermon was designed to lead this multitude away from a false concept of righteousness to a true concept of righteousness; from a false hope of entrance into the kingdom to a sure foundation for entrance into Messiah's kingdom.

While we recognize that the Sermon on the Mount in its historical setting was Christ's instruction to that generation to which He was offering Himself as Saviour and Sovereign, we realize that it has a present-day application. The holiness of God does not change from age to age. The demands of God's holiness do not alter from day to day. When the Sermon on the Mount is viewed as revealing the holiness of God, it becomes a guide as to demands that God's holiness makes on believers of all generations.

In no sense is the sermon a means of attaining righteousness; instead, it is a revelation of the righteousness of God and reflects the demands God's holiness makes on those who would walk in fellowship with Him and enjoy the benefits of the kingdom He is offering.

The purpose of miracles

We cannot ignore the fact that Jesus used miracles to authenticate both His identity and His message, and that even these miracles have a logical and reasonable place in the outworking of God's covenant program. Paul noted that the faith of the Israelites was always so weak they would not or could not believe unless what was told them was confirmed by a sign. In the Old Testament God frequently used signs in Israel's history to confirm the messenger as His messenger and the message as God's message.

Signs first occurred in the time of Moses. God set Moses apart as a redeemer and sent him to enslaved Israel with the joyful news of redemption. Because Israel would not believe the good news, God enabled Moses to perform miracles to authenticate himself as God's messenger and to validate his message as God's message (Ex. 4:1-9, 30). Moses was sent to Pharaoh with God's command to release His covenant people. Moses performed miracles before Pharaoh to convince him that he was God's messenger with God's message (3:20; 7:10-13). The plagues were both miracles and judgments designed to accomplish the redemption God had promised His covenant people.

Miracles did not occur again in Israel's history until the days of Elijah and Elisha. These were sent with a message that judgment was forthcoming if there was no repentance; and Elijah was confirmed as God's messenger with God's message by the miracles he performed (1 Kings 17:17-24). Similarly, Elisha was authenticated by his miracles (2 Kings 2:14-15).

Notably, miracles did not occur again until the time of the ministry of Christ. All that Jesus did was done to authenticate Himself as God's messenger, and to authenticate His offer of the kingdom (as well as Himself as the promised Messiah) as God's message to the people (John 8:28; 14:10). The miracles were not performed to attract attention, to create interest, or to draw a crowd (although they did all those things). They were performed first of all to authenticate His person. Jesus claimed to be the Son of God, and His miracles gave proof to that claim. In addition they proved the genuineness of His offer of Himself as Israel's Messiah/King and of His offer of the covenanted kingdom.

Further, Christ's miracles revealed the realms of authority committed to the Son as Messiah. In stilling storms He showed His authority over the earth. In healing the sick He showed His ability to remove the results of the curse. In raising the dead He showed He was the Author and Giver of life. In forgiving sin He demonstrated that he could deal with that which separated men from God.

Each miracle in the physical realm was a revelation of what Christ had come to do in the spiritual realm. In healing the blind He revealed he had come to remove spiritual blindness. In healing the lame he showed He had come to enable those who were incapable of walking to please God to walk so as to please Him. In raising the dead he affirmed that He had come to give eternal life to those who trusted Him.

Finally, the miracles reveal the conditions that will prevail in His kingdom when He reigns. It will be a kingdom in which there is no sickness, no hunger, no sin, no death. All creation will be under His control. These same conditions were predicted by the prophets in their descriptions of the messianic kingdom.

In brief, Christ did not ask the nation to accept Him on His Word alone, but authenticated that word by a multitude of signs. The nation was responsible then to make a response to that authenticated offer.

The spread of the good news

The nation of Israel was blanketed with the good news that God was faithful to His covenants and had sent David's Son, the Messiah, to institute the promised kingdom. At the inception of His ministry, "Jesus went into Galilee, proclaiming the good news of God. 'The time has come,' He said. 'The kingdom of God is near. Repent and believe the good news!'" (Mark 1:14-15)

Through the course of His ministry "Jesus went through all the towns and villages, teaching in their synagogues, preaching the good news of the kingdom and healing every disease and sickness" (Matt. 9:35). This was a continuing ministry of the message. Not only Israel but people in all the territories bordering the land heard the good news of the kingdom, and they likewise had that message authenticated by the miracles Christ performed.

This ministry of Jesus was supplemented by the ministry of the Twelve (9:35–11:1) who were commissioned to go to "the lost sheep of Israel" (10:6) to proclaim that "the kingdom of heaven is near" (v. 7) and to authenticate their message with the same miracles Jesus had been using to authenticate Himself.

Later the ministry and the message were expanded further through the ministry of the seventy who were sent to proclaim, "The kingdom of God is near you" (Luke 10:9). Their message likewise was authenticated by the miracles they were given power to perform. It is highly unlikely, therefore, that any either in the land of Israel or in the bordering countries did not hear the good news that the promised Messiah—He who was to be Saviour and Sovereign—had come, and that the covenanted kingdom was being offered. Its benefits were available, conditioned only on the repentance of the nation of Israel as a nation.

Response of the nation

This widespread knowledge placed a responsibility on the nation to weigh the evidence and to make a decision about Jesus and His offer of His kingdom. The invitation of Messiah, therefore, was extremely significant when He proclaimed, "Come to Me, all you who are weary and burdened, and I will give you rest. Take My yoke upon you and learn from Me, for I am gentle and humble in heart, and you will find rest for your souls. For My yoke is easy and My burden is light" (Matt. 11:28-30).

The rejection of John, his message, and his call to repentance (11:2-19) anticipated the nation's response to Jesus. From the initial rejection of His presentation of Himself as the promised Messiah while in the synagogue in Nazareth (Luke 4:16-30), throughout the course of His life, Israel stubbornly refused His offer of Himself as King in spite of all the evidence He presented (Matt. 13:54-58; John 7:12).

The decision of Israel's leaders—the duly appointed representatives of the entire nation—came to a climax in an incident recorded in Matthew 12:22-30.

On this occasion Jesus was confronted by a demon-possessed man who was both blind and dumb (v. 22). Christ delivered the man from Satan's bondage, removing the blindness and dumbness that had afflicted him. Besides the obvious benefit to the man individually, Christ's miracle was a very clear validation that He could do what He offered to do. He could lift the burden of Pharisaism from those in bondage if they would take His yoke upon them. He could fulfill His promise to give rest to their souls.

This miracle, however, caused the multitude to be filled with consternation. Their question, "Could this be the Son of David?" (v. 23), actually expected a negative answer. We could state it, "This couldn't be the Son of David, could it?" The question arose not because of insufficient evidence, but rather because the leaders had already indicated their rejection of Christ. Having been taught that they were sheep who should follow the shepherds, the people at large could not conceive of accepting Christ apart from the approval of the leaders. Therefore, a great conflict stirred in their minds over the evidence that Christ presented and the leaders' response to that evidence. The people professed a willingness to accept Christ if the leaders would also approve, but they felt they must reject Him since the leaders disapproved.

Thus the Pharisees quickly presented their explanation of the miracle that had so convinced the multitude, saying, "It is only by Beelzebub, the prince of demons, that this fellow drives out demons" (v. 24). The Pharisees did not attempt to deny that Jesus had performed a miracle. But the Pharisees had an alternate explanation for what appeared to be a miracle performed by the power of God.

In an unthinkable mockery of God's perfect kingdom program, the religious leaders attributed the works of God's promised King to the ruler of the false kingdom of darkness, Satan. It was an explanation that not only revealed the religious leaders' unrepentant, darkened hearts, but one that also ultimately sealed the fate of that generation of Israel.

Three proofs

Because the destiny of the nation hinged on its response to His person, Christ offered three proofs to show that the Pharisees' explanation was false. The first proof was that division leads to destruction and that unity is necessary for preservation. If He received power *from* Satan and used that power *against* Satan, then Satan's kingdom ultimately must fall (vv. 25-26). Satan would not confer authority to be used for his own destruction.

The second reason recognized the existence of exorcists in the nation of Israel. Some in Israel could cast out demons, and Israel deemed them to be God's gifts to the nation. Even the Pharisees acknowledged this manifestation of God's power and thanked God for the gift of the exorcists. Christ's argument was that since the Pharisees recognized the ability to drive out demons as coming from God, they should not charge Him with being demon-possessed when He drove out demons (v. 27). The implication of Christ's words was that if He cast out demons by Satan's power, He could not be offering the prophesied kingdom of God to them. "But," He said, "if I drive out demons by the Spirit of God, then the kingdom of God has come upon you" (v. 28). Since Christ did cast out demons by God's power, it must be concluded that His offer of the kingdom was genuine and He was its genuine King.

The third refutation reminded them that before a robber can enter a guarded citadel, the robber must have sufficient power to subdue the guard (v. 29). The inference was that if Christ could enter Satan's stronghold and deliver people from his control as He had just done, then it is evident that He is stronger than Satan. Satan could not give Christ a power greater than what he himself possessed.

With these three proofs, then, Christ sought to show the multitudes that the Pharisees' explanation of this miracle was false.

Blasphemy against the Holy Spirit

Christ then called on the multitude for a decision (Matt. 12:30). He warned them of the dire judgment that would come on that generation of Israel if they accepted the explanation of the Pharisees and rejected Him. He spoke here of blasphemy against the Holy Spirit as a sin for which there could be no forgiveness. Forgiveness of this sin could not occur in this age—that is, the age in which the king-dom was being offered—nor in the age to come—that is, the age in which all their messianic hopes would be realized.

Often the question has arisen: What is the blasphemy against the Spirit for which there is no forgiveness? Christ had made it very clear that entrance into the kingdom He was offering depended on faith in both His person as well as His word. Previously He had encouraged His hearers to hear His words and accept them (7:24, 26). However, if the nation rejected Jesus' testimony concerning Himself, they still might come to faith in His word through the word of His Father, who authenticated the person of Christ (John 14:10). Christ's works were the Father's works, and these works supported the Father's word given at Christ's baptism that the Fa-ther was well pleased with the life of His Son.

If, however, one rejected the word of Christ *and* the word of the Father, he might *still* be brought to faith in the person of Christ by the witness of the Holy Spirit. *The miracles were the Spirit's witness to Christ.* The Spirit bore the final witness to both the person and word of Christ—and if one rejected this final witness, there was no further witness God had to offer. While rejecting the word of Christ was sin, a person could be led to a confession of that sin and to acknowledge the truth by the witness of the Father. Rejecting the witness of the Father was a sin; yet one could be led to faith in Christ by the witness of the Spirit. If one rejected the final witness, however, there was no further witness to bring him to Christ. Hence there could be no forgiveness for the sin of attributing the work of Christ to the devil (exactly as the Pharisees had just done) when, in truth, the work had been performed by the Spirit.

It is evident that this sin of blasphemy against the Holy Spirit could only be committed while Christ was personally present on earth. The sin could only be committed when the nation was being given evidence concerning the person of Christ through the mir-acles which He performed by the power of the Holy Spirit. Those essential circumstances do not exist today; consequently, *this same sin simply cannot be committed today.*

Rejection would bring judgment

Christ was gravely warning that generation in Israel that if they rejected the Father's testimony and the Spirit's testimony to His person and His work, no further evidence would be given. Their sins would stand unforgiven and result in temporal judgment on that generation. That judgment ultimately fell in A.D. 70 when Jerusalem was destroyed by Roman forces under the command of Titus.

It is important to recognize that this sin of rejecting the covenanted Davidic king was not viewed as the sin of an individual, but rather as the sin of the nation. It was a sin that was committed by that generation of Israel through its religious leaders, thus bringing the whole generation under divine judgment. Even this rejection did not nullify God's covenant promises to Israel or abrogate the future fulfillment of those biblical covenants—but it did condemn that generation of the nation, as a nation, to a dreadful temporal judgment. The nation had rejected the King, so the King rejected that generation of the nation.

Christ demanded of His hearers what John demanded when he said, "Produce fruit in keeping with repentance" (Matt. 3:8). A tree's fruit reveals the tree's true nature. The Pharisees who confronted Christ claimed to be righteous. Jesus, therefore, demanded that they show their righteousness by producing good fruit. He warned them that "men will have to give account on the day of judgment for every careless word they have spoken" (12:36). The "careless word" of which Jesus spoke was not any idle jest, but rather referred to their words about the person of Christ. If the multitude who heard the Pharisaic explanation repeated that explanation, they would come under divine judgment. Response to the person of Christ would determine their destiny.

This incident, then, marked the great turning point in Christ's ministry and message. From this point to the Cross, the nation would be viewed in the Gospels as having rejected Christ as Messiah. And the unofficial rejection by the leaders would become official when finalized at the Cross. The Pharisees, the priests, and teachers of the Law knew full well that Jesus was claiming to be the heaven-sent Messiah. They were familiar with the multitude of miracles He had already performed to authenticate His identity. Even so, they came to challenge Him and to request a sign that would prove to them He was what He claimed to be (12:38-45). Christ explained the reason for their request. It did not arise from faith, but from unbelief. They had refused to believe His words and His signs, and this indicated that they were evil. They were "a wicked and adulterous generation" (v. 39).

Christ then declared that He had no sign—other than that of Jonah—to give to the nation to prove that He was the One He claimed to be. As Jonah was brought from the place of death so He would be resurrected from the dead. This resurrection would be the climactic proof of His person and the validation of His offer of the Davidic kingdom. Interestingly, by quoting the much maligned Prophet Jonah, Jesus put His undeniable stamp of authenticity on what is recorded in that Old Testament book.

Through another illustration Christ revealed the condition of the nation Israel at that time as a result of its rejection of Him and His offer (vv. 43-45). Jesus said that when an evil spirit leaves a man, it seeks rest and is unable to find it. Remembering the body in which it formerly dwelt, it determines to return. On its return it finds the man freed from evil spirits and determines to reenter, but rather than occupying that body alone it seeks seven other spirits more wicked than itself. Together these spirits move in and occupy that body as their dwelling place. Thus the man's condition after his initial deliverance is worse than before.

This illustration clearly revealed Christ's reflection upon the recent history of Israel. John the Baptist had come to find the house of Israel occupied by evil spirits—the nation was full of unrighteousness and sin. As a result of John's preaching, which brought about repentance and confession, the nation of Israel had been purged from its evil. Multitudes were awaiting the coming of the kingdom. But before the kingdom could be established, the nation of Israel had returned to the sin that had been removed by John's preaching—and now the nation was further from God. It was more wicked—and consequently under more severe judgment—than it had been before John began his ministry. The nation that professed to receive John's witness had turned in unbelief from the One whom John introduced.

Jesus, in a highly symbolic act, signified His rejection of the nation because of their rejection of Him. While He was addressing the multitude, Christ's mother and brothers sought to speak with Him, but the crowd was so great that they were unable to come near Him. Therefore word was conveyed to Christ that His mother and brothers were on the outer fringes of the multitude, or outside the house, and wanted to speak with Him. And that's when Jesus made a strange but very significant reply.

He raised the question, "Who is My mother, and who are My

brothers?" (v. 48) The natural response to that question would have been: those with whom He had a blood relationship. But rather than recognizing blood ties as constituting a true relationship, He pointed to His disciples, that is, those who by faith had accepted Him. He said, "For whoever does the will of My Father in heaven is My brother and sister and mother" (v. 50). This relationship was instituted not by natural birth but as a result of a supernatural birth. These were related to Him not by blood but by faith in His person.

The nation of Israel claimed an "automatic" relationship with the coming Messiah because of their common blood relationship to Abraham. But Christ rejected blood ties as constituting a true spiritual relationship. The only ones He would accept as being spiritually related to Him were those who were related to Him by faith. In that multitude were those who claimed a relationship to Abraham as a basis for entrance into the kingdom. But Jesus said the kingdom must be entered by faith in His person, not by physical birth.

This incident clearly anticipated God's setting aside of the nation Israel and prepared the way for the revelation of a new form of God's program for the kingdom.

Summary

In response to Christ's presentation of Himself as the covenanted Messiah, the populace who heard His message faced the requirements for kingdom entrance. Because they only knew righteousness as defined by the Pharisees, Christ in the Sermon on the Mount rejected Pharisaic righteousness as sufficient to bring them into the kingdom and offered them His righteousness, received by faith.

Jesus validated His offer of Himself as the Messiah by the miracles which He performed. When the people expressed a willingness to put faith in Him as the Messiah, the leaders offered an alternate explanation of His person: They said He came from hell and got His power from Satan. Though Christ warned of judgment on that generation if they persisted in their rejection, the leaders did indeed reject Him; and thus He withdrew His offer of the kingdom to that generation and announced judgment instead.

19

A New Form of the Kingdom Predicted

Jesus the Messiah had remained in the same house while three important matters took place. These were: (1) the incident of healing the demon-possessed man, which brought the Pharisees' accusation that Jesus was demon-possessed; (2) the request of the Pharisees for a miraculous sign to authenticate that He was who He claimed to be; and (3) Christ's rejection of that generation of the nation of Israel (Matt. 12). Jesus then withdrew Himself from the house where these incidents took place and retired to the seashore.

Parables to reveal and conceal

It may be that He sought rest from the arduous conflicts in which He had been engaged for so much of that day. Perhaps the size of the crowd caused Him to withdraw to the shore so everybody could gather together while He spoke to them. Matthew recorded that such large crowds gathered around Him it was necessary for Him to get into a boat and sit in it in order to teach the multitude.

When He taught, we read, "He told them many things in parables" (Matt. 13:3). Previously Christ had used parables infrequently in His teaching. His use of them on this occasion was so significant that when an opportunity presented itself, "the disciples came to Him and asked, 'Why do You speak to the people in parables?'" (v. 10)

In order to understand the disciples' question, we need to recognize that *a parable is a literary device used to teach by means*

215

of transference. In order to make it possible to discover truth in an unknown realm, something familiar is transferred from the known realm to the unknown realm. To accomplish this, a simple figure of speech such as a *metaphor* may be used: "I am the gate" (John 10:9). Or the figure might be a *simile* such as, "Be as shrewd as snakes and as innocent as doves" (Matt. 10:16). The figure may also be more complex, consisting of a parable which is a narrative and conveys one principal point of parallelism, even though there may be other incidental parallels.

Sometimes we find an allegory—a narrative in which there are many intended parallelisms. Our Lord used parables frequently, but employed allegories only on rare occasions (such as in John 10 where He used the analogy of the relationship between a shepherd and sheep). While an allegory may or may not be true to life, a parable is always true to life. Transference in an allegory is in the sphere of ideas, but in parables transference is always through a historical reality.

In order to interpret any literary figure, we must first clearly discern what is true in the antecedent (i.e., in the known realm). Having done that, we then can transfer the truth of the antecedent to the truth to be learned in the unknown realm. For instance, before we can learn any truth about Christ from His statement, "I am the gate" (John 10:9), we must understand the nature, function, and purpose of a gate in that time and culture. What a gate provided in the real realm is what Christ will provide in the spiritual realm. Facts from the known realm must be learned before they can be transferred to gain knowledge in the unknown realm.

In response to the disciples' questions, then, concerning why He spoke in parables, Christ replied that He used parables first *to reveal truth to some* and, second, *to hide truth from others* (Matt. 13:11-15).

Christ's answer would be unintelligible if we did not understand the historical situation. Through the course of His ministry Jesus had offered Himself to the nation as Saviour and Sovereign. The nation had seen that offer authenticated before them by the miracles Christ performed, and the nation was called on to respond to the evidence presented. The religious leaders, as representatives of the nation, indicated their purpose to reject the person of Christ and to discount His miracles, insisting His miracles were done by Satan's power. Therefore Christ had no further word for those who rejected and spurned Him and persisted in their unbelief.

On the other hand, some had believed His word and accepted His person, and these needed instruction. In short, Jesus was confronted by a mixed multitude comprising both believers and unbelievers—those who had received Him and those who had rejected Him. We see that He did not attempt to separate the unbelievers from the believers and then instruct only the believers. Rather, He constructed His teaching in such a way that those who had believed would understand, and those who had rejected—even though they heard—would not understand.

Believers have the key to knowledge and can interpret His teaching. Unbelievers do not possess that key and, therefore, cannot understand His word. The one who has the key of knowledge will use that key to gain more knowledge, but the one who does not have that key will lose such knowledge as he once possessed. This was the explanation Christ gave the disciples concerning why He used parables in His teaching.

Interpreting the parables

To properly interpret a parable it is necessary to study the historical context in which the parable was spoken. Jesus used parables to answer questions in the minds of those who heard Him teach, whether the questions were specifically stated or merely understood by Him. Jesus also used parables to solve problems concerning certain truths He sought to convey, but about which His hearers were having difficulty. It is necessary, then, in interpreting a parable to consider the question or problem with which our Lord was dealing. In some cases the question was specifically stated, but in others the question or problem was implied from some previous discussion.

The discovery of this question or problem safeguards interpretation, for if the truth gleaned from the interpretation does not answer the question or problem it is a false interpretation. Only that interpretation which answers the question or problem can be accepted. This principle will also determine at how many points in a parable an analogy should be drawn. It is legitimate to interpret parts of a parable only as long as they contribute to the answer of the question or problem being discussed.

In considering the interpretation of parables, it is most important to observe the following words of Christ: "The knowledge of the secrets of the kingdom of heaven has been given to you" (Matt. 13:11). The parables were designed to teach truth concerning God's kingdom program. Again and again our Lord used the formula, "The kingdom of heaven is like. . . ." Truth is *always* applicable to believers; therefore truth may be gained from a study of the parables and applied to persons living today. Yet we must never forget that based on our Lord's own words, His parables were designed to convey truth concerning the kingdom program.

The "secrets of the kingdom"

The Old Testament prophets had spoken about the fulfillment of God's covenant as given to Abraham (Gen. 12:1-3, 7; 13:14-16; 15:18; 17:6-8), to David (2 Sam. 7:16; Ps. 89:1-4), to Jeremiah (Jer. 31:31-34), to Ezekiel (Ezek. 36:25-30), and to Moses (Deut. 28–30). The nation of Israel eagerly awaited the coming of a Messiah who would fulfill these eternal and unconditional covenants. Messiah would redeem God's people from their sins, deliver them from the bondage of their oppressors, and institute a kingdom over which He would rule in peace and righteousness. Such was Israel's hope that was kept alive by the prophets God sent to encourage and comfort His people.

John's message arrested the attention of multitudes in the nation as he proclaimed, "The kingdom of heaven is near" (Matt. 3:2). To Israel this meant that John would introduce the promised King who would come in David's line, sit on David's throne, and rule over David's house. Christ proclaimed the same hope as, like John, He announced, "The kingdom of heaven is near" (4:17).

As Jesus ministered to His fellow residents of Nazareth during His first visit, after reading a messianic passage from Isaiah, He declared, "Today this Scripture is fulfilled in your hearing" (Luke 4:21). The response of the people in Nazareth on that occasion foreshadowed the response of the nation, for those who heard Him claim to be Messiah rejected His word and His person. They even sought to put Him to death. Thereafter the leaders of the nation consistently and persistently rejected Christ's word and person, with their rejection culminating in their response to the miracle of healing the demon-possessed man in Matthew 12.

On that occasion the leaders' rejection was indicated by their claim that Christ received His power from Satan. Christ warned the people at large against accepting that interpretation, noting that if the nation persisted in its rejection, it would come under severe temporal judgment. When the nation's response of rejection was clear, Christ set aside the nation—those related to Him by blood—and declared that He would accept only those related to Him by faith (vv. 48-50). In the mind of Christ, the destiny of the nation was sealed. Christ later would announce that the kingdom of God had been taken from Israel and would be given to a people who would produce the fruit of righteousness (21:43). Jerusalem would come under judgment (24:37-39) and would fall to the Gentiles (Luke 21:24). From this point on Christ no longer publicly announced that the kingdom was at hand; instead, He indicated that the kingdom had been postponed. He was not anticipating a throne, but instead foresaw a cross. What He had originally come to fulfill in God's covenant program for Israel had been postponed until another coming.

In light of all this, the following questions arise: What happens to God's kingdom—of which the Davidic millennial kingdom is only an earthly form—in this present age when the millennial kingdom has been postponed? What form does the kingdom take in this present age? What are the essential characteristics or features of God's kingdom in this present age?

In answer to this, Christ referred to "the secrets of the kingdom" (Matt. 13:11). He was not referring to the covenanted Davidic, or millennial, kingdom. That there would be such a kingdom was no "secret" in the Old Testament! It clearly revealed the essential features or characteristics of the millennial kingdom. But what the Old Testament had not revealed was that *an entire age would intervene between the offer of the kingdom by the Messiah and Israel's reception of the King and enjoyment of full kingdom blessings.*

It is very important we understand that Israel's Old Testament eschatology (doctrine of future things) viewed time in two ages: *the present age,* which was the age in which the nation awaited the coming of the Messiah; and *the age to come,* which was the age of blessing to be introduced by Messiah at His coming. The Old Testament, however, did not reveal that the offer of the "age to come" would terminate with Israel's rejection rather than reception, nor did it disclose that it would be necessary for the King to postpone until a future advent the blessings of His reign.

219

Features of the new program

With this background, we come to see that the time period covered by the parables in Matthew 13 extends from Israel's rejection until its future reception of the Messiah. Thus this new program began while Christ was still on the earth, and it will extend until His return to the earth in power and great glory.

This period includes within it the period from Pentecost in Acts 2 to the Rapture, that is, the age of grace (which we can also call the age of the Holy Spirit, or the age of the church). Although this period includes the Church Age, it extends beyond it, for the parables of Matthew 13 precede Pentecost and extend beyond the Rapture. Thus these parables do not primarily concern the nature, function, and influence of the church. Rather, they show the previously unrevealed form in which God's theocratic rule would be exerted in a previously unrevealed age, made necessary by Israel's rejection of Christ.

In this discourse there are eight parables, each one providing an essential characteristic of the kingdom in this present age. The *first* feature of this age is that it is *characterized by a sowing of the seed by sowers, and that there are varied responses to this sowing.* The scene described by Jesus was so familiar and well known to His hearers that He did not think it necessary to explain the action. But because the use of parables was new in Christ's teaching, He carefully interpreted two of them as a guide to the proper way of interpreting the others.

Because one third of what our Lord taught He taught through parables, consideration of our Lord's own interpretation is extremely important. Without His guide to interpretation we could easily go astray. In this parable, the seed (vv. 3-8) represents the word, or "the message about the kingdom," while the field represents the "heart" of the individual hearer (see v. 19). In Scripture, the "heart" often indicates the intellectual capacity of the individual. A message, then, was being proclaimed and heard. But to this proclamation there were varying responses. Some seed showed no sign of life at all (that sown by the wayside). Some produced no fruit (that sown on rocky places). Some seed gave promise of bearing fruit but was eventually fruitless (that sown among the thorns). Finally there was seed which produced a crop yielding a hundred, sixty, or thirty times what was sown (v. 23).

In each case the seed was the same, the sower was the same, and the place where the seed was planted was the same. What determined the outcome of the sowing was the preparation of the soil. While this parable is commonly called "The Parable of the Sower" (i.e., the NIV heading), it might perhaps better be entitled "The Parable of the Soils."

Through this parable Christ did several things. He explained the varied responses to His ministry as a Sower of good seed. The various responses were due to the preparation of the hearts of His hearers. Some refused to hear; some heard and received the message with joy but did not continue; some heard but the truth was soon forgotten because of the concerns of life or the desire for material gain. But some seed produced an abundant harvest because the soil had been adequately prepared.

As He taught these truths concerning the coming age, Christ not only explained the varying responses to His ministry but also revealed the future responses to the disciples' ministry. The response to their ministry would be the same as Israel's response to His. From this parable we see that an essential feature of this present age will be a sowing of the Word to which there will be different responses.

Mark recorded another parable by Jesus on the theme of sowing seed. This parable (Mark 4:26-29) was designed to teach that *the fruit depends not on the sower but on the life that is in the seed itself.* This illustration featured a man who sowed his field; then, regardless of what the man did, the seed germinated, sprouted, grew, produced grain, and eventually yielded a bountiful harvest, which the man reaped. Because the Eleven would be commissioned to proclaim a message to the ends of the earth (Matt. 28:19-20), it would be easy for them to feel that the harvest depended on their efforts. But Jesus wanted to make it clear that any harvest they saw would be the result of sowing the seed, and then allowing the life in the seed to manifest itself by growth and yield.

The *second* parable concerned weeds sown among wheat (13:24-29). It was designed to supplement the first parable and teach that *there would be a false sowing alongside the sowing of the Word of God.* The field had been sown with good seed, and the sower could anticipate a harvest for his labors. But later the sower was told of the false sowing, that an enemy had come in and sown the field with the seed of weeds.

This false sowing evidently took place immediately after the sowing of the good seed. Then both kinds of seed germinated and sprouted. In the process of waiting for the harvest, it became evident that weeds had been sown in the wheat field. The presence of weeds would crowd out the growth of the fruit-bearing wheat. The servants, concerned as they were with the results of their labors, suggested that they try to remove the weeds from the field. However, the owner of the field recognized that it would be impossible to remove the weeds without destroying the wheat. So the servants were commanded to let both ripen, and at the time of wheat harvest they would separate the good grain from the worthless weeds. The weeds could be burned and destroyed, while the wheat would be gathered into storage. Through this parable Jesus prepared these men to be on guard for Satan's work of sowing false seed, or false doctrine, while they were sowing the good seed. Satan's false kingdom would continue to exist alongside the new form of God's kingdom.

In this parable Christ is viewed as the Sower. He explained, "The One who sowed the good seed is the Son of Man" (v. 37). The field in this parable is the world, for it was Christ's purpose that His truth be disseminated throughout the world. The good seed sown throughout the world represents "the sons of the kingdom" (v. 38). Thus we see that those with knowledge of the truth would be scattered throughout the world so that the truth might be disseminated through them. At the same time, however, Satan would plant his emissaries around the world to carry on a countersowing. This parable anticipates a judgment at the end of the age to separate the unsaved from the saved since, as we have already seen, these parables concern the kingdom. The future harvest through the ministry of God's children will see many taken into the Lord's earthly millennial kingdom, which will be established at His second advent. But those who have rejected the good word and have followed the word of Satan will be excluded from that kingdom. Thus the "barn" into which the wheat will be gathered is Messiah's millennial kingdom that has been promised to Israel.

The *third* parable, the mustard seed, reveals that *this new form of the kingdom will have an almost imperceptible beginning* (vv. 31-32). The emphasis in the parable is on the contrast between the size of the seed and the plants that that seed produced. "Small as a mustard seed" was a Jewish proverb to indicate a very minute particle. But out of that insignificant seed in one year would grow a plant that became large enough for birds to nest in it. In Daniel 4:12 and Ezekiel 31:6, we find that the figure of a spreading tree in which birds lodge indicates a great kingdom that can protect and provide benefits for many peoples.

All previous empires had been established by military might. Babylon was crushed by the military might of Medo-Persia. Medo-Persia was destroyed by the military prowess of Alexander and his Greek armies. The Greek Empire fell before the military might of Rome. The history of empires, then, is that one empire has succeeded another by displaying greater might or power. However, that will not be true of the kingdom Jesus indicated will exist in this present age. From a small and insignificant beginning, it will go through a process of development until it reaches out its branches to provide blessing to all who take refuge in its shade. Christ would commission only eleven men to become His emissaries (John 17:18). This would seem to be an insignificant beginning, yet Christ predicted that the world would hear His message from such a small beginning. Thus the parable teaches that the new form of the kingdom, while it did have an insignificant beginning, would eventually spread out to the ends of the earth.

The *fourth* parable was designed to show *how the kingdom program would develop and operate in the present age.* Some have referred to this as "The Parable of the Leaven," but that title puts the emphasis on what leaven is or what leaven signifies. Actually, this is "The Parable of Leaven Hidden in Meal" (Matt. 13:33). In other words, the parable emphasizes what leaven does or how leaven works. In that culture, three measures of meal was the amount of flour a housewife baked into a loaf of bread for an average family. When the yeast was introduced into the flour, a process began that was steady, continuous, and irreversible. That process continued until the whole mixture was leavened. Thus Jesus was teaching that the kingdom would not be established by outward means, since no external force could cause the dough to rise. Rather, this new form of the kingdom would operate according to an internal force that would be continuous and progressive until the whole mixture had been leavened.

Here the emphasis was on the Holy Spirit and concerned His ministry to the world. Christ would again speak of this in John 15:26 and 16:7-11.

The *fifth* and *sixth* parables, taken together, reveal *what accrues to God through the kingdom in this present age*. In the "Parable of the Treasure Hidden in the Field" (Matt. 13:44), Christ revealed that a multitude from among the nation Israel will become God's purchased possession through this present age. Throughout the Old Testament, Israel was called God's "treasured possession" (Ex. 19:5; Deut. 14:2; Ps. 135:4). In the parables of Matthew 13, Christ had already interpreted the field to mean the world (v. 38). Therefore, this parable clearly pictures Israel, God's peculiar treasure, being taken out of their land because of discipline and scattered throughout the world. This condition became a reality when Titus invaded Jerusalem and expelled the people from the land. Now, in order for the man in the parable to regain the treasure of which he was deprived, it was necessary for him to purchase the field where the treasure was hidden. This Christ did by His death: "He is the atoning sacrifice for our sins, and not only for ours but also for the sins of the whole world" (1 John 2:2). And it will not be until the Second Advent that this treasure will become the possession of its rightful Owner (Matt. 24:31).

In the "Parable of the Merchant Looking for Fine Pearls" (13:45-46), Christ revealed that God will obtain a treasure not only from the nation Israel, but from the Gentiles as well. We understand this from the fact that a pearl comes out of the sea, and quite frequently in Scripture the sea represents Gentile nations. So once again we see that a treasure from among the Gentiles becomes God's by purchase.

The *seventh* parable reveals that *this new form of the kingdom will conclude in a judgment separating the righteous from the unrighteous*. The net drawn up from the sea brings with it all kinds of fish, some useful and some useless (vv. 47-48). Therefore, it is necessary to separate the useful from the useless. The useful are gathered into baskets, while the useless are thrown away. Through this parable Christ taught that the age will end in a judgment to determine who enters the future millennial kingdom and who is excluded from it.

Righteousness is a prerequisite for entrance into the kingdom. The righteous are taken into it, but the unrighteous are excluded. The destiny of the wicked is not the blessing of the kingdom, but rather is the judgment of eternal fire. This same truth concerning the judgment prior to the institution of the millennial kingdom is taught in Matthew 25:1-30, where Christ predicted judgment on the nation Israel, and in verses 31-46 where He described judgment on living Gentiles. The judgment predicted here is not a judgment on the dead but on the living, and it will take place at the time of Christ's second advent to the earth.

The *eight and final* parable of Matthew 13 is that of the house-holder (v. 52), which teaches that *some features of the new form of the kingdom are identical to features previously revealed about the millennial kingdom*. It also teaches that *other features are entirely new and have no correspondence to what had been revealed about the millennial form of the kingdom*.

In this parable the owner entered his storeroom and brought from there what would meet the needs of the household as he knew them. The truth Christ has been proclaiming is likened to the trea-sure of the owner of the house. Christ has presented some previous-ly revealed truths that could be called "old"; He has presented other truths not previously revealed, and therefore "new."

Kingdom promises not canceled

As we survey the parables of Matthew 13, then, we find that in light of Israel's rejection of the person of Christ, He foresaw postpone-ment of the millennial form of the kingdom. He announced the introduction of a new form of the kingdom, one that would span the period from Israel's rejection of Christ until Israel's future reception of Christ at the Second Advent. This present age—with its new form of the kingdom—is characterized by the sowing of the Word to which there will be varying responses, depending on the prepara-tion of the soil (the Parable of the Soils). The harvest that results from the sowing is the result of the life that is in the seed that was sown (the seed growing of itself). Concurrent with the sowing of the Word, there is a false countersowing (Parable of the Weeds). The new form of the kingdom had an insignificant beginning, but will grow to great proportions (Parable of the Mustard Seed). The power in the kingdom is not external but internal (Parable of the Leaven Hidden in Meal). God will gather a peculiar treasure to Himself through this present age (Parable of the Hidden Treasure and the Pearl of Great Price). The present form of the kingdom will end in a judgment to determine who are righteous and eligible to enter the future millennial form of the kingdom, as well as who are unrighteous and will be excluded from the millennial kingdom to come.

This revelation of the new form through which the theocracy would be administered in this present age was followed by a specific prophecy: "I will build My church" (16:18). The nature and function of the church is not explained here, but will be revealed in its historical development in the Book of Acts, with its doctrines explained in the Epistles.

This revelation was also followed by a notice of the withdrawal of the offer of the kingdom and its postponement until the King's future return. In Matthew 21:43 Christ said, "The kingdom of God will be taken away from you and given to a people who will produce its fruits." While some see the nation of whom Christ spoke as a reference to Gentiles in this present age, it seems better to understand it as a future generation in Israel which will repent as the Davidic form of the kingdom is instituted by the returning Messiah. Regardless, this passage clearly indicates a withdrawal of the offer of the kingdom to that generation.

Further, in the parable in Luke 19:11-28 Christ clearly taught not the cancellation of the kingdom promises, but the postponement of that covenanted form of the kingdom. As Jesus and His disciples made their way toward Jerusalem, the Twelve were confident that Jesus was going there to receive a crown, be acknowledged as a king, and institute the millennial kingdom. Therefore Christ told a parable in order to correct the misconception of the people, who "thought that the kingdom of God was going to appear at once" (v. 11).

John the Baptist had preached that the kingdom of heaven was near (Matt. 3:2). Christ had preached the same message as He began His ministry (4:17), and during His ministry Jesus had offered Israel a kingdom that would be established if the nation would receive Him as Saviour-Sovereign. But the nation had rejected Him and the kingdom had to be postponed. Christ had previously taught that the generation of His day would not see the kingdom (Luke 17:22), because the kingdom would be postponed indefinitely to some future time. The Lord's words did not nullify the genuine offer of the kingdom in His day, nor deny the concept of a literal kingdom in a future day. Rather, this parable was designed to teach the truth concerning *postponement* of the kingdom.

In this parable (Luke 19), a man of noble birth—and therefore eligible to rule—traveled to a distant country to have himself appointed king of a kingdom. He did not appoint himself, but rather he sought appointment by the one who had authority in the kingdom over which he expected to rule. Anticipating an extended absence while he received the appointment as king, he called ten of his servants and entrusted to them a sum of money that represented approximately three months' wages. These men were made stewards of this large sum and held accountable for their use of it. While the one who had the right to rule was absent, he was rejected by those over whom He had been appointed as ruler. In spite of the rejection by his rightful subjects, the king did return.

When he returned he asked his servants to give an account of their stewardship. The first servant reported that he had multiplied the sum of money entrusted to him ten times, and for this he was commended and rewarded. The king gave him administrative responsibility over ten cities. The second servant came and reported that his investment had been multiplied five times, and he also was commended and given responsibility to administer five cities. Then another servant came to give an account of his stewardship. He confessed that he feared both his master and the judgment into which his master might bring him; therefore he had been afraid to risk his master's money and had hidden it during his master's absence. He returned what had been entrusted to him but with no increase. The master reproved this man and took the money entrusted to him and gave it to the one who had been faithful and increased his investment tenfold. He then ordered the executions of all subjects who did not want him to be king (v. 27).

In this parable Christ taught that He who possesses the right to rule would be absent from the place over which He was appointed to rule. Those over whom He has a right to rule would rebel against Him and reject Him. In His absence and during His time of rejection, there would be those who claim to be His disciples and they would have a stewardship entrusted to them. He will hold them accountable for the discharge of that stewardship, and at His return He will call them to give an account. Those who have proven themselves to be good stewards by their faithfulness will be rewarded with positions of authority in the kingdom. But those who by their unfaithfulness have proved that they are not His stewards will be cut off from the kingdom.

The nation Israel was appointed as the King's stewards but proved to be unfaithful. Only those found faithful to Him from among the nation will be admitted at the King's coming into His kingdom.

Summary

Following the rejection of Christ's offer of Himself as the Messiah by the leaders in the nation, Christ revealed a new form in which the theocratic kingdom would be administered in the age falling between Israel's rejection of Christ as Messiah, the Son of God, and the nation's future acceptance of Him as Messiah at His second advent. Christ revealed the essential features of the new form of the kingdom in the parables which He taught, recorded mainly in Matthew 13.

In the chapter that follows, we will survey the parables specifically in light of the doctrine of the kingdom and all that Christ revealed concerning the kingdom as He taught in parables.

20

The Doctrine of the Kingdom in the Parables

In response to the disciples' questions, "Why do You speak to the people in parables?" (Matt. 13:10) Jesus replied, "The knowledge of the secrets of the kingdom of heaven has been given to you" (v. 11). Here Christ made it clear that the parables were designed to reveal truth concerning the theocratic kingdom program of God. Many times He introduced His parables with the formula, "The kingdom of heaven is like" (13:24, 31, 33, 44-45, 47; 18:23; 20:1; 22:2; 25:1). Using the individual parables, Christ revealed various facets of truth concerning the theocratic kingdom.

Therefore it will benefit us greatly to arrange the parables thematically in order to develop an understanding of the kingdom based on this portion of Christ's teaching.

The offer of the kingdom

The uniqueness of Christ's offer
Because of the covenants and promises of the prophets, the nation of Israel anticipated a kingdom over which David's Son would rule· They expected a literal kingdom containing literal people. However, because of their indoctrination by the Pharisees, they had come to believe that they were already in the kingdom. Christ spoke the *Parables of the Patched Garment and the Wineskins* (Luke 5:36-39) in order to show that He had not come to build on Pharisaism. He would not fulfill God's unconditional covenant promises by perpetu-

229

ating the doctrine of the Pharisees; rather, He had come to offer a kingdom that was new and unique and had no relationship whatsoever to the concept of the kingdom as it was taught by the religious leaders.

Christ the Good Shepherd

Because His right to assume the messianic role was rejected and His claims debated, Jesus spoke the *Parable of the Shepherd and His Sheep* (John 10:1-18). He wanted to prove that since He had come in the way the prophets had predicted, that He was truly the Messiah. He then revealed that those who are truly His—and consequently are a part of the true kingdom—would recognize Him even though the nation rejected Him. He would lead His own out of the bondage of Pharisaism and bring them into the liberty that characterized His kingdom.

The welcome for sinners to enter the kingdom

The Pharisees had a perverted and distorted concept of the character of God. Recognizing that God is holy, they concluded that He could not and would not receive sinners into His kingdom. They reasoned that one's goal in life should be to produce enough righteous works to gain admission into the kingdom. They taught that God hated sinners and rejoiced in a sinner's death, because then the sinner was removed from His presence forever.

In order to correct this wrong teaching, our Lord taught the *Parables of the Searching Shepherd, the Searching Housewife, and the Welcoming Father* (Luke 15:1-32). In the Parables of the Lost Sheep and the Lost Coin, Jesus put the emphasis on the diligent search conducted by the owners until what was lost had been found, and then He stressed the joy that came to the owners when what was lost was restored to them. In the third parable, our Lord emphasized the heart of the father. Even though there was no worthiness in the son, the father eagerly awaited the son's return and had prepared a robe, a ring, and sandals to confer authority on the son. In addition, the father had prepared a banquet through which he revealed his joy at his son's return.

Christ told these parables, then, to emphasize that any sinner is welcome to avail himself of the offer that He was making and to enter into the kingdom in the way that He—as the Messiah—had prescribed.

Warning against rejection
The people in the nation looked to the Pharisees for leadership in religious matters. The Pharisees were considered as the shepherds of Israel, and the people felt obligated to follow their lead. In the *Parable of the Blind Man Leading a Blind Man* (Luke 6:39), Jesus warned against following the Pharisees, who had already indicated their intent to reject Him. Because the religious leaders were spiritually blind, if the people followed them they would be destroyed. This parable, then, recognized the possibility of the nation's rejection since He already had been rejected by the leaders.

The announcement of the kingdom
In the *Parable of a King Who Prepared a Wedding Banquet for His Son* (Matt. 22:1-14), Christ indicated that an invitation was being given to that generation to enter the covenanted kingdom. The original announcement had been sent to the friends of the bridegroom at the time of the betrothal. Then some twelve months passed and the marriage was ready to be completed. According to the custom of the day, a second invitation was extended to those invited at the time of the betrothal in order that they might attend the wedding banquet and share the bridegroom's joy. The fact that a second invitation was being announced shows that the wedding was at hand. Since Christ was using the wedding banquet as a figure of His millennial kingdom, we know this parable teaches the offer of the kingdom. However, not all who were invited chose to attend; therefore the invitation was extended a second time, and even a third time, in order that the banquet hall might be filled with guests. It is clear that the covenanted and prophesied kingdom was being offered to that generation. Jesus taught the same truth in the *Parable of the Man Who Was Preparing a Great Banquet* (Luke 14:16-24), where the guests also had received a previous announcement and later were told that the banquet was ready and that they were invited to come.

Invitation in the light of His offer of the kingdom
In the light of His offer, Christ extended the following invitation: "Enter through the narrow gate. For wide is the gate and broad is the road that leads to destruction, and many enter through it. But small is the gate and narrow the road that leads to life, and only a few find it" (Matt. 7:13-14). Christ then gave a warning that revealed

the danger of neglecting the invitation He had just given.

In the *Parable of the Wise and Foolish Builders* (vv. 24-27), Christ likened His words to a rock on which a person may build. A house built on such a secure foundation will stand through every storm. Christ then likened the teaching of the Pharisees to sand. If a person builds on this foundation, the structure will collapse when a storm comes. The nation was faced with a decision. On one hand, they could accept Christ's words and enter the kingdom through trusting in Him. If, on the other hand, they rejected His words and accepted the doctrine of the Pharisees, they would be excluded from the kingdom. Thus the invitation to enter the kingdom was coupled with a warning not to try to enter the kingdom any other way than through Christ Himself.

Rejection of the offer

In a number of His parables Jesus indicated that the nation would reject His offer. Therefore in the *Parable of the Physician Who Was Called on to Heal Himself* (Luke 4:23), Christ perceived the unbelief of the nation. They would ask Him to prove that He was the Messiah since He so claimed to be. No one would consult a physician who could not heal. The inference was that Christ was a sinner; before He could offer salvation as a prerequisite for entrance into the kingdom, He needed to deal effectively with His own sins.

The *Parable of the Wedding Banquet* (Matt. 22:1-14) not only emphasized the offer of the kingdom, but revealed the response of the invited guests to the invitation that had been extended to them. The guests were occupied with personal pursuits and refused to be interrupted in order to respond to the invitation. In like manner, in the *Parable of the Great Banquet* (Luke 14:16-24), the invited guests "began to make excuses" (v. 18). In these parables, invitations had been extended and received; the recipients considered their response and chose to ignore the banquet to which they had been invited.

The rejection of the kingdom was further revealed in the *Parable of the Landowner Who Planted a Vineyard* (Matt. 21:33-44). The landowner, anticipating the harvest of his vineyard, sent servants to collect the fruit. However, the tenants beat, stoned, and killed the servants. This part of the parable revealed the attitude of the nation in times past toward the prophets, who exhorted the people to repent in view of the promise of the Davidic kingdom. The land owner finally sent his son to claim the harvest, but the tenants killed him also. Again, this revealed the response of the nation to the kingdom offer Jesus the Messiah was making.

Postponement of the kingdom

The millennial kingdom was to be the fulfillment of the unconditional and eternal covenants that God gave to the nation of Israel. In His covenant promises to Abraham (Gen. 12:1-3; 13:14-17; 15:18-20; 17:4-8), God said that Abraham's physical descendants would inhabit the land God had permanently deeded to Abraham. In His covenant with David (2 Sam. 7:16), God promised that a descendant of David would sit on David's throne and rule over his house. This covenanted program was offered to Israel, but was rejected by the nation. Because the covenants are eternal, unconditional, and therefore irrevocable, the Davidic kingdom program would not be cancelled. It could, however, be postponed.

Christ spoke the *Parable of the Ten Minas* (Luke 19:11-27) in order to teach that the kingdom offer was being withdrawn from that generation and the Davidic form of the theocracy postponed. The Lord told of a nobleman who "went to a distant country to have himself appointed king and then to return" (v. 12). Because the man was of noble birth, he had the right to rule. His absence from the realm did not abrogate his right. When he returned from his journey, he would exercise the rights that belonged to him. In this manner Jesus affirmed that Israel's rejection of Him as Messiah did not set aside His royal rights, nor did His absence mean that He had relinquished those rights. In his own time He would return to exercise the reign that is rightly His.

Christ inferred this same fact in the *Parable of the Watchman at the Door* (Mark 13:34-37). Christ spoke of the owner of a household who was leaving his domain for an extended absence. This portion of the parable emphasized Christ's postponement of the kingdom and His absence from the realm in which the kingdom would be instituted at His return.

Christ further taught this truth in the *Parable of the Landowner Who Planted a Vineyard* (Matt. 21:33-34). Because the tenants produced no fruit to give to the landowner, he decided to take the vineyard from them and give it to other tenants. Christ interpreted this portion of the parable, saying, "The kingdom of God will be taken away from you and given to a people who will produce its fruit" (v. 43). The main teaching is the same despite a difference of opinion among Bible teachers concerning whether the people to whom the kingdom will be given are the Gentiles through whom God will work in the present age, or a future generation of Israel to whom the kingdom will be reoffered during the Tribulation. Christ's central teaching was that the Davidic kingdom would be postponed until a future time.

Judgment on that generation because they rejected Messiah

In a number of parables, Jesus spoke of the judgment that would fall on that generation because of their rejection of Him. In the *Parable of the Landowner Who Planted a Vineyard* (Matt. 21:33-34), Christ had pictured Himself as the stone that the builders rejected (v. 42), and then He had announced that "on whom it [the stone] falls will be crushed" (v. 44). Christ pictured Himself as a Judge who would mete out judgment to the guilty.

In the *Parable of the Cleansed Household* (vv. 43-45), Christ depicted the nation as having undergone a cleansing through the ministry of John the Baptist. However, that cleansing was not permanent. The unclean spirit that had left the house took seven other spirits that were more wicked than itself, and they entered and occupied the house that had been cleansed. Christ said, "The final condition of that man is worse than the first" (v. 45). By this He meant that the state of the nation was lower as a consequence of the rejection of Him than it had been before John began his ministry of calling the nation to repentance. Christ said, "That is how it will be with this wicked generation" (v. 45). Jesus meant that just as the man's condition was worse at the end than at the beginning, so the same was true of Israel. This parable shows that while an offer had been made that, if accepted, would have removed judgment, the nation had rejected the offer and so judgment must come.

The new form of the kingdom

The promised and Davidic form of the theocracy offered to that generation by Jesus Christ was rejected. He therefore passed judgment on that generation, and the offer of the Davidic kingdom was withdrawn. However, because the kingdom is based on an eternal, unilateral, and unconditional covenant, it cannot be nullified or abrogated; instead, it has been postponed to some indeterminate future time.

Christ chose to reveal through parables the form of the theocracy through which God would evidence His sovereign authority during this present age. As noted earlier, the parables were designed to reveal truth to believers while concealing truth from unbelievers. And, as discussed at length in the previous chapter, many of the parables which reveal features of the new form of the kingdom are found in Matthew 13. By way of review, in the *Parable of the Soils* (vv. 3-23) Christ revealed that this age will be characterized by a sowing of seed that He interpreted as the "Word of God" (Luke 8:11), by a Sower who is Himself, followed by a sowing by those He would appoint to this ministry. The sowing would be done throughout the world (rather than primarily in Israel), and to this sowing there would be varied responses, depending on the condition of the soil.

Through the *Parable of the Weeds* (Matt. 13:24-30), Christ revealed that Satan will try to defeat the program of God and exercise his "right" to rule by sowing weeds among the good seed the Sower has sown. Since Satan is an imitator, the weeds he sows bear a striking resemblance to the real thing; and it is not possible until the harvest to distinguish between the wheat and the weeds.

Turning to the internal characteristics of the kingdom, in the *Parable of the Seed Growing by Itself* (Mark 4:26-29) Christ called attention to the way physical seed germinates and grows because of the essential life in the seed. Similarly, said Jesus, when the new form of the kingdom is introduced by the sowing of the seed of God's Word, that kingdom will develop by the power in the seed that was sown. In the unfolding of the kingdom program, the development of the kingdom will not depend on human agency but on the power of the Word as it is proclaimed.

In the *Parable of the Mustard Seed* (Matt. 13:31-32), Christ revealed that the kingdom would begin in seeming insignificance but grow to great proportions. His emphasis here was to contrast the size of the mustard seed with the plant it produces. The new form of the kingdom began essentially with eleven men; from that insignificant beginning it grew so extensively that one could say by the time the Book of Acts closed, the whole world had heard the Gospel (cf. Rom. 1:8; Col. 1:6).

In the *Parable of the Yeast Mixed into a Large Amount of Flour* (v. 33), Jesus revealed that when the new form of the kingdom began, it would work irreversibly, persistently, and pervasively throughout the present age. Just as yeast introduced into flour continues to work until the mixture is ready for baking in an oven, so when the kingdom message was introduced, it would work continuously throughout the age.

In the *Parables of the Hidden Treasure and the Pearl* (vv. 44-45), Christ revealed God's purpose for the kingdom in this present age. His emphasis was on the value of the treasure and the pearl that the purchaser obtained through great personal sacrifice. Through His death Christ would become a propitiation (satisfaction of God's wrath) for the sins of the world (1 John 2:2). As a result of Christ's propitiatory act, the world was reconciled to God (2 Cor. 5:18-19). God's plan, then, in the present age is to acquire for Himself a treasure. Since the field or the land in Scripture frequently refers to Israel, the *Parable of a Treasure Hidden in a Field* may emphasize that God will receive to Himself some from among Israel during this present age (Rom. 11:5). Since the pearl comes out of the sea, and the sea is used in Scripture to represent Gentile nations (see Isa. 57:20), the second parable may emphasize that God will call many from among the Gentiles as His own possession (this is the basis of Paul's doctrine of the church in Eph. 2:11-22).

The *Parable of the Net* (Matt. 13:47-48) reveals that at the end of this age a judgment will separate the good from the bad, and the useful from the useless, in the same way a fisherman divides his catch. Prior to the inception of the millennial kingdom, there will be a judgment to exclude the unsaved and to invite the saved to participate in the joys and blessings of Christ's reign.

Finally, in the *Parable of the Household* (v. 52), Jesus likened Himself to the custodian of a storehouse who brings forth the items that will meet the needs of the household. The custodian may bring forth old grain or new grain, or old wine or new wine. But through what he brings forth, he fully meets the needs of the household. Here Christ was revealing that some aspects of the new form of the kingdom would be like previous forms of the kingdom; and some aspects would be entirely new. The fact that there would be a kingdom was clearly revealed in the Old Testament; but an aspect that was new was that it would be proclaimed throughout the world. The kingdom in the Old Testament was for Israel, even though

Gentiles would be blessed in the kingdom. However, a new truth was that Jews and Gentiles would participate equally in this new form of the kingdom. Thus in the new form of the kingdom, we do find some features that are similar to the old, but we also discover other features that are unique to the new.

Exhortations in view of Christ's return to establish the millennial kingdom

In response to the disciples' question concerning the signs that would forewarn of the end of the age and the coming of the King, our Lord enumerated many signs (Matt. 24:4-25) that would find their fulfillment in the seven years of the Tribulation. These signs will be given to alert a disobedient people to whom the kingdom will be offered again (v. 14) concerning the approach of the Judge. To stress the importance of these signs, Christ spoke the *Parable of the Fig Tree* (vv. 32-35). Just as the first shoots on a fig tree, or any tree (Luke 21:29), indicate the arrival of spring and herald the advent of summer, so the appearance of these signs will warn the nation Israel of the momentous event that they forecast, that is, the return of Messiah.

The response that these signs were designed to produce is revealed in several brief parables. In the *Parable of the Doorkeeper* (Mark 13:33-37), Christ emphasized that the servant assigned to keep watch at the door is to be faithful to this assignment because the servant does not know precisely when the master will return. It is incumbent on that servant, therefore, to diligently watch without interruption. Thus in this parable Jesus emphasized faithfulness in light of the unexpectedness of His return.

In the *Parable of the Watchful Owner* (Matt. 24:42-44), Christ again emphasized watchfulness and preparedness. If a thief served notice when he would arrive to plunder a home, the owner would not need to secure his household until the appointed hour arrived. However, since a thief gives no notice, a theft could occur at any time; and the owner of the house must keep the household secured. By this parable Christ emphasized the necessity of being prepared and being faithful in view of the unexpectedness of Messiah's return.

In the *Parable of the Wise and Wicked Servants* (vv. 45-51), Christ emphasized the need for faithfulness to the assigned responsibilities in view of the approach of the Lord's return, as indicated by the signs. A wise servant will fulfill assigned responsibilities, but a foolish servant will neglect assigned duties and live to indulge the flesh. Such a faithless servant will be deprived of the joys of the kingdom when the master returns.

In these brief parables, then, Christ gave exhortations to watch-fulness, preparedness, and faithfulness in view of His return as indicated by the signs that will be given.

Events preceding the establishment of the millennial kingdom

In the parables revealing the characteristics of the present age, Christ revealed that this age will end in judgment. However, no details were given at that time. In the lengthy parables of Matthew 25, Jesus did reveal details concerning this judgment program.

Judgment on living Israel
Following Messiah's second advent to the earth (Matt. 24:30), angels will regather living Israel from the four corners of the earth where they will be scattered during the Tribulation (v. 31). These will be brought back into the land given by irrevocable covenant to Abraham (Gen. 12:7). The Old Testament made it clear that repentance and restoration to fellowship with the God against whom the Israelites had sinned was a prerequisite for the enjoyment of the covenanted kingdom blessings (Deut. 30:1-10). Thus it was revealed that no unsaved person would enter the promised kingdom.

This judgment on living Israel is described in the *Parable of the Wise and Foolish Virgins* (Matt. 25:1-13). Immediately preceding this parable, Christ had exhorted His hearers to be watchful, faithful, and prepared. This Parable of the Wise and Foolish Virgins, then, revealed that there will be a judgment to determine the preparedness of those in Israel alive at the time of the second advent of Messiah. We need to understand here that the virgins in the Oriental wedding refer to the guests at the banquet, in contrast to the bride who appears with the bridegroom. The invitation had been extended to the nation to prepare themselves to enter the millennial kingdom, which could be expected imminently (24:14). The nation was now assembled and was expecting to enjoy the wedding banquet, which is the Lord's literary figure for the Davidic, millennial kingdom.

When the announcement was made that the bridegroom was

approaching, the assembled guests lit their lamps in order that they might go to meet him. The wise were prepared for the bridegroom's return and had brought supplemental oil to replenish their lamps. The foolish, however, had made no preparation, and so were unprepared when the bridegroom returned. The prepared guests were accepted into the millennial banquet; the unprepared guests, however, sought to prepare themselves, then found that the door to the banquet hall was shut and they were denied admission. Thus in this parable Christ taught that living Israel would be brought back to the land of judgment to determine who is prepared and who is unprepared. Those who are prepared will be accepted into the Messiah's millennial kingdom, but the unprepared will be excluded.

Judgment on living Gentiles

In the *Parable of the Sheep and Goats* (Matt. 25:31-46), Jesus revealed that Gentiles will also be gathered to judgment. They will be divided into two groups. Those classified as sheep will be accepted into the kingdom, but those called goats will be excluded from it. The sheep will be received because of what they did for Christ. In response to the surprise registered on His right hand, Christ explained that the treatment afforded His brothers was done for Him. The term *brothers* (v. 40) seems to make reference to either the nation of Israel as a whole, or to the chosen ones from among Israel (Rev. 7) who will proclaim the Gospel during the Tribulation. These will not be accepted because of their works, for no man is saved by works; rather, their works will prove the genuineness of their faith. Having demonstrated a faith validated by works, they will be accepted into the kingdom. Conversely, those on the left will not have produced works, and this lack will reveal the absence of saving faith.

In this parable, then, Christ explained the tests to be given the Gentiles to prove the state of their preparedness as individuals. Those on the right will be accepted into the kingdom, but those on the left will be excluded from the kingdom. Thus in these two judgments the whole world will be brought to judgment in preparation for the establishment of the millennial kingdom.

Judgment for reward

In the *Parable of the Talents* (Matt. 25:14-30), our Lord revealed that there will be a judgment prior to the millennial kingdom to test one's faithfulness. A master assigned to his servants responsibilities for which they were held accountable. At the master's return, the servants were called to account. Those found faithful were admitted into the master's domain and given positions of responsibility in the administration of his affairs. Conversely, one servant was found unfaithful and was cast out of the household and excluded from any responsibility in the master's domain.

In this parable Christ revealed that not only one's preparedness but also one's faithfulness will be tested. The unfaithful will reveal their lack of faith by their unfaithfulness and will be excluded from the kingdom. By their faithfulness, others will reveal the existence of their faith, and they will not only be received into the kingdom but will also be given responsibilities to be exercised in the Kingdom Age to come.

These judgments, then, will be preparatory to the institution of the millennial kingdom. The wicked will be excluded from the kingdom, while the righteous will be received into it. Judgments were anticipated because Christ had just before said, "Two men will be in the field; one will be taken [away in judgment] and the other left [to go into the kingdom]. Two women will be grinding with a hand mill; one will be taken [away in judgment] and the other left [to go into Messiah's kingdom]" (24:40-41). There will also be a judgment to distribute to the faithful rewards that will be enjoyed during the Messiah's millennial reign.

Life in the kingdom

The parables thus far have dealt with the kingdom program. In them Christ taught concerning the offer of the kingdom to Israel, the judgment on that generation because of the rejection of the offered kingdom, and the new form of the kingdom. Christ gave exhortations in view of the coming of the King and outlined events preceding the establishment of the Davidic form of the theocracy.

But many parables were directed to the disciples to instruct them concerning life in His kingdom. These parables reveal what the King expects of His subjects.

Obedience
In the *Parable of the Two Sons* (Matt. 21:28-32), Christ taught that obedience is a test of sonship. This parable counteracted the popular teaching of the Pharisees that all of Abraham's physical descendants

were already in the kingdom by virtue of their blood relationship to the patriarch. In this parable Christ revealed that a person's right to enter the kingdom will be determined not by his outward profession, but by his obedience to the King. Obedience will not only be a test of eligibility, but it will be required of those who are in the kingdom. They must be subject to the rule of the King.

Love

During the course of His earthly life, Christ had demonstrated the compassion of God toward the poor, the sick, the sorrowing, the outcast, and the sinful. Compassion such as He demonstrated will be required of those who are His subjects in the kingdom. In the *Parable of the Two Debtors* (Luke 7:41-50), Christ taught the basis for love. This parable was spoken in the house of a Pharisee where a sinful woman lavished her devotion on the person of Christ. The Pharisee could neither understand why the woman would love Him, nor why He would accept such attention and devotion from her.

In the parable, Christ told of two debtors who had been forgiven; one of a large debt, and the other of a small debt. Christ then asked the Pharisee who would love the forgiving creditor the most. The obvious answer was that the one who had been forgiven most would love the most. In this parable Jesus explained to the Pharisee why the woman loved Him. She was a notorious sinner who had been forgiven much. The parable also answered the Pharisee's question concerning why Christ would accept her devotion. The answer was that her devotion arose out of the love that was generated because of the forgiveness she had received.

From this parable, then, we learn that love for Christ will be shown by the one who has experienced His gracious forgiveness. Further, we see that Christ will accept that love when it flows from one who has received His forgiveness.

In the *Parable of the Good Samaritan* (10:30-37), we discover that mercy that is a manifestation of love is to be demonstrated to anyone who is our neighbor. From the parable we learn that our neighbor is anyone in need, whose need we know and whose need we are able to meet. The fact that Christ commanded the scholar in the Law to go and do as the Samaritan had done reveals that such mercy is a mark of those who are in the kingdom, because it is a fulfillment of the righteousness demanded by the Law. The subjects of the King in the kingdom, then, must not only demonstrate love toward God, because of the forgiveness that has been received, but also love toward their neighbors.

Thus life in the kingdom must fulfill the requirements of the Law, which said, " 'Love the Lord your God with all your heart and with all your soul and with all your strength and with all your mind'; and, 'Love your neighbor as yourself'" (v. 27). These two parables dealing with love describe an important characteristic of life in the kingdom.

Prayer

Prayer is primarily an act of worship in which the one praying submits to the authority of the One to whom the prayer is offered. Through prayer one registers total dependence on the One to whom the prayer is addressed. These facts concerning prayer suggest that it will play an important role in the kingdom. Therefore our Lord addressed several crucial aspects of prayer, including:

(1) The basis of prayer: In the *Parable of the Pharisee and the Tax Collector* (Luke 18:9-14), Christ revealed the basis on which one may approach God in prayer. The Pharisee thought he could approach God on the basis of his works and so he reiterated in his prayer the evidence of his righteousness. However, works are rejected as a basis on which one may address prayer to God.

On the other hand, the tax collector recognized that there was nothing in himself to commend himself to God. He gazed toward the ground and beat his breast in humiliation. By faith he put himself under the propitiating blood that was provided on the Day of Atonement and under which the unworthy could take refuge. Because he put himself under blood, Christ said he "went home justified before God" (v. 14). Thus in this parable Christ gave instructions concerning the basis on which people will approach God to offer worship, praise, thanksgiving, petition, and intercession in the kingdom.

(2) Persistence in prayer: In several parables Christ taught the necessity of persisting in order to obtain an answer to prayer. In the *Parable of the Persistent Widow* (Luke 18:1-8), Christ revealed that even a hard-hearted, indifferent judge can be moved by the persistence of a widow to grant her request. The judge was not moved by the justice of her claim, and he did not react emotionally to her need. He granted her request because of her persistence.

In the *Parable of the Persistent Friend* (Luke 11:5-13), Christ had stressed this same truth. Hospitality placed a responsibility on the host that he, because of the late hour, was not able to fulfill; however, the host knew one who could meet the need and asked for that friend's help. Because of the lateness of the hour, the friend refused to disturb the entire household in order to grant the request. But the host persisted until the need was met. The application that Christ drew was (using a literal translation of v. 9): "Keep on asking and it will be given to you; keep on seeking and you will find; keep on knocking and the door will be opened to you. For everyone who keeps on asking receives; he who keeps on seeking finds; and to him who keeps on knocking, the door will be opened."

The use of wealth

The Pharisees counted wealth as a certain sign of God's blessing. They strove to accumulate material possessions to assure themselves that they were righteous to a degree that rendered them acceptable to God. It became necessary, therefore, for Jesus to devote much teaching to correct this wrong attitude toward wealth. In telling parables about the use of wealth, Jesus was revealing characteristics of life in the kingdom. He specifically taught:

(1) The use of present opportunities: In the *Parable of the Shrewd Manager* (Luke 16:1-13), Jesus stressed that a righteous person will not misuse a stewardship selfishly, thinking only of the present; instead, a righteous person will act wisely and with a view to a future reckoning in the stewardship. Christ related that when the unfaithfulness of a manager caused the loss of his privileges, he wisely used the position he held, not for selfish indulgence in the present, but wisely with a view to the future. By reducing the indebtedness of his master's debtors, he won favor for himself. Christ did not approve of the manager's devious conduct, but He did commend the manager for wisdom in using present opportunities, not for the present only, but for the future.

Jesus applied this principle to the use of wealth. He asked, "If you have not been trustworthy in handling worldly wealth, who will trust you with true riches?" (v. 11) Thus He taught that a mark of life in the kingdom will be the wise use of material possessions.

(2) The temporary nature of material things: In the *Parable of the Rich Man and the Beggar* (Luke 16:19-31), Christ revealed that material wealth is not permanent but only temporary. The rich man who died left all his material possessions behind. The soul of the

rich man continued to exist, but the end of this earthly life meant he no longer could use his material wealth.

The parable further teaches that wealth is not a basis of salvation. No doubt the wealthy man was schooled in the Pharisaic doctrine that held out the hope that he was acceptable to God because he possessed wealth. The parable revealed that the poor beggar was accepted, not the wealthy man. This leads to the observation that a rich man, according to biblical concepts, is not one who has great material riches, but one who loves what God has given and trusts his wealth for salvation. The parable also reveals that, contrary to the Pharisaic concept, poverty is not necessarily an evidence of God's displeasure or punishment for sin. The beggar was not accepted into heaven because he was poor; but his poverty was no barrier to his entrance into true riches.

(3) The reward of covetousness: The *Parable of the Rich Fool* (Luke 12:16-21) shows that one's use of wealth will reveal whether one is righteous or unrighteous. The parable concerns a man, already wealthy, whose riches were greatly increased by an abundant harvest that his land produced. The extensive harvest gave the man an opportunity to demonstrate that he fulfilled the righteousness of the Law by distributing his wealth to his neighbors in need. However, he refused to do this and instead set the goods aside for his own use. By such a use of his wealth, the man showed he was unrighteous according to the demands of the Law. Thus in this parable Christ was stressing that wealth must be rightly used during this life if it is to provide any benefits in the life to come.

Faithfulness

The *Parable of the Faithful and Wise Manager* (Luke 12:42-48) emphasizes that privilege brings responsibility and that responsibility entails accountability. If one is appointed to a position of authority and then misuses that authority, that one will forfeit the authority. When Paul taught, "It is required that those who have been given a trust must prove faithful" (1 Cor. 4:2), he reiterated the truth that Christ spoke in this parable. Faithfulness to privileges and responsibilities will be a characteristic of life in the kingdom.

Humility

In the *Parable Concerning Seats at the Wedding Feast* (Luke 14:7-11), Christ warned against seeking preeminence for oneself.

True honor is not what one confers on oneself, but what others confer in recognition of worthiness. Therefore, Christ commanded that one is to take a lower seat as a sign of humility and let the host confer the honor on the one who deserves it.

In the Beatitudes (Matt. 5:3-12), Jesus gave the characteristics of righteous people. From the features that characterize life in the kingdom as revealed in the parables, we observe that those characteristics required in the Beatitudes will be realized in those who are citizens of the kingdom.

Summary

We can see, then, that from the parables we can develop an understanding of the theocratic kingdom, tracing the offer by Messiah, its rejection by Israel, its consequent postponement to a future time, the resultant judgment on the generation that rejected His offer, the new form of the theocracy to be developed in the present age, the events preceding the establishment of the coming messianic kingdom, and the characteristics of those who are in the kingdom.

21

The Kingdom
and Israel's Future

Anticipating the final rejection of His offer and His person, as indicated by the leaders' accusation that He received His power from Satan (Matt. 12:24), Christ gave stern warnings of judgment (vv. 31-32) but also pronounced judgment on that generation of Israel:

> Then Jesus began to denounce the cities in which most of His miracles had been performed, because they did not repent. "Woe to you, Korazin! Woe to you, Bethsaida! If the miracles that were performed in you had been performed in Tyre and Sidon, they would have repented long ago in sackcloth and ashes. But I tell you, it will be more bearable for Tyre and Sidon on the day of judgment than for you. And you, Capernaum, will you be lifted up to the skies? No, you will go down to the depths. If the miracles that were performed in you had been performed in Sodom, it would have remained to this day. But I tell you that it will be more bearable for Sodom on the day of judgment than for you" (Matt. 11:20-24).

Again:

> This is the time of punishment in fulfillment of all that has been written. How dreadful it will be in those days for pregnant women and nursing mothers! There will be great distress in the land and wrath against this people. They will fall by the sword and will be taken as prisoners to all the nations. Jerusa-

lem will be trampled on by the Gentiles until the times of the Gentiles are fulfilled (Luke 21:22-24)·

Or again:

O Jerusalem, Jerusalem, you who kill the prophets and stone those sent to you, how often I have longed to gather your children together, as a hen gathers her chicks under her wings, but you were not willing. Look, your house is left to you desolate. . . . I tell you the truth, not one stone here will be left on another; every one will be thrown down (Matt. 23:37-38; 24:2).

Christ was vividly predicting the coming destruction of Jerusalem by Titus, the Roman general who in A.D. 70 brought either death or exile to that generation of Israel living in the land. This was the physical temporal judgment meted out to the generation that rejected Christ and refused to repent in order to receive the benefits of His offer of the covenanted kingdom and to meet its prerequisites.

The destruction of the city and the temple seemed to declare the cancellation of all Israel's hopes. Without these there could be no nation, there could be no kingdom. It is understandable that many unanswered questions surged through the minds of the Twelve. So in His great prophetical/eschatological discourse of Matthew 24–25, Christ outlined the chronology of prophetic events preceding the second advent of Messiah and the establishment of the covenanted kingdom.

Let's consider this discourse in some detail.

The question—Matthew 24:1-3

Christ's announcement of coming judgment on the city and the nation left the disciples stunned and perplexed. They evidently had withdrawn from Jesus to discuss the matter among themselves. As Jesus left the temple and was walking toward the Mount of Olives, the disciples came to Him, still very puzzled. They wanted a further explanation of Christ's words. They called attention to the temple buildings that Herod had begun fifty years before and that would not be completed for another generation. Herod, a master builder, had planned for his buildings to outlast the pyramids. What he had constructed seemed very permanent. How, the disciples wanted to know, could the permanence of these buildings be reconciled with Christ's message concerning judgment?

Jesus very specifically replied, "Not one stone here will be left on another; every one will be thrown down" (v. 2). This statement, though extremely clear to us, was incomprehensible to the disciples. They walked in silence with Jesus from the temple area through the Kidron Valley to the slopes of the Mount of Olives. Though nothing was said, the disciples must have been struggling to understand what Jesus had meant. When they were alone with Him on the Mount of Olives, they asked, "Tell us . . . when will this happen, and what will be the sign of Your coming and of the end of the age?" (v. 3)

The questions showed that they had arrived at certain conclusions. The Prophet Zechariah had described the advent of Messiah to institute His kingdom (Zech. 14:4). This coming was to be preceded by an invasion of Jerusalem (12:1-3; 14:1-3). Jerusalem would be totally destroyed and the majority of the people in the land would be slaughtered (13:8-9). To these men, then, Christ's words concerning the destruction of Jerusalem equaled the destruction predicted by Zechariah that would precede the advent of the Messiah.

Remember, as mentioned earlier, Jewish eschatology recognized two ages: The first was this present age, the age in which Israel was waiting for the coming of the Messiah; and the second was the age to come, the age in which all of Israel's covenants would be fulfilled and Israel would enter into her promised blessings as a result of the Messiah's coming. The present age would be terminated by the appearance of Messiah, while the coming age would be introduced by His advent. The present age, then, was to end in judgment, and the coming age must be preceded by this devastation.

The disciples concluded that the judgment Christ predicted was the one that would terminate this present age. After this judgment Messiah would come to introduce the age to come. Therefore they asked, "When will this happen, and what will be the sign of Your coming and of the end of the age?" (Matt. 24:3)

We must note that *Jesus was revealing the prophetic program for Jerusalem, the nation Israel, and the people of Israel.* He made *no* reference to the church or the prophetic program for the church. Jesus did not speak here of events that will precede the consummation of the program for the church at the Rapture (John 14:1-4; 1 Cor. 15:51-52; 1 Thes. 4:13-17). Rather, He dealt with the future Tribulation, or seven-year period that will complete the prophetic program for Israel as revealed in Daniel 9:27. Because of its Jewish context, therefore, this portion of Scripture *must* be interpreted with reference to Israel and not to the church.

The Tribulation—Matthew 24:4-26

We earlier observed that the disciples addressed two questions to Jesus. The first was "When will this happen?" that is, "When will Jerusalem be destroyed?" (v. 3) In His discourse, Jesus forewarned when destruction would fall on Jerusalem. And Luke's record of Christ's words calls special attention to the answer to the disciples' *first* question (Luke 21:20-24).

Christ anticipated the approach of the Roman armies under Titus, the instrument through whom God's judgment on that generation would be executed. When those in Jerusalem were aware of Rome's approach, said Jesus, they were to leave Judea and flee to the mountains (v. 21). They were to flee in haste because the destruction would not be delayed for long. Multitudes would be slain by Titus' soldiers (v. 24) in connection with the invasion. And, noted Jesus, "Jerusalem will be trampled on by the Gentiles until the times of the Gentiles are fulfilled."

The "times of the Gentiles" refers to an extremely important period in biblical prophecy. The expression refers to a time period that began with Nebuchadnezzar's overthrow of Jerusalem. This assault began in 606–605 B.C., was continued in a second invasion in 597 B.C., and was consummated in the utter destruction of Jerusalem in 586 B.C. Jerusalem, according to chapters 2 and 7 of Daniel's prophecy, would be occupied in turn by four world empires: the Babylonian, the Medo-Persian, the Grecian, and finally the Roman.

The times of the Gentiles would end when Christ the Messiah (referred to as a smiting "rock" in Dan. 2:34-35, 45) would destroy the nations that ruled over Jerusalem and liberate that city, land, and people from bondage to the Gentiles. The times of the Gentiles, then, began in the days of Nebuchadnezzar and will continue until the second advent of Jesus the Messiah to this earth. When He returns He will smite the nations and "rule them with an iron scepter" and "dash them to pieces like pottery" (Ps. 2:9). At that time it will be said, "The kingdom of the world has become the kingdom of our Lord and of His Christ, and He will reign forever and ever" (Rev. 11:15). Thus Luke's record emphasized the details that our Lord provided in answer to the first question concerning when Jerusalem would be destroyed.

Meanwhile, Matthew in his record of Christ's discourse directed attention to the disciples' *second* question, "What will be the sign of Your coming and of the end of the age?" (Matt. 24:3) The disciples did not ask two questions here, but one. They believed, having read the Old Testament, that Messiah's coming would terminate the present age in which they were waiting for His appearance. Quite simply, when He came, He would introduce the age to come. So Jesus devoted the first great portion of His discourse, as recorded in Matthew 24:4-28, to answering this question.

In His discourse, Jesus spoke of signs that will forewarn the nation Israel of the approaching advent of Messiah to the earth for a second time.

The first half—Matthew 24:4-8
In verses 4-8, Jesus described events that will fall within the seven years of what Jeremiah called "a time of trouble for Jacob" (Jer. 30:7). Jesus referred to the rigors that Israel will undergo in this period as "birth pains" (Matt. 24:8). They will be the sufferings that precede the birth of the new age to come.

Daniel indicated that this seven-year period will be divided into two parts of equal length (Dan. 9:27). In light of that, Jesus described signs that will be given to the nation Israel in the first half of the Tribulation (Matt. 24:4-8). One sign will be that false messiahs will appear (v. 5). Another sign will be reports of war (vv. 6-7). Another will be natural catastrophes—famines and earthquakes (v. 7).

In Revelation 6, John described events of the first half of the Tribulation by disclosing what was hidden under the seals on a scroll. The parallels between Christ's signs in Matthew 24:4-8 and what John revealed in Revelation 6 suggest that both accounts fall within the first half of the Tribulation. John's first seal has to do with a rider on a white horse (v. 2), who is a false messiah. As the result of the rise of this one, peace will be taken from the earth and war will ensue (v. 4). As a result of war there will be widespread famine (v. 6) that will result in widespread death (v. 8). Even so, Christ revealed that as rigorous as these judgments may seem, they will be only "the beginning of birth pains" (Matt. 24:8).

In this portion, then, Christ described the judgments of the first half of the Tribulation. He told of signs that would be given to Israel to forewarn them of the approach of the Judge.

The second half—Matthew 24:9-14
Next Christ mentioned signs that will fall in the second half of the Tribulation (vv. 9-14). There will be widespread persecution and death (v. 9). Many will turn from Christ to worship the political dictator whom John called the "beast" (Rev. 13:1-10) and Paul called "the man of lawlessness" (2 Thes. 2:1-4). And many false prophets will appear and deceive many.

John wrote about a particular false prophet (Rev. 13:11-18) who, by Satan's power, will perform miracles to persuade the world to worship the first beast, the political dictator described in verses 1-10. This false prophet will begin his ministry in the middle of the Tribulation. The beast will extend political power over the world and assume the prerogatives of Deity in the religious world.

Note that all these activities will be signs which fall in the second half of the Tribulation to forewarn Israel of the approaching advent of Christ. The beast will become a persecutor (v. 7), and many will lose their lives. This no doubt will tempt many to renounce Christ and give allegiance to the beast. But Christ promised, "He who stands firm to the end will be saved" (Matt. 24:13). (In the context, the salvation referred to here is from persecution, that is, salvation from the beast's control by the appearance of the Deliverer—Rom. 11:26).

During the time that the politico-religious system of the beast is in absolute control, the Gospel of the kingdom will be preached throughout the whole world (Matt. 24:14). The "Gospel of the kingdom" is what was preached by both John and Jesus (3:2, 4-17). This "Gospel" was the Good News that the kingdom was near, and was a message with both a soteriological (salvation) and an eschatological (prophetic) emphasis. This Gospel directed sinners to "the Lamb of God, who takes away the sin of the world" (John 1:29) and promised the expectant ones that "the kingdom of heaven is near" (Matt. 3:2). When John and Jesus called on the people of the nation to repent, they were asking them to acknowledge their sinful state and their need of salvation. They were inviting the people to turn in faith to

251

God, who had promised to send a Saviour.

In light of this, the Gospel of the kingdom as preached in the Tribulation will have two emphases. On one hand it will announce the good news that Messiah's advent is near, at which time He will introduce the messianic age of blessing. On the other hand it will also offer men salvation by grace through faith based on the blood of Christ.

The Book of Revelation indicates that this Gospel will be preached by 144,000 set apart from the tribes of Israel (Rev. 7:1-8), all descendants of Abraham. They evidently will be brought to faith in Messiah the same way Saul of Tarsus was brought to faith in Christ on the Damascus road. They will be given a revelation of the person of Christ and they, like Saul, will be set apart to be God's messengers to the Gentiles. The result of their ministry will be that "a great multitude that no one could count, from every nation, tribe, people and language" (v. 9) will "[wash] their robes and [make] them white in the blood of the Lamb" (v. 14).

God will also send two "witnesses," or prophets, to the nation Israel (Rev. 11:1-12). This pair will point many to salvation by grace through faith based on the shed blood of Christ, and a remnant will be redeemed from Israel. Consequently, throughout the Tribuation as a result of the preaching of the Gospel of grace, coupled with a warning that judgment is imminent, many Jews and Gentiles will be brought to faith in Christ.

Repetition and explanation—Matthew 24:15-26

Christ then directed His attention to the sign that will forewarn Israel of His approaching second advent. He referred to the one "spoken of through the Prophet Daniel" (v. 15). Daniel 7:8 speaks of a "horn, a little one."

This introduces us to a prophetic figure who will be elevated to a position of authority over ten nations that had their origin in the disruption of the old Roman Empire. This one, the same person John called "the beast," will come to power, not by military conquest, but by common consent (Rev. 17:13). From chapter 7 on in Daniel's prophecy, this individual plays the prominent role. He is referred to—and his activities are described—by the name of a "stern-faced king" (Dan. 8:23). He is mentioned again as "the ruler who will come" (9:26). He also is called "the king [who] will do as he pleases" (11:36). Still another reference to him is "the abomination that causes desolation" (12:11). It is to this person Christ referred in Matthew 24:15.

According to Jesus, the appearance of this dictator will herald the beginning of the Tribulation. What Titus did to Jerusalem in A.D. 70 merely foreshadowed what this abominable one who desolates will do to Jerusalem and to the land of Israel in the Tribulation. Just as in Luke 21:20-24 Christ instructed the people to flee the land when Titus approached, so here in Matthew 24:16-18 He gave similar warning to those who will hear of the approach of the armies of this dictator in the Tribulation. The need for haste will be so great that it will cause undue difficulties for those who are hindered because of pregnancy (v. 19), or who for other reasons have problems traveling (v. 20).

As a result of this final invasion of the land, Christ said, "There will be great distress, unequaled from the beginning of the world until now—and never to be equaled again" (v. 21). As great as has been Israel's sufferings in days past, unprecedented suffering awaits them in this period. But God has determined to preserve a remnant in Israel, even though Satan will seek to exterminate every physical descendant of Abraham in order to prevent the fulfillment of the covenant God gave to him. John described this persecution (Rev. 12:13-17), and it is only the willingness of Gentiles to harbor the fleeing Jews that will prevent their utter destruction.

Christ promised that the Tribulation would be "cut short" and spoke of "those days" (Matt. 24:22). Here His promise has been misunderstood by some. Daniel spoke of the Tribulation as a "seven," that is, a seven-year-period (Dan. 9:27). John gave its duration in months (Rev. 11:2), and even in days (v. 3). Therefore some have asked, "How could those days be shortened? Can Christ's words mean that the days will be decreased in number?"

The phrase *cut short* can mean "to terminate." In other words, if those days with their awful judgments were allowed to continue indefinitely, the human race would be totally destroyed. But Christ pointed out that God will allow that period to run its course, but will terminate it according to His timetable so that a remnant will be spared.

So great will be the desperation of those experiencing the rigors of this judgment that they will seek some deliverance. They will turn to false Christs and false prophets for help (Matt. 24:24). Thus the beast will extend his power, and many will turn to him when they see miracles the false prophet will perform to persuade the world to worship him as God (Rev. 13:11-18). They will accept these miracles as proof he is God.

Ultimately this one will want to be recognized as Messiah, but Christ warned men not to submit to him. Men will be able to discern the true Messiah when He comes, for His coming will be as lightning (Matt. 24:27). Darkness will envelope the earth throughout the latter part of the Tribulation, as the sun, moon, and stars will fail to give their normal light (Rev. 8:12). This darkness will suddenly be illuminated by the shining of the brightness of the glory that belongs to Jesus Christ. This revealed glory will identify the true Messiah.

Jesus further implied that He will return first in the role of a Judge when He said, "Whenever there is a carcass, there the vultures will gather" (Matt. 24:28). He thus viewed the nation Israel as a lifeless corpse, which He will judge.

The second advent—Matthew 24:27-30

Having described the Tribulation (Matt. 24:4-26), Christ moved on to describe the next event in Israel's prophetic program, speaking of His return to the earth (vv. 27-30). Zephaniah had already foretold the darkness of the Day of the Lord (Zeph. 1:14-17). Now Christ foresaw physical darkness as well as moral and spiritual darkness, and indicated that it will be against this darkness that "the sign of the Son of Man will appear in the sky" (Matt. 24:30).

All through the Old Testament, God revealed His presence among His people by the shining of light. When Immanuel returns, His presence will be heralded by the shining of the essential glory that belongs to Him, and the peoples of the earth "will see the Son of Man coming on the clouds of the sky, with power and great glory" (v. 30). The transfiguration of Christ was a premature disclosure of the glory to be revealed at the second advent of Christ. God gave to man the authority to rule as His representative over the earth (Gen. 1:28). The Holy Spirit led David to reaffirm that destiny (Ps. 8:6-8). It is not surprising, then, that at His second advent Christ will come as "the Son of Man" (Matt. 24:30) to subject the earth to His authority so that He might fulfill the destiny that God assigned to man.

According to Jesus, this coming will be both bodily and visible. Christ's feet shall touch the Mount of Olives as predicted in Zechariah

14:4, and He will return in the same manner that He ascended into heaven (Acts 1:11).

The regathering of Israel—Matthew 24:31

Christ then proceeded to describe the third great prophetic event in Israel's program—the restoration of the nation Israel back to the land. Since His entire discourse had been devoted to the prophetic program for Israel, the reference to "His elect" (v. 31) could not possibly refer to the church. Instead, it must refer to the nation God had chosen (Ex. 19:5-6).

During the Tribulation Israel will be scattered out of the land by military invasions (Rev. 12:14-16), and the Israelites will flee and find refuge among the Gentile nations. Supernaturally God will bring the people back to the land through the instrumentality of angels, which will be the final restoration anticipated in the Old Testament (Deut. 30:1-8).

Parenthetical exhortations—Matthew 24:32-51

The fig tree—Matthew 24:32-44
Before resuming the chronology of prophetic events (25:1), the Lord paused to give certain parenthetical exhortations concerning watchfulness and preparedness (24:32-51), and He applied His teaching to those who will witness the great events of which He had previously spoken.

He first exhorted the people to "keep watch" (v. 42). In response to the disciples' question, He said a multitude of signs had been given that a future generation of Israel will see. These signs will forewarn them of the approach of the Judge and of coming judgments. Now to show the importance of these signs as indicators of coming judgment, Christ used an illustration from nature.

Anyone who passed through the rigors of a cold Judean winter would eagerly anticipate the coming of summer. When one would see the first green shoots appearing on a fig tree, he would have an indication of the season in which he was then living (v. 32). He could anticipate the passing of the cold and the coming of spring. Christ applied this simple principle, saying, "When you see all these things, you know that it is near, right at the door" (v. 33). In the context "these things" refers to the signs of verses 4-28. Those who will see the signs will know that He, the Messiah, or it, Messiah's judgment, is at the door. Since these signs will all occur in the seven years of Daniel's seventieth week, the generation that sees the beginning of these signs will "not pass away until all these things have happened" (v. 34), for they all will fall within a brief span of time.

Notice that these will *not* be signs given to a generation preceding the Rapture. Instead, these signs will be given to a generation that cannot begin until after the church has been translated.

To remove any doubt as to the certainty of these events, Christ said, "My words will never pass away" (v. 35). God's predetermined program to pour out judgment before believers experience the blessings of the Millennial Age must come to pass. While no one knows the specific day or hour in which Jesus Christ will return, people who properly understand and interpret the signs will know that they are living in the last days. We might suppose that this consciousness would deliver people from complacency and indifference, but that apparently will not be the case.

Christ likened those future days in which the signs will unfold to the days of Noah. Noah announced a coming judgment and offered people a way of escape from it. However, people ignored Noah's warnings of judgment and went on occupying themselves with their normal course of life. They were "eating and drinking, marrying and giving in marriage" (v. 38) right up until the very day Noah entered the ark. When the Flood came, people who had ignored the warning of coming judgment were unprepared for the Flood and had not availed themselves of the way of escape. Hence they were swept away in the judgment. So it will be in the Tribulation. The signs will forewarn of the coming of the Judge and His destroying judgment. But when He comes, "two men will be in the field; one will be taken [away in judgment] and the other left [to go into the millennial kingdom]. Two women will be grinding with a hand mill; one will be taken [away in judgment] and the other will be left [to go into the kingdom]" (vv. 40-41).

In the light of this, Christ exhorted those in that generation to "keep watch" (v. 42). It will be important for them to watch because of the uncertainty of the actual time when Messiah will appear. To clarify His teaching, Christ used a parable. He said if a thief gave advance notice of when the theft would occur, the owner of a house would not have to stand guard until the appointed time arrived. But since a thief gives no advance notice, the owner of the house must continally watch. In applying this parable, Christ said, "So you also must be ready, because the Son of Man will come at an hour when you do not expect Him" (v. 44). The exact time of His coming will not be known.

The faithful servant—Matthew 24:45-51

Next Christ gave an exhortation concerning faithfulness in view of the fact that believers do not know just when He will return. He likened a prepared disciple to a servant who was put in charge of his master's household. The servant's responsibility was to administer his master's goods for the benefit of his master's servants. His responsibility demanded faithfulness even though the master was not present to supervise him. If when the master returned he found the servant had been faithful, the master would reward him. But if the servant was faithless when his master was away, he would be punished if the master unexpectedly returned and discovered his faithlessness.

As pointed out earlier, Christ used this parable to teach that at His return those who call themselves His servants will be tested; those who are faithless will be rejected in spite of their profession, but those who are faithful will be accepted because their faithfulness will validate their faith. In this parenthetical section, then, Christ exhorted those who will witness the signs to be watchful, to be prepared, and to be faithful in view of His coming.

Judgment on Israel—Matthew 25:1-30

The ten virgins—Matthew 25:1-13

Christ next resumed His revelation of the chronology of prophetic events for Israel. He taught that following His return (24:30) and the regathering of the nation Israel to their land (v. 31), the nation would be brought under judgment (25:1-30).

Christ used two parables to teach that the regathered nation will be judged to determine who is saved and who is unsaved. The purpose of this judgment will be to exclude the unsaved from, and to receive the saved into, the kingdom He will establish following His second advent.

The first parable was that of the ten virgins (vv. 1-13). While Paul used the figure of a virgin in reference to the church (2 Cor. 11:2), the Jewish context here shows that the church is not in view. In His discourse Jesus was developing the eschatological program for the nation Israel. And, as we saw in previous chapters, the parable was based on the marriage customs of our Lord's day. And, as we have seen, in this parable our Lord taught that during the interval in which He will be absent, those who anticipate His coming should be prepared and should be watching.

His return will terminate the opportunity for people to prepare themselves to enter the millennial kingdom, and only the prepared will be accepted. No unsaved (unprepared) person will be admitted into Christ's millennial kingdom. This is made very clear in Psalm 24, which tells of prilgrims proceeding to Jerusalem for a festival. They are seen approaching the city with the hope that they might on that occasion meet Messiah and welcome Him to His kingdom. But as they proceed, some ask, "Who may ascend the hill of the Lord? Who may stand in His holy place?" (v. 3), that is, who will be accepted into Messiah's kingdom? Others give the answer: "He who has clean hands and a pure heart, who does not lift up his soul to an idol or swear by what is false" (v. 4).

Thus only the pure in heart shall see God (Matt. 5:8).

Talents—Matthew 25:14-30
In the second parable (vv. 14-30), Christ again taught that following His return and Israel's regathering, the nation must undergo judgment. This again will be a judgment to determine on one hand who is saved and therefore to be accepted into the kingdom; and on the other hand who is unsaved and to be barred from entering the kingdom.

In this parable the Lord taught truth similar to what He had taught in Luke 19:11-27. In that parable in which there was equal distribution, Christ taught equal opportunity; here, however, where there is an unequal distribution, He taught individual responsibility. Since we have already covered this parable in detail, we can let it suffice to observe that Christ used this parable to reveal that the nation Israel, which had been set aside as God's servant (Ex. 19:5-6), received a responsibility for which they were answerable.

In the Old Testament, Israel was designed to be God's light to the Gentile world. In fact, the candlestand in the tabernacle was to be a perpetual reminder of Israel's function. But because Israel was faithless to that function, God promised that another Light would come to bring light to the Gentiles (Isa. 60:1-3).

Christ came as the "true light" (John 1:9; 8:12)—but God will set apart Israel again during the Tribulation to be His light to the world (Rev. 7:1-8). When Christ comes the second time, the nation will be judged to determine individual faithfulness to that appointment. Faithfulness will indicate faith in the person of Christ. Those who prove themselves faithful will be accepted into His kingdom. But those who are faithless will be excluded from His kingdom.

Thus in these two parables Christ described the judgment that will come on the nation Israel following their regathering after His second advent.

Judgment on Gentiles—Matthew 25:31-46

Finally, Christ concluded His discourse by speaking of the final prophetic event preceding the actual establishment of His millennial kingdom. The Gentile nations must be judged to determine who from among the living Gentiles will be accepted into His kingdom and who will be rejected.

As we have already seen, this is the revelation that Jesus gave in the judgment of the sheep and the goats (vv. 31-46). When Christ comes the second time, He will be enthroned in heavenly glory (v. 31). He will sit on David's throne (2 Sam. 7:16; Luke 1:32-33), and while on David's throne, Messiah will rule not only over Israel but over the Gentiles as well. Since no unsaved person can enter His millennial kingdom, it will be necessary to separate the saved from the unsaved in the Gentile nations.

Therefore after Israel has been judged, "All nations will be gathered before Him" (Matt. 25:32). This will not be a judgment of nations as national entities, but of individuals from the nations. If this were a judgment of national entities, it is obvious that some unsaved would be included in an accepted nation and some saved would be excluded because they were in a rejected nation. Therefore, we must conclude that this will be a judgment of individuals, not of nations.

When the Gentiles appear before Christ, they will be separated into two groups. Without a spoken word the ones called "sheep" will be put on His right hand, and the others called "goats" will be put on His left hand. To the sheep on His right hand Christ will speak a word of welcome: "Come, you who are blessed by My Father, take your inheritance, the kingdom prepared for you since the creation of the world" (v. 34). They will be included because of their works done for Christ in His name (vv. 35-36).

But the sheep, who are called "righteous" (v. 37), will question that they had even seen Christ. How could they, then, have done things for Him that would gain them admission into His kingdom? Christ will explain, "Whatever you did for one of the least of these brothers of Mine, you did for Me" (v. 40).

The reference to "these brothers" indicates there will be a third group there in the presence of Christ. That phrase may refer to those who are Christ's brothers after the flesh, that is, the nation Israel; or it may refer to those chosen messengers, the 144,000 of Revelation 7, who will bear witness of Him during the Tribulation. These 144,000 will be under a death sentence by the beast. They will refuse to carry the beast's mark, and so they will not be able to buy and sell. Consequently, they will have to depend on those to whom they minister for hospitality, food, and support. Only those who receive the message will jeopardize their lives by extending hospitality to the messengers. Therefore, what is done for them will be an evidence of their faith in Christ, that is, what is done for them will be done for Christ. These will not be accepted because of their works, since no man is ever saved by works. But their works will demonstrate their faith in the person of Christ, which renders them acceptable to Him.

Christ then will turn to those on His left hand and command, "Depart . . . into the eternal fire prepared for the devil and his angels" (Matt. 25:41). The basis of this judgment will be their works (vv. 42-43). They will reply that since they had never seen Christ, they had never had an opportunity to do anything for Him. They will try to show that their judgment is not just. But Christ will reply "whatever you did not do for one of the least of these, you did not do for Me" (v. 45). When these stand before Christ, they will have heard the message of the messengers; and they will have shown their rejection of the message by refusing to give the messengers hospitality. Their lack of faith in Christ will be evident in that they did not receive His messengers. Christ will view what was withheld from the messengers just as if it had been withheld from Him. Their lack of faith in Christ will be evidenced by their lack of works, causing them to be excluded from the millennial kingdom. And such "will go away to eternal punishment, but the righteous [will go] to eternal life" (v. 46).

Thus the righteous will be accepted into Messiah's earthly kingdom, but the unsaved will be rejected from it. Those who are received into the kingdom will be those received into eternal life. Those rejected from the kingdom will be those excluded from eternal life due to failure to believe in Christ.

Following this great discourse, events moved rapidly toward his trial and death, which He had been predicting since the leaders in the nation committed themselves to their explanation of His person as having been empowered by Satan.

It was as a king that Christ was on trial before Pilate (Matt. 27:11; Mark 15:2; Luke 23:3; John 18:33). It was as king that Jesus was rejected by the Jews. "When Pilate heard this he brought Jesus out. . . . 'Here is your king,' Pilate said to the Jews. But they shouted, 'Take Him away! Take Him away. Crucify Him!' 'Shall I crucify your king?' Pilate asked. 'We have no king but Caesar,' the chief priests answered" (John 19:14-15).

And even though He was declared innocent six times by both Pilate and Herod, He was delivered over to death. According to Roman customs, the charge for which a criminal was being executed would be prominently displayed. Pilate therefore had the charge written in Aramic, Latin, and Greek: "Jesus of Nazareth, the King of the Jews" (vv. 19-20).

The rejection of the King and His offered kingdom was then finalized and that generation was delivered over to judgment and the kingdom postponed, until that day when a remnant will cry: "Blessed is He who comes in the name of the Lord" (Matt. 23:39).

It would appear that Satan and his counter-kingdom had triumphed over the true King appointed to rule over the kingdom of the God of heaven on earth. The resurrection of Christ, however, proclaimed His victory over Satan and the kingdom of darkness, just as it guaranteed the eventual establishment of His kingdom here on the earth—that realm over which the prince of darkness now rules.

Summary

Christ's announcement of judgment on Jerusalem undoubtedly was understood by the disciples in its prophetic context as a judgment preceding the second advent of Messiah to the earth. They asked when the judgment would come and what signs would be given to the nation Israel. Christ explained the signs in detail (Matt. 24:4-26), outlining the events of the first half of the Tribulation (vv. 4-8), and also the events of the second half (vv. 9-14). He then described the climactic sign (vv. 15-26).

Christ then moved on to the next eschatological event, His second advent to the earth (vv. 27-30), followed by the regathering of Israel (v. 31). In a parenthetical statement in unfolding the eschatological events, He gave exhortations concerning watchfulness, preparedness, and faithfulness (vv. 32-51). He then resumed the eschatological revelation, pointing out that following Israel's regathering, Israel will be judged to separate the saved from the unsaved. The saved will be received into the kingdom but the unsaved will be excluded (25:1-30).

In conclusion, He spoke of the judgment of living Gentiles to separate the saved from the unsaved. Again, the saved will be received into the kingdom but the unsaved will be excluded (vv. 31-46).

It is evident from this consideration of Christ's eschatological discourse that *He does not view Israel's covenants as having been cancelled,* nor her kingdom hopes abandoned, but only postponed until a future generation to whom the good news of the kingdom is proclaimed will be brought to faith and repentance. The Lord Jesus Himself will then assume David's scepter and mount David's throne and reign in the covenanted kingdom.

22

The Kingdom
and the Apostles

Things pertaining to the kingdom

In the forty days between His resurrection and ascension, Jesus spent time instructing the eleven He had chosen and designated as His apostles. Luke summarized the content of Christ's instruction by writing, "After His suffering, He showed Himself to these men and gave many convincing proofs that He was alive. He appeared to them over a period of forty days and *spoke about the kingdom of God*" (Acts 1:3, italics mine).

If this was the focus of Christ's teaching following His resurrection and preceding His ascension, it is essential that we have a clear understanding of what Luke had in mind when he spoke of the things "about the kingdom of God." Some understand this to mean that Christ gave further revelation concerning the future earthly Davidic kingdom. However, close examination of what is recorded of the postresurrection ministry of Christ shows that He provided instruction concerning the new form of the kingdom which had been revealed in the parables of Matthew 13 and included the prophecy concerning the formation of the church in 16:18.

These men were being sent into the world not to announce the imminence or the inauguration of the Davidic kingdom, but rather to proclaim a new message based on the death and resurrection of Jesus Christ. Mark recorded the Lord's commission to them, "Go into all the world and preach the good news to all creation" (Mark 16:15). Luke records the commission given to them, "Repentance and forgiveness of sins will be preached in His name to all nations, beginning at Jerusalem" (Luke 24:47). This message was based on the death and the resurrection of Jesus Christ (v. 46). And the specific instruction was, "You are witnesses of these things" (v. 48). These men were not authorized as was John the Baptist to announce that the kingdom was at hand; rather, they were to proclaim salvation through the death and resurrection of Jesus Christ.

Their commission was based on the fact that "All authority in heaven and on earth has been given to Me" (Matt. 28:18). Commissioning these men was an exercise of the God-given authority that belonged to Jesus Christ, and based on that He commanded them, "Therefore go and make disciples of all nations" (v. 19). To disciple nations means to bring nations under the sovereign authority that belongs to Jesus Christ. Therefore they could come under His authority only by identifying themselves (being baptized) with the Father and the Son and the Holy Spirit. This would be possible only as they were instructed in the things that Christ had commanded (v. 20).

The purpose of signs

In these commissions, then, we see that Jesus Christ was not sending these men into the world as He had sent them previously to proclaim the imminence of the kingdom (Matt. 10:7). Instead He was sending them to proclaim a new message of salvation based on the death and resurrection of Jesus Christ. And just as the message these men had previously proclaimed was authenticated by the signs they performed (v. 8), so the new message they were now sent to proclaim would be authenticated by signs that they would perform (Mark 16:17-18). These signs were given specifically to the apostles to authenticate them as God's messengers with God's new message of salvation based on the death and resurrection of Jesus Christ.

It is important to recognize that these signs were not given generally to all believers, but exclusively to the apostles. That's why Paul could appeal to the signs he performed as an authentication of his apostleship (2 Cor. 12:12). Had those signs been given to all believers, they could not have authenticated Paul as a genuine apostle of Jesus Christ.

These signs were not to authenticate an offer of the Davidic kingdom as before, but were intended to authenticate the new message

God was proclaiming to the world through the apostles. The message the apostles were commissioned to preach, then, became the message of the kingdom of God of which Luke spoke (Acts 1:3). That message is the heart of the new form of the kingdom which would be administered in the present age which falls between the death of Christ and Messiah's second advent back to earth.

Gospel sources

Later, after receiving this instruction concerning this new form of the kingdom of God, two recipients of this instruction wrote their Gospels—Matthew and John. In a study of these Gospels we see that during this forty-day interval in which they received the Lord's instructions, they came to understand the transition in the kingdom program as it was to be developed here on the earth in this present age.

As a result of this understanding, Matthew wrote not to prove to the Jews that Jesus actually was the Messiah—as his Gospel is so frequently interpreted. Rather, he wrote to explain why—after the true Messiah came and was introduced to Israel by the appointed forerunner and authenticated Himself and His offer of the kingdom by the miracles that He performed—the kingdom He came to establish was not instituted in fulfillment of the covenants and promises. In his Gospel Matthew traced the nation's response to Christ's offer of Himself and His kingdom and he showed that the kingdom failed to be established, not because it was not a legitimate offer by a legitimate Messiah, but because the nation knowingly rejected Jesus as Messiah and spurned His offer of the covenanted kingdom.

Matthew then recorded the revelation of a new form of the kingdom in which the church would play a significant role. In the great discourse of Matthew 24 and 25, Christ outlined future events for the nation of Israel leading up to the second advent of Christ and the establishment of the promised kingdom on earth. Clearly Matthew's understanding of the transition from the offer and rejection of the Davidic form of the kingdom to the establishment of a new form of theocratic administration must have come to him as a result of Christ's instruction during the forty days following His resurrection.

As John wrote his Gospel he made it clear that he was not writing to authenticate the messiahship of Jesus, or to teach that the present form of the kingdom is somehow the fulfillment of the Davidic

Covenant, but rather to demonstrate that Jesus Christ is the Son of God so that those who believe He is the Son of God might have life through His name (John 20:31). John's message does not have to do with the reign of Christ in this present age, but rather with the salvation that was made available through the death and resurrection of the Son of God.

During the course of His postresurrection ministry, then, Jesus explained to the Eleven the transition from an offer of the covenanted Davidic kingdom to a new form of the kingdom, and He prepared these men to be His representatives in proclaiming a new message offering salvation to all men based on His death and resurrection. This instruction constituted Christ's teaching concerning the kingdom of God.

Christ understood these men and knew that in spite of His instruction they would not perceive what He had communicated to them. In fact it would not be until after the advent of the Holy Spirit, who would come as a Teacher (John 14:26), that these men would understand what Christ had been teaching them (16:12-14).

Acts: Book of transition

As we understand this progression of events, then we can see that the Book of Acts is a book of transition, and that the entire period from the death of Christ to the destruction of Jerusalem by Titus in A.D. 70 is a transitional period.

Positionally, the old order was done away at the death of Christ, as signified by the tearing of the veil of the temple (Matt. 27:51). Positionally, the new order began with the coming of the Holy Spirit to indwell the body of believers as recorded in Acts 2. Positionally, the entire transition took place within the span of those few days.

Experientially, however, the transition covered nearly four decades. The transition was extensive. Ethnically, there was a transition from dealing primarily with Jews to dealing with both Jew and Gentile without distinction. There was also a transition in the people with whom God was dealing, from Israel to the church. Likewise, there was a transition in the principle on which God was dealing with men, from Law to grace. There was a transition from the offer to Israel of an earthly Davidic kingdom to the offer to all men of salvation based on the death and resurrection of Jesus Christ. There was a transition from the prospect of Messiah's coming to the historical fact that the promised One had come. There was a transition from the promise that the Spirit would be given to the historical fact that the Spirit had come.

Again, all these transitions were made positionally in the brief period of time from the death of Christ to the Day of Pentecost. Yet experientially these truths were understood and entered into only over a span of some four decades. The Book of Acts records the positional transition as well as the experiential transition in the development of the theocratic kingdom program.

The promise of the Spirit

According to God's revelation given to Israel through the cycle of the levitical feasts, two divine works were essential before Israel could experience the covenanted kingdom blessings.

As revealed in Passover, the Lamb of God must be sacrificed to take away the sin of the world. And according to the Feast of Pentecost, the Holy Spirit must be given to unite the people of God just as the flour was united into a loaf. The Spirit also would enable those who were God's people to walk in obedience to the demands of God, in order to be eligible for the blessings God had covenanted to give to them. Because the Feast of Pentecost was counted off fifty days after Passover, these two acts were viewed as two parts of a single divine provision.

Clearly the death of Christ fulfilled that which was anticipated in the Feast of Passover (1 Cor. 5:7); but the full divine work would not be fulfilled until the Holy Spirit had been given. During the latter portion of Christ's earthly ministry, He spoke frequently concerning His approaching death (Matt. 20:17-19; Mark 10:32-34; Luke 18:31-34). In the upper room on the eve of His crucifixion, however, Jesus spoke not concerning His approaching death, but rather concerning the coming of the Holy Spirit in which the Feast of Pentecost would be fulfilled. He told the men gathered with Him there that He would return to His Father (John 16:17). He also had informed them that after He returned to the Father, He would ask the Father to send the Holy Spirit to them (14:16). He then gave the promise that the Spirit who had been with them would be in them (v. 17). This Spirit would join with them in their testimony concerning the person of Jesus Christ and to the salvation that He had provided through His death and resurrection (15:26-27).

After His resurrection, Jesus reiterated the promise of the coming of the Spirit in the symbolic act of breathing on them. "He breathed on them and said, 'Receive the Holy Spirit' " (20:22). The Eleven did not receive the Holy Spirit at that time; instead this was a promise that they would receive that of which He had spoken. Just before His ascension Jesus "gave them this command: 'Do not leave Jerusalem, but wait for the gift My Father promised, which you have heard Me speak about' " (Acts 1:4). If the Spirit had been given when Christ breathed on them it would have not been necessary for them to await the fulfillment of that which the act of breathing on them symbolized.

Question about the kingdom

After Christ had instructed the Eleven to await their ministry for Him until after the Holy Spirit had been given we read, "They asked him, 'Lord, are You at this time going to restore the kingdom to Israel?' " (Acts 1:6) This question reveals the thinking of the Eleven. Jesus had frequently predicted His forthcoming death and resurrection (Matt. 20:17-19; Mark 10:32-34; Luke 18:31-34). He had further announced the forthcoming judgment on the nation (Matt. 23:37–24:2; Luke 21:24). He had outlined the detailed eschatological program that would befall the nation prior to the institution of the future earthly Davidic kingdom (Matt. 24–25). Along with this program for the nation Christ had predicted that when the kingdom was instituted, "You who have followed Me will also sit on twelve thrones, judging the twelve tribes of Israel" (19:28). These men were assured positions of administrative authority in the kingdom that Christ will establish on earth at His return.

In spite of all Jesus had taught these men during the course of His ministry and during His postresurrection ministry, they had not yet grasped the fact that the kingdom they were anticipating had been postponed to some future time. They were correct in their anticipation that as Messiah Christ will again restore the kingdom to Israel. They rightly anticipated the restoration of the Davidic kingdom in fulfillment of the promises of the Davidic Covenant (2 Sam. 7:16; Ps. 89:3-4). And it is extremely important to notice that Jesus did not change their concept of the coming kingdom. Instead, He dealt with their understanding of the timing of when this kingdom will be instituted. They had asked, " 'Lord, are You at this time going to restore the kingdom to Israel?' " And Christ responded to their question by telling them that the timing was not for them to know (Acts 1:7).

This present age—in which the prophesied program concerning the new form of the kingdom will run its course, and in which the church Christ promised has been formed—is indefinite in its duration. The disciples could not know when Messiah would return to establish the millennial kingdom. This passage makes it clear that while the covenanted form of the theocracy has not been cancelled and has only been postponed, this present age is definitely *not* a development of the Davidic form of the kingdom. Rather, it is a period in which a new form of theocratic administration is inaugurated. In this way Jesus not only answered the disciples' question concerning the timing of the future Davidic kingdom, but He also made a clear distinction between it and the intervening present form of the theocratic administration.

The promise fulfilled

Christ indicated that their time of waiting would be brief when He said, "In a few days you will be baptized with the Holy Spirit" (Acts 1:5). Christ earlier had instructed these men to petition the Father to fulfill His promise (Luke 11:13). That of which Christ had spoken in the upper room and in His postresurrection ministry was the same thing the Father had promised in Ezekiel 36:26-27 and Joel 2:28-29. The promise of God reaffirmed by Jesus Christ became the foundation of their faith as they prayed. And after the Ascension when the Eleven gathered into an upper room, "They all joined together constantly in prayer" (Acts 1:14). Without doubt they were united in praying for the fulfillment of that which the Father had promised and was confirmed to them by Christ's promise.

That prayer was answered as the historical events recorded in Acts 2 took place. On the Day of Pentecost a fact took place. That fact is stated in verse 4: "All of them were filled with the Holy Spirit." The personal pronoun *them* of verse 4 refers back to verse 1 and on back to the eleven apostles of 1:26. The filling referred to was the initial act by which the Holy Spirit indwelt the corporate body of believers as His temple. Paul asserts, "In Him the whole building is joined together and rises to become a holy temple in the

Lord. And in Him you too are being built together to become a dwelling in which God lives by His Spirit" (Eph. 2:21-22). Further, the Spirit who indwelt the corporate body of believers also indwelt believers individually: "Do you not know that your body is a temple of the Holy Spirit, who is in you, whom you have received from God?" (1 Cor. 6:19)

So we see that what transpired on that momentous day was that the Holy Spirit whom the Father had promised had come to indwell believers corporately and individually as His temple.

There were three attestations to this fact: The *first* was *audible:* "Suddenly a sound like the blowing of a violent wind came from heaven and filled the whole house where they were sitting" (Acts 2:2). This tornado-like audible sound was given as evidence that the powerful Spirit had come.

Second, "They saw what appeared to be tongues of fire that separated and came to rest on each of them" (v. 3). This experience of the Eleven may be compared with the experience of Moses as recorded in Exodus 34:29. After Moses had been in the Lord's presence he experienced a transfiguration in which his countenance reflected the *shekinah*, the glory of the God in whose presence he had been. This same type of experience was a *visible* sign to the Eleven as they became the instruments through whom God would reveal Himself in order that He might be glorified among men.

The *third* sign was an *experiential* sign. They "began to speak in other tongues as the Spirit enabled them" (Acts 2:4). The biblical record of the event makes it clear that these other tongues were known languages (vv. 6, 8, and 11), as representatives of the many nations assembled there to observe this feast heard the apostles speaking in their own mother tongues. And these three signs—the audible, the visible, and the experiential—were obviously beyond the human power of the Eleven; note the reaction of the multitude that witnessed them: "Amazed and perplexed they asked one another, 'What does this mean?' " (v. 12)

An explanation from Joel

Supernatural manifestations demand an explanation. When Christ performed miracles that were obviously supernatural, the leaders attributed the power for these miracles to Satan (Matt. 12:24). Here the skeptics attributed these signs—particularly the sign of speaking in languages known to hearers but unknown to the speakers—to intoxication by alcohol. Peter quickly refuted that explanation, pointing out that the third hour of the day, particularly of a holy feast day, was too early for men to have become intoxicated.

But another explanation was in order; so Peter attributed the supernatural phenomenon they had witnessed to be an evidence that God had fulfilled that which He had promised in Joel 2:28-32, the passage Peter quoted to the audience.

When Joel's prophecy is examined we find that it centers around a fact. The fact was that God promised, "I will pour out My Spirit on all people." Moreover, there would be certain results of the fulfillment of that promise: "Your sons and daughters will prophesy, your old men will dream dreams, your young men will see visions. Even on My servants, both men and women, I will pour out My Spirit in those days."

According to the context of Joel's prophecy, these results would be enjoyed when David's Son takes David's scepter and sits on David's throne and institutes the covenanted kingdom blessings. That day would be "the great and glorious Day of the Lord" (Acts 2:20). Before the Day of the Lord would come, said God, "I will show wonders in the heaven above and signs on the earth below, blood and fire and billows of smoke. The sun will be turned to darkness and the moon to blood" (vv. 19-20). These are the signs that would be fulfilled in that period that our Lord refers to as the Great Tribulation (Matt. 24:21), a period of divine discipline on a disobedient nation to bring them to repentance and to faith in Jesus Christ so that they can receive the blessings of the covenant. Joel's prophecy, then, gave the *promise*, showed the *results* flowing from the fulfillment of that promise, and depicted the *signs* that will prepare a remnant to receive the benefits of the coming of the promised Spirit.

With that in mind, when Peter said, "This is what was spoken by the Prophet Joel" (Acts 2:16), he was referring only to the promise contained in Joel's prophecy and was asserting that that promise of the Father which had been confirmed by Christ has taken place. Just as the death of Christ was the fulfillment of Passover, so the event taking place here was the fulfillment of the Feast of Pentecost.

But because of their unbelief, the nation of Israel had not entered into the benefits of the coming of the Spirit, just as they (because of unbelief) had not entered into the benefits of the death of Christ.

Therefore the disciplinary signs of which Joel spoke will be given in some future day to bring a remnant to repentance so they may reap the benefits of both the death of Christ and of the Spirit who has been given.

Therefore we can see that Scripture affirms that the supernatural signs the multitude witnessed on this day were the results of the Spirit having been given. This does not in any way imply that the church had become Israel, or that the church is a substitute for Israel in the fulfillment of Joel's prophecy. Nor does it imply that the Davidic kingdom has somehow been established. It does, however, indicate that the supernatural signs were the work of the Spirit, and that the Spirit had been given.

Peter closed his quotation from Joel's prophecy with the words, "Everyone who calls on the name of the Lord will be saved" (v. 21), and then he moved into a discourse on the resurrection of Jesus Christ to show how men can be saved.

"What shall we do?"

In his discourse Peter gave an explanation of the sign of Jonah Christ had given to the leaders of the nation as the climactic sign that He was God's Son, Israel's Messiah. Peter affirmed the fact of resurrection (Acts 2:24) and showed that the resurrection of Christ was predicted by David (vv. 25-31). He supported the fact of resurrection by citing those who had seen the resurrected Christ (v. 32), and then concluded his argument with the fact of the ascension of Christ (vv. 33-35), for one who was still dead could not have ascended physically, literally, and bodily into heaven to be enthroned at the right hand of God.

Christ's enthronement at the time of His ascension was not to David's throne, but rather was a restoration to the position at His Father's right hand (Heb. 1:3; Acts 7:56), which position He had given up at the time of the Incarnation (Phil. 2:6-8). It was for this restoration that Christ had prayed to His Father in John 17:5. Since Christ had never occupied David's throne before the Incarnation it would have been impossible to restore Him to what He had not occupied previously. He was petitioning the Father to restore Him to His place at the Father's right hand. Peter, in his message, establishes the fact of resurrection by testifying to the Ascension, for one who had not been resurrected could not ascend.

Peter quotes from Psalm 16, not to teach that Christ is on the Davidic throne, but rather to show that David predicted the resurrection and enthronement of Christ after His death. The enthronement on David's throne is a yet-future event while the enthronement at His Father's right hand is an accomplished fact.

The Resurrection anticipates the eventual enthronement of Christ on David's throne, for at the Ascension the Father promised, "I will give You the holy and sure blessings promised to David" (Acts 13:34). The Father did not say, "I am hereby giving You that promised to David," but asserted that those blessings would come to Him in the future.

The Resurrection is then an assurance of the perpetuity of the Davidic Covenant which will be fulfilled through Christ.

Peter's conclusion was that the Resurrection proves Jesus is "both Lord and Christ" (2:36). In fact the evidence was so convincing that no objection was raised in the multitude! Rather, out of the conviction that settled on them they cried, "What shall we do?" (v. 37) It could be stated this way: "In light of the fact that the Resurrection proves we as a nation are guilty of the crime of crucifying the One who truly is the Son of God, the Messiah, what shall we do now?"

Peter first of all called on them to repent. This repentance would be an acknowledgment of their sin in rejecting Christ. This was the sin concerning which Christ had given sober warning (Matt. 12:31-32). Second, Peter called on them to be baptized. Baptism was a sign of identification with Jesus Christ; therefore this public act of identification would be an outward demonstration of their faith in the One whom the nation had rejected. In short, they were to repent and be baptized with a view to the remission of sins.

Remember, this generation of Israel through their rejection and crucifixion of Christ had committed that sin for which Christ said there would be no forgiveness (v. 32). That generation consequently had come under a physical, temporal judgment that would eventually be carried out through Titus in his invasion and destruction of Jerusalem. But while the nation as a whole could not escape that judgment, individuals by faith in Jesus Christ could separate themselves from that nation and thus escape the judgment that had been pronounced on the nation.

That's why Peter exhorted them, "Save yourselves from this corrupt generation" (Acts 2:40). If a Jew submitted to public baptism in the name of Jesus Christ, identifying himself with the despised and

273

rejected One, he would be cut off from any relationship to that nation. By identifying himself with Jesus Christ and severing connection with the nation he could escape that forthcoming physical, temporal judgment. If on the other hand he continued as a member of that nation, he would come under the judgment that fell on the nation.

Thus Peter was addressing an invitation to individuals in a nation under judgment to place their faith in Jesus Christ, and to validate that faith by publicly identifying with Christ by baptism. Only this manifestation of true repentance would deliver them from the judgment that was to come.

As a result of Peter's explanation through the use of Joel's prophecy; Peter's vindication of the person of Christ by His resurrection; and Peter's invitation to put faith in Jesus Christ in order to escape the coming judgment, "Those who accepted his message were baptized, and about three thousand were added to their number that day" (v. 41).

Reoffer of the kingdom?

Christ had promised the Eleven that to validate their witness to the salvation provided by His death and resurrection, they would perform many signs. In Acts 3 one of these signs was performed when Peter and John confronted the lame man in the temple. They performed one of the miracles that Christ had so frequently performed during the course of His ministry and caused the lame man to walk. Most in the temple recognized this as a supernatural sign, so an explanation was in order lest the sign attract attention to the two who had been instrumental in performing it.

Peter in his explanation pointed away from himself and toward Jesus Christ. He reminded them: "You disowned the Holy and Righteous One and asked that a murderer be released to you. You killed the Author of life, but God raised Him from the dead. We are witnesses of this. By faith in the name of Jesus, this man whom you see and know was made strong. It is Jesus' name and the faith that comes through Him that has given this complete healing to him, as you can all see" (vv. 14-16).

After pointing this curious multitude to Jesus Christ, Peter said, "Repent, then, and turn to God, so that your sins may be wiped out, that times of refreshing may come from the Lord, and He may send the Christ, who has been appointed for you—even Jesus. He must remain in heaven until the time comes for God to restore everything, as He promised long ago through His holy prophets" (vv. 19-21). Here Peter was *not* reoffering the kingdom to the nation, nor was he telling them that if the nation repented the kingdom would be instituted at that time. Rather he was telling the nation—the same nation that had committed the sin for which there is no forgiveness—what they must do as a nation in order to enter into the benefits of the kingdom that had been covenanted and promised to them. In a word, they must "repent."

It had been made very clear throughout the Old Testament as well as through the ministry of John and Jesus that enjoyment of the covenanted blessings was conditioned on the nation's repentance (Deut. 30:1-10; 2 Chron. 7:14). And when the nation one day puts its faith in Jesus the Messiah, it will experience forgiveness of sins, and then the times of refreshing shall come from the presence of the Lord. "Times of refreshing" is a reference to the covenanted kingdom blessings that Messiah will provide when He reigns. Only after faith producing repentance brings about forgiveness of sins will God send the Messiah back to this earth to reign.

Notice that Peter pointed out that Christ's enthronement at His Father's right hand in heaven is of indefinite duration, and that He will not return to the earth to take the Davidic scepter and mount the Davidic throne and reinstitute the covenanted Davidic kingdom until the nation does repent.

The time "for God to restore everything," to which Peter refers in Acts 3:21, is the same restoration referred to in 1:6. Therefore, this statement does not constitute a reoffer of the kingdom, since the necessary prerequisites are not at hand. Jesus Christ is not personally present and offering Himself to the nation. Only He could make a genuine offer of the kingdom. And while the apostles were His representatives, they were never authorized to reoffer the kingdom to Israel. A genuine offer could not be made to the nation until after it had met the precondition of repentance.

That generation had come under a divine judgment which was irreversible. That judgment must be carried out, and since it would not be carried out until Titus came four decades later, no genuine offer could be made. Christ had predicted the establishment of the church and the proclamation of the Gospel to the ends of the earth; and until the church had been established and the Gospel been proclaimed, that kingdom could not genuinely be offered. Christ in His great eschatological discourse in Matthew 24–25 had outlined the prophetic events leading up to the establishment of the covenanted kingdom; and until those events had been fulfilled, a genuine offer could not be made.

Thus we must conclude that Peter was not offering the kingdom to Israel, nor was he stating that the kingdom had already been instituted; instead he was stating the conditions by which the nation will eventually enter into their covenanted blessings. The very fact that Peter anticipated the institution of the Davidic kingdom at some future time shows that the promise had not been abrogated because of Israel's rejection, but only postponed.

Thus the present program must be viewed as a new form of the kingdom program falling between Israel's rejection of Christ and the nation's future reception of Christ at His second advent.

In orderly fashion

By divine arrangement, the good news of salvation through the death and resurrection of Jesus Christ was to go in orderly fashion from Jerusalem and Judea to Samaria and then to the ends of the earth (Acts 1:8). Peter in his message (2:39) recognized that the message he proclaimed was not only for those in Jerusalem and Judea but even "for all who are far off—for all whom the Lord our God will call."

While Peter was the principal instrument in proclaiming the Gospel to those living in Jerusalem and Judea, a new instrument was selected to carry that Gospel to the Samaritans. Philip was one of those set apart by the apostles to assist in the ministries entrusted to them in the care of the church (6:5-6). When Philip went to Samaria to preach, he did so with apostolic authority that had been conferred on him by the laying on of the hands of the apostles. When Philip came to Samaria he "proclaimed the Christ there" (8:5). As a result of this preaching, "When they believed Philip as he preached the good news of the kingdom of God and the name of Jesus Christ, they were baptized, both men and women" (v. 12).

It is interesting to note that Philip's preaching of Christ is called the "good news of the kingdom of God." Philip was not preaching concerning the earthly Davidic kingdom; rather, he was preaching the message of salvation through Jesus Christ, which was called the good news of the kingdom of God. This reveals that the "kingdom of God" as it is used here is a reference to God's program in this present age of bringing men to Himself through the preaching of the death and the resurrection of Jesus Christ. The kingdom of God is made up, then, of all who by faith have received Jesus Christ as personal Saviour. The kingdom of God as used here is soteriological (salvation-related), not eschatological (prophecy-related). And those who believed the message became a part of that present form of the theocracy.

Those who believed publicly identified themselves with Jesus Christ by baptism. They were a part of the kingdom of God. When the report of the Spirit's work in Samaria reached Jerusalem, the apostles sent Peter and John to verify that work. The promise had been given that the Holy Spirit would indwell all believers as His temple. But up to this point it was only Jews or proselytes who had been received into the church and thus constituted the Spirit's temple. By laying hands on the Samaritans who had believed, those believers were officially brought into the body as a group. And having been received into the body, they received the Holy Spirit (v. 17). The gift of the Spirit was not for Jewish believers alone but for all who responded to the message that had been preached. The church, as a part of the kingdom of God, was thus composed of both Jews and Samaritans.

After they had received the Samaritans as a separate group into the body, and "when they had testified and proclaimed the Word of the Lord, Peter and John returned to Jerusalem, preaching the Gospel in many Samaritan villages" (v. 25). Again we see that preaching the things concerning the kingdom of God meant preaching the Word of the Lord and the Gospel of salvation by faith in Jesus Christ.

No mention was made of the future millennial form of the kingdom of God. Rather, the preaching of salvation through Jesus Christ constituted the preaching of the kingdom of God. In order to take the Gospel beyond the Jews and the Samaritans to the whole world, a new messenger was sovereignly prepared by God. Paul of Tarsus was brought to faith in Jesus Christ through a special revelation of the resurrected Christ. He was set apart as "My chosen instrument to carry My name before the Gentiles and their kings and before the people of Israel" (9:15). And as a result of that revelation, Paul was baptized (v. 18) to identify himself with Jesus Christ and "at once he began to preach in the synagogues that Jesus is the Son of God" (v. 20).

The church in Antioch assumed the responsibility of reaching the Gentiles with the message of the Gospel. In response to the Holy Spirit's direction they commissioned Barnabas and Saul for this ministry (13:2). Again we see that there was satanic opposition against this messenger of the Gospel and the kingdom of God. It came through unbelieving Jews who were instruments Satan used to thwart the proclamation of the message of the kingdom (vv. 6-13, 44-45; 14:2, 19). After the opposition, which culminated in the stoning of Paul, we find that "they preached the good news in that city and won a large number of disciples. They then returned to Lystra, Iconium and Antioch, strengthening the disciples and encouraging them to remain true to the faith. 'We must go through many hardships to enter the kingdom of God,' they said" (vv. 21-22). Here we see that preaching the Gospel and the kingdom of God are equated. When he referred to the kingdom of God, Paul was not speaking of the future earthly millennial kingdom, but rather of that relationship to Jesus Christ into which men enter through faith in the Gospel that was preached to them.

The present form of the kingdom

Notice that entering into the present form of the kingdom will involve suffering for the Gospel's sake. Christ sent the apostles into the world. As those sent to proclaim the Gospel, He warned them of the sufferings that would be involved (John 15:18–16:4). Paul, on his first missionary journey, had partaken of those sufferings for the Gospel's sake.

Notice too that the kingdom of God in this present age formed through the preaching of the Gospel would be made up of Jews, of Samaritans, and of Gentiles. This was made clear to Peter in the vision given to him in Acts 10, where his hunger was to be satisfied through eating of all that was contained in the vessel that descended from heaven. It contained all kinds of animals that according to the levitical Law were unclean. Yet Peter was commanded to kill and eat from that which was in the vessel. When Peter, in obedience to the levitical Law, refused to eat that which was unclean, he was told, "Do not call anything impure that God has made clean" (v. 15). To make sure there was no misunderstanding of the message, this command was repeated three times. It later became apparent that Peter understood that the distinctions inherent in the levitical Law had been removed, for when he was in the house of Cornelius he declared, "I now realize how true it is that God does not show favoritism but accepts men from every nation who fear Him and do what is right" (vv. 34-35).

Peter felt free to proclaim the Gospel of the death and resurrection of Jesus Christ to the Gentiles assembled there in the house of Cornelius. And in response to their faith, "The Holy Spirit came on all who heard the message" (v. 44). The evidence that Gentiles had received the Holy Spirit was that they spoke with tongues (v. 46). Tongues were evidence to the apostles of the genuineness of the conversion of the Gentiles and of the inclusion of Gentiles in the body of believers. In response to this verification these Gentiles showed their identification with Jesus Christ and the company of believers by their baptism.

Even so, Jerusalem needed to be convinced of the acceptance of Gentiles into the church and into the kingdom of God. So Peter testified to the genuineness of their conversion by recounting what had happened. And those in Jerusalem, "When they heard this, they had no further objections and praised God, saying, 'So then, God has granted even the Gentiles repentance unto life'" (11:18).

Afterward a question was raised concerning whether it was necessary for the Gentiles who had believed and had been brought into the church to abide by the precepts of the Mosaic Law. Judaizers insisted that in order to please God as believers and members of the kingdom of God, it was necessary for all men to live under the precepts of the Mosaic Law. This question was submitted to the apostles in Jerusalem, and Peter testified to the salvation of the Gentiles by faith in Jesus Christ apart from the Law (15:7-11). His testimony is further corroborated by Barnabas and Paul (v. 12), and James who presided at this council hearing rendered the decision of the council. It was evident that God for the first time in dealing with men was dealing with Gentiles as Gentiles "taking from the Gentiles a people for Himself" (v. 14).

James found this in keeping with the prophetic program. In Amos 9:11-12 it was prophesied that after the period in which Israel was disciplined because of disobedience (vv. 1-10) and the Davidic throne left empty for a time, the Davidic throne would be restored and the Davidic kingdom would be instituted. When it is reinstituted, the kingdom will include not only the physical descendants of Abraham, but also a multitude of Gentiles as well. Therefore the restored Davidic kingdom under its rightful Davidic king would be composed of both Jews and Gentiles. In that kingdom Gentiles would not be made into Jews; instead they would be in the kingdom as Gentiles.

This allowed James to conclude that if God had a program for Gentiles as Gentiles in the future Davidic kingdom established here on the earth, there was no reason to deny that God could include Gentiles as Gentiles in this present form of the theocracy. Therefore the issue was settled—the Gentiles did not need to be circumcised and bring themselves under the Mosaic Law in order to participate in the present form of the kingdom. Rather, apart from the Mosaic Law, through faith in Jesus Christ they are equal participants with believing Jews in the present form of the kingdom of God.

When Paul visited Ephesus later he told the Ephesian elders, "And now, compelled by the Spirit, I am going to Jerusalem, not knowing what will happen to me there. I only know that in every city the Holy Spirit warns me that prison and hardships are facing me. However, I consider my life worth nothing to me, if only I may finish the race and complete the task the Lord Jesus has given me—the task of testifying to the Gospel of God's grace" (Acts 20:22-24).

Paul's life was dedicated to the preaching of the grace of God. But then he went on to say, "Now I know that none of you among whom I have gone about preaching the kingdom will ever see me again" (v. 25). Paul clearly equated preaching the Gospel of the grace of God with the preaching of the kingdom of God. Once again we see that the two terms are used interchangeably, as in 28:23 when Paul arrived in Rome and "they arranged to meet Paul on a certain day, and came in even larger numbers to the place where he was staying. From morning till evening he explained and declared to them the kingdom of God and tried to convince them about Jesus from the Law of Moses and from the Prophets." Again the preaching of the Gospel was referred to as testimony concerning the kingdom of God. And in verses 30-31 this identification was again made where "for two whole years Paul stayed there in his own rented house and welcomed all who came to see him. Boldly and without hindrance he preached the kingdom of God and taught about the Lord Jesus Christ."

Thus as we survey Paul's ministry as recorded in the Book of

Acts, we see that he was an ambassador of the kingdom of God—but his message was salvation through the death and the resurrection of Jesus Christ. No reference is made to support the notion that the earthly Davidic kingdom had been established. Rather, the message concerns entrance into a present form of the kingdom of God by faith in Jesus Christ.

Summary

Christ, following His resurrection, spent time with those whom He had chosen (John 15:16), instructing them concerning the new form of the kingdom and preparing them for their ministry of introducing the new form of the kingdom to Jew and Gentile alike. He reiterated His promise of empowerment by the Holy Spirit for the discharge of their ministry. On the Day of Pentecost the promised Spirit was poured out and came to indwell believers as His temple. In the Book of Acts their ministry of proclaiming the new message of the new form of the kingdom is recorded, by which the Gospel was proclaimed and spread throughout the world.

23

The Kingdom
in the Epistles

Uses of "the kingdom"

While there are many references to the kingdom in the New Testament Epistles, on closer examination we find that the term *the kingdom* is used in several different ways.

First, it is used of the *future earthly Davidic kingdom* to be established at the second advent of Jesus Christ to the earth. In 2 Timothy 4:1 Paul wrote, "In the presence of God and of Christ Jesus, who will judge the living and the dead, and in view of His appearing and His kingdom, I give you this charge." This must refer to the earthly Davidic kingdom which will be established on the earth, since that's the kingdom that will follow the second advent of Jesus Christ and the judgments associated with that momentous event (Matt. 25:1-46).

Paul also wrote, "Christ, the firstfruits; then, when He comes, those who belong to Him. Then the end will come, when He hands over the kingdom to God the Father after He has destroyed all dominion, authority and power" (1 Cor. 15:23-24). Here Paul outlined a resurrection program that began with the resurrection of Christ and will continue with the resurrection of those that are Christ's at His second advent. The completion of the resurrection program does not come until after the reign of Christ here on earth following His second coming. At the conclusion of that resurrection program, Christ will have delivered up the kingdom to God (v. 24). It is quite obvious, therefore, that the kingdom referred to here is the millennial kingdom over which Christ reigns on earth following His second advent. Thus the idea of a future earthly Davidic kingdom is not at all foreign to the thinking of the apostle.

Second, we find that the *future eternal kingdom* is referred to in the Epistles. In 2 Timothy 4:18 Paul declared, "The Lord will rescue me from every evil attack and will bring me safely to His heavenly kingdom." Paul obviously was anticipating the eternal reign of Christ in His eternal kingdom.

Peter declared, "You will receive a rich welcome into the eternal kingdom of our Lord and Saviour Jesus Christ" (2 Peter 1:11). Peter likewise was anticipating his participation in that eternal reign of Christ.

Elsewhere in his epistles Paul wrote, "Flesh and blood cannot inherit the kingdom of God, nor does the perishable inherit the imperishable" (1 Cor. 15:50). Here Paul seems to be using the term *kingdom of God* in reference to the eternal state of the believer. Thus the term *kingdom* or *kingdom of God* may refer to the eternal reign of Christ.

While the term *kingdom* is used in these two senses in the Epistles, its *third* and most common use by far is in reference to the present form of the kingdom, that into which a believer enters by faith in Jesus Christ. Paul stated that God "has rescued us from the dominion of darkness and brought us into the kingdom of the Son He loves, in whom we have redemption, the forgiveness of sins" (Col. 1:13-14). Here it is evident that the phrase "the kingdom of the Son He loves" is equated with the redemption and the forgiveness of sins that we receive by faith in Jesus Christ.

In Galatians 5:19-21 Paul listed the works of the flesh and then declared "that those who live like this will not inherit the kingdom of God." Paul made a similar statement in Ephesians 5:3-5, where he listed grievous sins of the flesh and then stated that those who practice such things do not have "any inheritance in the kingdom of Christ and of God" (Eph. 5:5). This concept is also found in 1 Corinthians 6:9-10. And in these passages Paul is saying that men who are characterized by these sins are not saved, because it is evident they have never received by faith the salvation that comes through Jesus Christ. Therefore they are not participants in the kingdom of God. Thus we see again that the term *kingdom of God* is equated with salvation and it must refer to participation in or exclusion from the present form of the kingdom.

Believers are exhorted to "live lives worthy of God, who calls you into His kingdom and glory" (1 Thes. 2:12). Here Paul seems to be referring to the participation of believers in the present form of the kingdom, who consequently are to walk worthy of that position. Paul commended the Thessalonians for their faithfulness and patience in the midst of persecutions and testings (2 Thes. 1:4), which validated their membership in the kingdom of God. By that conduct they were deemed "worthy of the kingdom of God, for which you are suffering" (v. 5). Paul was not encouraging them to patience and faithfulness in order to participate in a future millennial kingdom, but rather to conduct themselves in a manner worthy of their participation in the present form of the kingdom.

Paul declared to the Corinthians, "The kingdom of God is not a matter of talk but of power" (1 Cor. 4:20). In other words, if those in Corinth were actually saved and in the kingdom of God, they would demonstrate that by manifesting the power of the kingdom of God in their daily lives. Mere profession was not a sufficient demonstration of salvation or participation in the kingdom of God; that relationship must be demonstrated by the works of the Holy Spirit who is the power in the present form of the kingdom of God.

James made reference to the kingdom in James 2:5 where he asserted that entrance into that kingdom is for those who are "rich in faith." A popular Jewish concept said that he whom the Lord loves He makes rich, and that those who had material wealth received it because God approved of their righteousness. Therefore, many sought riches as a basis for assurance of their acceptance by God. James, however, said that it is not those who are rich in this world's goods but those who are rich in faith who will "inherit the kingdom." Like Paul and Peter, James equated participation in the kingdom with salvation received by faith.

As a final note, according to Colossians 4:11 Paul considered himself a laborer on behalf of the kingdom of God and saw those faithful servants who worked with him as fellow workers in the kingdom of God.

From this survey, then, we see the most frequent reference to the "kingdom" or the "kingdom of God" in the Epistles is a reference to the present form of the kingdom in which individuals by faith in Jesus Christ, and because of His death and resurrection, receive salvation and the gift of eternal life. All these are a part of the kingdom of God.

The covenants in the Epistles

As we have already seen, the biblical covenants dominated the thinking of the writers of Old Testament Scripture. And while those covenants play a prominent role in the Gospels, little reference is made to the covenants in the New Testament Epistles. This observation supports the fact that during this present age, in which a new form of the kingdom is being developed, God has temporarily set aside the nation Israel, His covenant people, and is developing a new kingdom program.

Romans

We must also recognize, however, that the New Testament writers most certainly recognize the existence of the biblical covenants and refer to them when appropriate. For example, Paul in his great Epistle to the Romans wrote to vindicate the righteousness of God. Paul, writing under the inspiration of the Holy Spirit, argued that God is righteous in judging sinners (1:18–3:20). He is righteous in justifying men by faith (3:21–5:21). He is righteous in providing for a believer's sanctification by identifying him with Christ in His death and resurrection (6:1–8:27). And He is righteous in providing for the believer's ultimate glorification (vv. 28-39).

Paul then moved on to show that God is righteous in dealing with the nation Israel (chaps. 9–11). Paul proved this by pointing out that Israel's hope is based on the covenants and promises God gave to that people (9:4), but that those promises will only be realized by those who have Abraham's faith (vv. 6-13). God is sovereign in His display of mercy (vv. 14-24), and God's mercy may be extended even to the Gentiles (vv. 25-33). Therefore, Israel's covenanted promises are not realized, not because God is unfaithful, but because Israel refused to acknowledge their sin and to believe God (10:1-21).

Paul also presented the fact that though Israel has been set aside and is not now experiencing the fulfillment of the covenants, that does not mean God is unfaithful, for there are those in Israel who are experiencing the blessings of salvation (11:1-6). In fact, the setting aside of Israel opens the door of opportunity to the Gentiles to find the salvation provided through Israel's Messiah (vv. 7-12). Israel, in keeping with the sovereign purposes of God, had been put in the place of blessing and became the channel through which God would accomplish His purposes in the world. Israel is viewed as a branch in a tree drawing its life from the root of that tree. But because the nation was an unproductive branch it was cut off and wild branches, that is the Gentiles, were grafted in. The Gentiles were put in the place of blessing and could by grace draw life from the root.

Warning was then given to the Gentiles that if they prove unfruitful branches, they could be removed just as Israel had been removed. But the apostle assured us that the setting aside of the nation Israel was not permanent, but only temporary. Paul wrote, "If you were cut out of an olive tree that is wild by nature, and contrary to nature were grafted into a cultivated olive tree, how much more readily will these, the natural branches, be grafted into their own olive tree!" (v. 24) Paul assured his readers that, "The Deliverer will come from Zion; He will turn godlessness away from Jacob. And this is My covenant with them when I take away their sins" (vv. 26-27).

We can clearly see that in the analogy of the olive tree, Paul was viewing the root as the covenant that put Israel in a privileged position and guarantees restoration to that position when the Deliverer comes out of Zion and turns away ungodliness from Jacob. God's covenant program was prominent in the apostle's thinking as he vindicated the faithfulness of God in dealing with His people Israel.

Hebrews
Since the writer to the Hebrews was writing to Jewish believers, it's not surprising that we would find reference to the covenants in that epistle.

In Hebrews 5, in order to contrast the priesthood of Christ with the Aaronic priests, the writer referred to Psalm 110:4 where Christ was appointed a High Priest after the order of Melchizedek (Heb. 5:10). The Melchizedekian priesthood of Christ was then developed in chapters 7-8. The author went on to point out that the Aaronic priests derived their authority from the Mosaic Covenant, but of the priesthood of Christ the author says, "The ministry Jesus has received is as superior to theirs as the covenant of which He is mediator is superior to the old one, and it is founded on better promises" (8:6).

Some feel that the "superior covenant" here is a reference to the

New Covenant of Jeremiah 31:31-34, which was instituted for the house of Israel and the house of Judah by the death of Jesus Christ. This understanding may have some validity.

However, the better covenant also may refer to the covenant God the Father made with God the Son at the time of His ascension into glory. There are two aspects to this covenant. *First*, in Psalm 2:6-9 we read, " 'I have installed My King on Zion, My holy hill.' I will proclaim the decree of the Lord: He said to Me, 'You are My Son; today I have become Your Father. Ask of Me, and I will make the nations Your inheritance, the ends of the earth Your possession. You will rule them with an iron scepter; You will dash them to pieces like pottery.' " Here the psalmist recorded a decree or covenant that God the Father made with God the Son which guarantees the Son the right to rule. The begetting of the Son referred to (v. 7) has to do with appointment to authority; this authority was conferred on Christ at the time of His enthronement at the right of the Father following His ascension.

The *second* aspect of the Father's covenant with the Son is recorded in Psalm 110, where we read the words with which the Father welcomed the Son into glory at the time of His ascension. There He was seated at the Father's right hand until the time comes for Him to exercise the authority that was conferred on Him. There He also was appointed "a Priest forever, in the order of Melchizedek" (v. 4). In other words, by the Father's covenants with the Son, the Son was given authority to rule as a King-Priest.

It may well be this covenant to which the writer of Hebrews refers in 8:6. The covenant which was the basis of the authority of the Aaronic priest was a conditional covenant, but the covenant which constituted Jesus Christ as a King-Priest forever was an unconditional covenant, and therefore it is considered a better covenant which was established on better promises.

The writer to the Hebrews does make specific reference to the New Covenant in verses 7-13, where he quoted Jeremiah 31:31-34. And while some say that the writer was quoting Jeremiah's New Covenant in order to assert that the church supplants Israel as a covenant people and that there is no future for the nation Israel, a careful study of the context reveals that this is not the author's intent at all.

Some to whom the author was writing still believed the Mosaic Covenant was a permanent covenant, and that men therefore were bound by the Mosaic Law. It was the author's intent to show that even during the period in which the Mosaic Law operated, it was viewed as a temporary—not a permanent—arrangement. He did this by quoting Jeremiah 31:31-34, to show that when God served notice that He would take away the Mosaic Covenant and institute a New Covenant with the house of Israel and of Judah, He was serving notice that the Mosaic Covenant was a temporary and transitory covenant.

This is the point the writer was making when he said, "By calling this covenant 'new,' He has made the first one obsolete; and what is obsolete and aging will soon disappear" (Heb. 8:13). The writer made no attempt whatsoever to show that while the "old" covenant was made with Israel, the New Covenant was made with the church so that believers today become God's people in place of Israel. However, he did effectively demonstrate that the Mosaic order was a temporary arrangement and consequently is not binding on believers who are participants in the new form of the kingdom.

In 10:16-17, the writer again made reference to the New Covenant, quoting portions of Jeremiah 31:31-34. In that covenant God promised, "Their sins and lawless acts I will remember no more." The author was pointing out in this chapter the limitations of the Old Testament sacrifices. At best they could provide only a temporary covering for sins, referring of course to that which was accomplished on the Day of Atonement. In contrast to that, however, through the one sacrifice made by Jesus Christ, sins were permanently put away.

Therefore, instituting the New Covenant with Israel by the death of Christ means there is no further need for the animal sacrifices required under the Mosaic Law. This is the point the writer was making when he wrote, "Where these have been forgiven, there is no longer any sacrifice for sin" (Heb. 10:18). The answer to those who felt that animal sacrifices might continue to be efficacious was to refer to the New Covenant of Jeremiah 31:31-34 and recognize that what was promised there had been instituted. Sins have been put away so there is no further need for animal sacrifices. The writer further asserted in Hebrews 12:24 that Jesus is "the Mediator of a New Covenant." Consequently God is not dealing with sins on the basis of animal sacrifices, but on the basis of the all-sufficient sacrifice of Jesus Christ.

Another reference to the covenant is made by the writer of Hebrews in 13:20-21, when he said, "May the God of peace, who through the blood of the eternal covenant brought back from the dead our Lord Jesus, that great Shepherd of the sheep, equip you with everything good for doing His will, and may He work in us what is pleasing to Him, through Jesus Christ, to whom be glory forever and ever. Amen." The covenant here must of necessity refer to the New Covenant of Jeremiah 31:31-34, since the blood of that covenant brings the believer to perfection or maturity. That covenant is referred to here as an "eternal covenant." This New Covenant is in contrast to the Mosaic Covenant which, as the writer of Hebrews has already shown, was viewed even during its time of operation as a temporary covenant.

This New Covenant is an everlasting covenant. It is on the basis of the blood of this covenant that God will deal with sin. The work of Christ was to provide salvation and to bring all things into subjection to God's authority so that covenant will never need to be superseded by a better covenant.

While the writer to the Hebrews dealt principally with the New Covenant, he did make reference to the Abrahamic Covenant in 6:13-20. There he dealt with the believer's assurance of salvation. He referred to the covenant God made with Abraham, and indicated that Abraham's confidence concerning the Promised Land and seed depended on the faithfulness of God—not the faithfulness of Abraham—to His covenants and promises. The writer further asserted that Abraham's expectation was certain because, "It is impossible for God to lie" (v. 18). Therefore, our confidence of salvation—like Abraham's—is based on the character of God, and we who have "fled to take hold of the hope offered to us" (v. 18) are confident and secure. Why? Because the God who could not lie concerning that which He covenanted to Abraham cannot lie in that which He has promised to us.

In short, the writer's concept of the unconditional nature of the Abrahamic Covenant and the faithfulness of God to His covenants and promises becomes the basis of the believer's assurance of his salvation. Thus much of the author's doctrine and practical exhortation is based on his understanding of the eternal and unconditional nature of the covenants which God gave to His covenant people.

It must be noted that though reference is made to Israel's covenants in writing epistles to believers in the church it does not mean that the church becomes Israel or deprives Israel of a future fulfillment of the covenants made with that nation.

Whenever Israel is used in the Scriptures, whether in reference to an individual (Rom. 11:1) or a nation (9:4) without exception it refers to those who are physical descendants of Abraham. Paul makes this clear when he defines an Israelite as "a descendent of Abraham" in 11:1. Gentiles, by faith in Christ and by virtue of their relationship to Christ, who is a descendant of Abraham, are called the seed of Abraham (Gal. 3:29). The covenants were made with the physical descendants of Abraham. Those related to Abraham by faith may receive benefits from the covenants God gave that people, but they do not supplant the nation as recipients of the covenants.

The covenants did provide for universal blessings which are applicable to Gentiles and to the church. Universal blessing was promised in the Abrahamic promises (Gen. 12:3) which are fulfilled through Christ as Abraham's seed. Universal blessings are promised through the Davidic Covenant, for Gentiles will be a part of the kingdom ruled over by David's Son (Luke 2:10). These blessings come on the Gentiles who will participate in Messiah's earthly rule. Universal blessings are promised through the New Covenant (Joel 2:28-32). These blessings will be experienced by Gentiles when the Spirit is poured out on all flesh so that "everyone who calls on the name of the Lord will be saved" (v. 32). However, the enjoyment of these blessings that flow from Israel's covenants does not mean that that nation will not eventually enjoy the fullness of those blessings into which we enter by faith today.

In Galatians 6:16 Paul distinguishes between the Gentiles, "who follow this rule" and the saved Jews, whom he calls "the Israel of God." While there is no privilege given to the Jew above the Gentile in the church today (3:28)—which certainly was not true in the Old Testament—there is a recognition of the ethnic backgrounds from which the individuals came. Both receive blessings from the covenants, but the reception of these benefits in no way withdraws the promises for the application of these blessings to the nation Israel in the future.

Summary

Though the Davidic form of the covenanted kingdom was postponed until the second advent of Christ because of Israel's rejection, the New Testament writers make frequent reference to the kingdom of

God. At times it is used in reference to the coming Davidic kingdom, sometimes in reference to the eternal kingdom, but most
frequently it is used in reference to the new form of the theocracy
predicted by Christ in Matthew 13. The Old Testament covenants
are referred to, to show that the spiritual blessings that are ours
stem from the universal aspects of the covenants that God gave to
Israel. While God's program would be administered by the nation
Israel and flow through them to those in the nations of the earth, yet
God had provided for blessing for the world through His covenant
people. We thank God for the blessings that are ours while we
anticipate blessings the covenant people will experience in the
future when they turn by faith to Him in repentance.

24

The Administration of God's Kingdom in the Present

Successive administrations

Our sovereign God, in every period of theocratic administration, has ruled through those to whom He assigned His authority. In the garden, Adam was the appointed theocratic administrator whose responsibility it was to subject all creation to himself, so that through him creation might be subject to the authority of God. When this form of administration failed, God brought a judgment and expelled Adam and Eve from the garden.

God instituted a new form of theocratic administration in which He wrote His law in the hearts of men and subjected man to His law. That law was man's conscience (Rom. 2:15), and as men subjected themselves to the rule of conscience, they were in subjection to the authority of God. But that too failed. And when men rebelled against that form of theocratic administration, God wiped the human race off the face of the earth by a flood.

God then instituted a new form of theocratic administration in which authority was given to human government (Gen. 9:6). It was the responsibility of human government to curb lawlessless and to bring man in subjection to the authority of God. Again, however, man failed miserably. And when men organized in open rebellion against God, "The Lord scattered them from there over all the earth, and they stopped building the city. That is why it was called Babel—because there the Lord confused the language of the whole world" (11:8-9).

With the call of Abraham, God introduced a new form of theocratic administration and instituted the Abrahamic Covenant that promised Abraham a land, seed, and blessing. Throughout the Old Testament—through that expanding covenant program—God administered His theocracy here on earth. But when His covenant people rebelled against His authority and turned aside from His law of administration, God brought judgment. The northern kingdom of Israel fell captive to Assyria in 722 B.C., while the southern kingdom of Judah was exiled in 589 B.C.

From that point on, God administered His kingdom through the Gentile nations. It was revealed to Nebuchadnezzar in Daniel 2, and to Daniel in Daniel 7, that four Gentile empires in succession would be the instruments God would use not only to discipline His covenant people, but also to be the channel through which He would administer the affairs of His kingdom here on the earth. That is why Nebuchadnezzar and Cyrus could be called God's servants or God's anointed ones (Isa. 45:1).

Later, when Jesus Christ came as the anointed Messiah to offer the covenanted kingdom to Israel, He called on the people to repent, to put faith in His person, and to show the genuineness of their faith by their works. This the nation as a nation refused to do, with the result that Messiah's offer of the kingdom was withdrawn and its establishment postponed until some future time when the nation would repent and place faith in Jesus Christ.

Four realms of authority

At that point a new form of theocratic administration was instituted. Rather than investing authority in one individual who would exercise authority in every realm of life, authority was assigned to administrators in four different realms in which we all live: the civil realm, the realm of the home, the realm of employment, and the religious realm. Those in authority in these four realms are effectively God's administrators, and to them is given the responsibility of curbing lawlessness in those realms and bringing man into subjection to God's authority in each of them.

Civil government
The *first* realm is that of *civil government*. Paul in Romans 13:1-7 and Peter in 1 Peter 2:13-14 set forth a universal principle that all

men are to be in subjection to governmental authorities. The reason obedience is commanded is because these authorities are God's ministers (Rom. 13:4).

Obviously a governmental authority is not a minister of the Gospel; he is, however, an administrator of the theocracy in that portion of the kingdom to which he has been assigned. It is therefore the responsibility of the civil authority to curb lawlessness, to punish evildoers, to reward those who obey the law, and to provide an atmosphere in which righteousness may flourish and men may live in peace without fear. The authority of the civil ruler extends even to the removal of the lawless by death, the sword being the symbol of that power. As these civil administrators exercise their God-given authority and provide benefit for men as they exercise that authority, they are to be supported by taxes and are to be respected because of the position they hold as God's administrators in His kingdom.

The home

The *second* sphere of authority, the sphere of *the home,* was developed by Paul in Ephesians 5:21-33 and by Peter in 1 Peter 3:1-7. These writers make it clear that the responsibility to curb lawlessness in the home is placed on the husband. Wives are commanded to be in subjection to their own husbands, because in subjecting themselves to their husbands, they are showing subjection to the Lord. Similarly, responsibility is placed on children to recognize the authority of parents and to submit themselves to the rule of their parents. In so doing they are subjecting themselves to the rule of God. Sarah's submission to Abraham is given as an example of the submission that God requires (v. 6), and where these principles of submission are practiced, the Lord will be ruling in that home. That home, in short, will constitute a miniature theocracy.

Relationships in this sphere were designed according to God's principles of marriage which were laid down in the Garden of Eden to show the relationship existing between a believer and God. The husband or father portrays the authority that belongs to Christ, and he is to exercise his responsibilities in such a way that reflects the love and care Christ exercises over those who are His own. Likewise the wife represents the believer, and as the believer is rightly subject to the authority of Christ, so she portrays this relationship by subjection to her husband.

A home is not a Christian home because all in that home are Christians. A home cannot be considered a Christian home and a model of the theocracy unless those in the home are rightly related to each other according to God's established laws of marriage. Peter pointed out that one of the practical results of this relationship will be that an unbelieving husband may be brought to the Lord by the gracious submission of the wife to His authority.

It is crucial to recognize that the wife was *not* subjected to the authority of her husband as a punishment imposed on Eve for her rebellion against the revealed law of God. Rather, it was as a protection for her. She was relieved of the responsibility of making decisions. That responsibility is placed on her husband. Her responsibility is to submit to his protection and oversight. In this arrangement, the more difficult responsibility is given to the husband, who is commanded to love his wife as Christ also loved the church (Eph. 5:25).

Employer/employee

The *third* realm in which lawlessness may abound and in which God assigns administrative authority is in the sphere of *employment*.

Paul dealt with this issue in Ephesians 6:5-9, while Peter addressed it in 1 Peter 2:18-20. The apostles commanded slaves and hired servants to recognize and to submit to the authority of their masters or employers because God has given administrative responsibility in the present form of the theocracy to the employer in that realm. The submission that is given by the employee to the employer is the same submission he is expected to give to Christ. In submitting to Christ's administrator he is in fact submitting himself to Christ. Consequently any service that the employee renders his employer is viewed as a service for Christ.

Of course, an employer is responsible to treat employees as Christ would treat them, and in fact he is reminded that he is a servant of a Master who is in heaven. Thus they are Christ's representatives in that realm as theocratic administrators.

The church

The *fourth* and final realm in which lawlessness may occur is within the religious realm or in the church itself. Peter in 1 Peter 5:1-7 deals with this sphere.

The elders with whom Peter identified himself were overseers of the flock. The flock refers to the body of believers, meaning that the elders are responsible to oversee the flock so as to curb lawlessness and to bring those in the flock into subjection to the authority of Christ. It is their responsibility to feed the flock. The word *feed* includes the thought of taking care of every need the flock may have. They need to be fed, they need to be watered, they need to be led and guided, and they need to be corrected or disciplined. These are the responsibilities resting on those who are administrators in this part of the theocracy.

Peter commanded the younger ones (and this would refer to the members of the flock) to submit themselves to the elders (v. 5). Logically, submission given by the members of the flock to their shepherds is submission to Christ; and when this proper relationship exists in the church we find a perfect miniature theocracy.

Thus we see that by dividing authority into the civil realm, the realm of the home, the realm of employment, and the realm of the church, administration is provided in all the spheres in which we live. The principle is the same in each sphere: *Submission to the administrator is submission to Christ.* And through this process Christ is effectively ruling through these delegated representatives to provide a kingdom in which peace prevails and righteousness persists, in which lawlessness is curbed, and in which those living in that kingdom can enjoy the blessings of Christ's rule.

Limited authority

It should be pointed out that while the authority given to leaders in these four realms is absolute within each realm, authority is limited to the realm to which they have been assigned. In other words, if the ruler in one realm steps outside of his realm and seeks to exercise his authority in another realm, it is no longer necessary to submit to that assumed authority.

For example, Peter, who wrote so clearly on the responsibility of man to submit to the authority of government, himself refused to submit. In Acts 4 those who exercised authority in the civil realm commanded Peter and John not to speak at all or teach in the name of Jesus. But Peter and John answered and said to them, "Judge for yourselves whether it is right in God's sight to obey you rather than God. For we cannot help speaking about what we have seen and heard" (vv. 9-20). Had those in the civil realm given command concerning the responsibility of Peter and John in that realm, the disciples would have been responsible to obey. But when they stepped out of their realm and moved into a realm in which they had no given authority, they no longer needed to be obeyed.

We must notice that the obedience commanded in these four realms is not enjoined necessarily because those in authority are believers. Whether or not they are believers, if they discharge God-given responsibilities within the realm to which they have been assigned, they are to be obeyed. The believing wife may not refuse to submit to a husband simply because he is an unbeliever. However, should he demand what is contrary to the Word of God, he then needn't be obeyed. A believing child may not rebel against the authority of a parent because the parent is an unbeliever. The only reason to disobey is if the parent demands that which is contrary to the Word of God.

The government that fulfills the function of government is viewed by the Bible as a legitimate government, and men are commanded to be in subjection to that government. However, should the government command or approve that which is contrary to the Word of God, then that government need not be obeyed.

In assigning authority in these four realms, the authority is limited and those who exercise the authority are bound by a higher authority. That is, they are ultimately bound by and responsible to the authority of the Word of God and the character of the one who has assigned them positions of responsibility.

Rebellion against authority

In surveying this present form of theocratic administration, we can readily see the attacks of the false ruler in a false kingdom against the kingdom of the God of heaven on earth. Satan, who is lawless and a rebel, has led men in lawless rebellion against all four aspects of theocratic administration.

Men have taken to themselves the right to rule and subject their rulers to themselves. Men feel free to rebel against the authority of government. We have passed through decades of lawless rebellion against constituted authority in the civil realm. This is an attack by the prince of the kingdom of darkness against the kingdom of God.

Further, we see rebellion against constituted authority in the home. Wives refuse to submit to the authority of husbands, and children refuse to submit to the authority of parents. Demands for equal rights and liberties amount to rebellion against constituted authority and are another attack by the kingdom of darkness against the kingdom of God.

Again, there is rebellion against constituted authority in the realm of employment. Employees have organized to take to themselves the authority that belongs to the employer so that lawlessness prevails on a wide scale in this realm. Again, this is an attack on the part of the kingdom of darkness against the kingdom of God.

And finally, there is rebellion on the part of members of the congregation against their shepherds, while the shepherds themselves fail to exercise their God-given responsibilities of guarding, guiding, protecting, and disciplining the flock under their oversight. Satan has entered this realm to promote lawless rebellion and has engineered an effective attack against the kingdom of God.

It is incumbent on believers, therefore, to recognize these forms of theocratic administration and to show themselves citizens of the kingdom of God by subjecting themselves to the administrators in the respective realms in which God has placed them as His theocratic representatives.

Summary

God, in previous forms of theocratic administration, had centralized the authority in one individual or one arrangement (as in human government). However, in the present age He has divided authority in four different realms, thus limiting the area committed to any administrator in the kingdom. The responsibilty of those administrators is the same in any previous form: to bring those under their authority into submission to God, to maintain law and order, and to provide an atmosphere in which men may live in peace because they are in subjection to appointed human authority and consequently to divine authority.

25

The Kingdom in the Book of Revelation

The righteous Judge

The Book of the Revelation gives us an eyewitness report of the events leading up to the enthronement of Jesus Christ as King of kings and Lord of lords in the covenanted kingdom, the administration in which the theocratic program will come to its ultimate fulfillment here on earth.

In Revelation 1:5, Jesus Christ—who will ultimately rule—is introduced to us as the One who is the Faithful Witness. That is, He has come to reveal the Father and to bring the Father's plan and purpose for man and for this earth to its ultimate conclusion. He is the Firstborn among the dead, which emphasizes that He is the Author of life and the One in whom the dead will be resurrected. Third, He is the Prince of the kings of the earth, that is, the One who has been given the authority to rule.

In John 5 Jesus was challenged by the Jews concerning His authority. And He replied by saying, "I tell you the truth, a time is coming and has now come when the dead will hear the voice of the Son of God and those who hear will live. For as the Father has life in Himself, so He has granted the Son to have life in Himself. And He has given Him authority to judge because He is the Son of Man" (John 5:25-27).

The power to create belongs to God alone. Likewise, the right to judge belongs exclusively to God. Therefore, since Jesus Christ has been given the authority to resurrect and to judge, we must conclude that He is God. Similarly, the right to rule necessitates judgment on all who would oppose His rule, so in Revelation 1 Jesus Christ is revealed in His role as a Judge (vv. 12-18). In chapters 2–3, Christ is seen as the Head of the church exercising judgment on the seven churches. And in chapters 4–11, the One who has given the authority to judge is judging the earth.

The judgments through the breaking of the seals (6:1–8:1) and the judgments through the blowing of the trumpets (8:2–11:15) are viewed as preparatory to the subjugation of the nations to the authority of Christ, and to the enthronement of Christ as Ruler in the kingdom of the God of heaven on earth. Judgments are seen to issue from the throne on which the God of heaven sits (4:2), and a description given of this throne (v. 3) is so similar to the throne of the God of heaven described in Ezekiel 1, there can be no doubt that God is the one who judges man on the earth.

The judgments, however, are executed by one who is called "the Lion of the tribe of Judah, the Root of David" (Rev. 5:5). When we study these names we find that "the Lion of the tribe of Judah" is a reference to Genesis 49:10, while "the Root" is a reference to Isaiah 11:1. With David (see 2 Sam. 7:16, Ps. 89:3) it was covenanted that one of his Sons would sit on David's throne and rule over David's kingdom. Therefore, these references in regard to the Judge make it very clear that the judgments are preparatory to the fulfillment of the Davidic Covenant.

In fact, the judgments revealed through the breaking of the seals closely parallel the judgments Christ revealed in Matthew 24:4-8 as signs in the first half of the seven years of the Tribulation period, preceding the second advent of Messiah.

The trumpet judgments revealed in Revelation 8–9 are judgments that fall in the second half of Daniel's seventieth week, or the Tribulation period. The seventh trumpet (11:15) is the second advent of Jesus Christ to this earth, as the announcement is made: "The kingdom of the world has become the kingdom of our Lord and of His Christ, and He will reign forever and ever." The second advent of Messiah brings blessing to believers—yet that coming is God's climactic judgment on unbelievers, on Satan, and on this world. The fact that Jesus Christ comes the second time as a Judge is clearly revealed in verse 15.

The nature of the judgment associated with the second advent of Christ is not revealed until Revelation 16, where the emptying of the bowls of the wrath of God on the earth is recorded. Since the bowl judgments must span some period of time, we must view the second advent of Christ as an event that encompasses a period of time. In that regard, we find an interesting chronological note in Daniel 12:11-12: "From the time that the daily sacrifice is abolished and the abomination that causes desolation is set up, there will be 1,290 days. Blessed is the one who waits for and reaches the end of the 1,335 days." Twelve hundred ninety days span the second half of Daniel's seventieth week, and that time period brings us to the end of the Tribulation period. But the blessings of Messiah's reign are not enjoyed until some forty-five days later. Therefore, it is suggested that the forty-five day period is the period in which the judgments associated with the second advent of Christ are poured out on the earth. And that entire forty-five day period, then, could be called the second advent of Christ.

Further, it is suggested that the 1,290 days come to their completion with the appearance of the sign of the Son of Man in heaven (Matt. 24:30). The judgments of Revelation 16 follow in a forty-five day period and are concluded with the physical descent of Jesus Christ to the earth. Hence, Revelation 11:15 brings us to the second coming of Jesus Christ back to the earth at which time He will experience the fulfillment of the Father's promise: "Ask of Me, and I will make the nations Your inheritance, the ends of the earth Your possession. You will rule them with an iron scepter; You will dash them to pieces like pottery" (Ps. 2:8-9). We would expect that a description of our Lord's millennial reign would follow immediately—yet that event is not recorded until Revelation 20. Why?

In Revelation 10:11 John was told, "You must prophesy again about many peoples, nations, languages and kings." John, who had brought us to the conclusion of the seven years of the Tribulation period and the return of Jesus Christ to the earth (11:15), will now survey that period a second time from a different viewpoint. In chapters 12–19 John will portray the important personalities and movements that play a significant role in the Tribulation period.

In Revelation 12 our attention is focused on the nation of Israel. That nation is the one from which came forth "a male child, who will rule all the nations with an iron scepter" (v. 5). Since this is a quotation from Psalm 2, the male child can be none other than Christ Himself. The nation from which Christ sprang according to the flesh will be subjected to the most severe persecution that nation has ever undergone. Satan will seek to exterminate every physical descendant of Abraham on the face of the earth, because if he could accomplish that, then the Abrahamic Covenant could not come to fulfillment. Satan has such respect for the faithfulness of God to His covenant that he seeks by their deaths to prevent establishment of the covenanted kingdom with that people, for he recognizes that Messiah's kingdom can only be established through the overthrow of his own kingdom and dominion of darkness.

The Antichrist

While the Tribulation period from a divine viewpoint will be a period of judgment on the earth, it will also be a period in which the prince of the kingdom of darkness will be permitted to manifest his kingdom in that realm over which Christ will ultimately triumph and reign. It has long been Satan's purpose to bring all things into subjection to himself in order to rule over that realm in which all authority has been given to Jesus Christ. To do this, Satan intends to present the world with his masterpiece of deception. He will offer the world a substitute for Jesus Christ who, by Satan's power, will appear to give the world everything that Jesus Christ will give when He assumes His rightful role as King.

John recognized this as Satan's purpose when he wrote, "Every spirit that acknowledges that Jesus Christ has come in the flesh is from God, but every spirit that does not acknowledge Jesus is not from God. This is the spirit of the antichrist, which you have heard is coming and even now is already in the world" (1 John 4:2-3). John knew that Satan was attempting to bring the world under his control through clever deceptions. Paul asserted the same when he said, "For the secret power of lawlessness is already at work; but the One who now holds it back will continue to do so till He is taken out of the way. And then the lawless one will be revealed, whom the Lord Jesus will overthrow with the breath of His mouth and destroy by the splendor of His coming" (2 Thes. 2:7-8).

That wicked one Paul anticipated is the masterpiece of deception Satan will offer to the world as a substitute for Messiah. In every generation Satan has had his instrument prepared should permission be granted him to put his plan in operation. However, as Paul reminds us, "Now you know what is holding him back, so that he may be revealed at the proper [God's] time" (v. 6). God's restraint by the work of the Holy Spirit is exercised on Satan so that Satan will not be able to introduce his masterpiece of deception until God's appointed time. Thus it will be in the Tribulation period that Satan's kingdom will have its greatest manifestation here on this earth.

The instrument whom Satan will empower and through whom he will work to establish his kingdom here on the earth is described in Revelation 13. This one referred to as the beast, whom we popularly nickname the Antichrist, will seek to imitate the reign of Christ and provide those in his kingdom with the benefits only Christ can truly provide when He establishes His kingdom.

But by Satan's power (13:2), Antichrist will be given political power over all the earth (v. 7). By establishing a one-world government, he will imitate the worldwide authority that will belong to Jesus Christ in His kingdom: "He was given authority over every tribe, people, language and nation." Further, he will introduce a one-world religion: "All inhabitants of the earth will worship the beast" (v. 8), which will be an imitation of that authority which Jesus Christ will exercise as King-Priest when He reigns.

In addition he will introduce a one-world economy: "He also forced everyone, small and great, rich and poor, free and slave, to receive a mark on his right hand or on his forehead, so that no one could buy or sell unless he had the mark, which is the name of the beast or the number of his name" (vv. 16-17). When Christ reigns there will be no hunger, no famine, no poverty. Thus in order to imitate the reign of Christ, Satan's masterpiece of deception will institute a regulated economy so that there will be an "equal" distribution of the world's goods to the world's people.

More about the beast

Scripture has a great deal to say concerning the individual who will appear in the end time as the head of the Gentile powers in their ten-kingdom federation. His person and work are presented in Ezekiel 28:1-10; Daniel 7:7-8, 20-26; 8:23-25; 9:26-27; 11:36-45; 2 Thessalonians 2:3-10; and Revelation 13:1-10; 17:8-14. A synthesis of the truths in these passages will reveal a number of facts concerning his activities, including:

(1) He will appear on the scene in the latter times of Israel's history (Dan. 8:23)

303

(2) He will not appear until the Day of the Lord has begun (2 Thes. 2:2-3).

(3) His manifestation is being hindered by He who restrains (vv. 6-7).

(4) This appearance will be preceded by a departure (v. 7), which may be interpreted either as a departure from the faith or a departure of the saints to be with the Lord (v. 1).

(5) He will be a Gentile. Since he will arise from the sea (Rev. 13:1), and in Scripture the sea depicts Gentile nations (17:15), he will be of Gentile origin.

(6) He will rise from the Roman Empire, since he will be a ruler of the people who destroyed Jerusalem (Dan. 9:26).

(7) He will be the head of the last form of Gentile world dominion, since he is like a leopard, a bear, and a lion (Rev. 13:1; compare Dan. 7:7-8, 20, 24; Rev. 17:9-11). As such he will be a political leader. The seven heads and ten horns (13:1; 17:12) will be federated under his authority.

(8) His influence will be worldwide, for he will rule over all nations (13:8). This influence will come through the alliance he will make with other nations (Dan. 8:24; Rev. 17:12).

(9) In his rise to power, he will eliminate three rulers (Dan. 7:8, 24). One of the kingdoms over which he will have authority will be revived, for one of the heads—representing a kingdom or a king—will be healed (Rev. 13:3).

(10) His rise to power will come through his peace program (Dan. 8:25).

(11) He personally will be marked by his intelligence and persuasiveness (7:8, 20; 8:23), and also by his subtlety and craft (Ezek. 28:6), so that his position over the nations will be by their own consent.

(12) He will rule over the nations in his federation with absolute authority (Dan. 11:36). He is depicted in Scripture as doing his own will. This authority will be manifested through a change in laws and customs (7:25).

(13) His chief interest will be in might and power (11:38).

(14) As the head of the federated empire he will make a seven-year covenant or treaty with Israel (9:27), which will be broken after three and a half years (v. 27).

(15) He will introduce an idolatrous worship (v. 27) in which he will set himself up as god (11:36-37; 2 Thes. 2:4; Rev. 13:5).

(16) He will bear the characterization of a blasphemer because of his irreverent assumption of Deity (Ezek. 28:2; Dan. 7:25; Rev. 13:1, 5-6).

(17) This one will be energized by Satan (Ezek. 28:9-12; Rev. 13:4), will receive his authority from him, and will be controlled by the pride of the devil (Ezek. 28:2; Dan. 8:25).

(18) He will be the head of Satan's lawless system (2 Thes. 2:3), and his claim to power and to Deity will be proved by signs effected through satanic power (vv. 9-10).

(19) He will be received as god and as ruler because of the blindness of the people (v. 11).

(20) This ruler will become the great adversary of Israel (Dan. 7:21, 25; 8:24; Rev. 13:7).

(21) There will come an alliance against him (Ezek. 28:7; Dan. 11:40,42) which will challenge his authority.

(22) In the ensuing conflict, he will gain control over Palestine and adjacent territory (v. 42) and will make his headquarters in Jerusalem (v. 45).

(23) This ruler, at the time of his rise to power, will be elevated through the instrumentality of the "harlot," the corrupt religious system, which consequently will seek to dominate him (Rev. 17:3).

(24) This system will be destroyed by the ruler so that he might rule unhindered (vv. 16-17).

(25) He will become the special adversary of the Prince of princes (Dan. 8:25), His program (2 Thes. 2:4; Rev. 17:14), and His people (Dan. 7:21, 25; 8:24; Rev. 13:7).

(26) While he continues in power for seven years (Dan. 9:27), his satanic activity will be confined to the last half of the seven-year period of the Tribulation (7:25; 9:27; 11:36; Rev. 13:5).

(27) His rule will be terminated by a direct judgment from God (Ezek. 28:6; Dan. 7:22, 26; 8:25; 9:27; 11:45; Rev. 19:19-20). This judgment will take place as he is engaged in a military campaign in Palestine (Ezek. 28:8-9; Rev. 19:19), and he will be cast into the lake of fire (v. 20; Ezek. 28:10).

(28) This judgment will take place at the second advent of Christ (2 Thes. 2:8; Dan. 7:22) and will constitute a manifestation of His messianic authority (Rev. 11:15).

(29) The kingdom over which the beast ruled will pass to the authority of Messiah and will become the kingdom of the saints (Dan. 7:27).

Names for the beast

Many names and titles are given to this individual in the Scriptures. Arthur W. Pink in his book *The Antichrist* (pp. 59-75) lists these: The bloody and deceitful man (Ps. 5:6); the wicked one (Ps. 10:2-4); the man of the earth (v. 18); the mighty man (52:1); the enemy (55:3); the foe (74:8-10); the head of many countries (111:6); the violent man (140:1); the Assyrian (Isa. 10:5-12); the king of Babylon (14:4); the sun of the morning (v. 12); the destroyer (16:4-5; Jer. 6:26); the peg (Isa. 22:25); the branch of the terrible ones (25:5); the profane wicked prince of Israel (Ezek. 21:25-27); the little horn (Dan. 7:8); the ruler who will come (9:26); the vile person (7:8); the willful king (11:36); the idol shepherd (Zech. 11:16-17); the man of sin (2 Thes. 2:3); the son of perdition (v. 3); the lawless one (v. 8); the Antichrist (1 John 2:22); the angel of the bottomless pit (Rev. 9:11); and, of course, the beast (11:7; 13:1). To these could be added: the one coming in his own name (John 5:43); the king of fierce countenance (Dan. 8:23); the abomination of desolation (Matt. 24:15); and the desolator (Dan. 9:27).

Thus we see just how extensive is revelation concerning this individual. It is not surprising that this one is Satan's great masterpiece in the imitation of the program of God.

The identity of the beast

Frequently people will ask, "Will the Beast be a resurrected individual?" This question arises because, on the basis of Revelation 13:3 and 17:8, some expositors have taught that the beast who will rule will gain a tremendous following because he will have experienced death and resurrection at the hands of Satan. Some have held that the beast will be the reincarnation of Nero. Others have insisted that the beast will be Judas restored to life. Some have simply contended that he will be a resurrected individual without attempting to identify him.

The question before us, then, is whether this is a resurrected individual in whom the miracle of Christ's death and resurrection will be counterfeited. Even though it is stated that this one will come to power by satanic activity (13:2), and it is also said that he will have a deadly wound that was healed (v. 3), and that he comes out of the abyss (17:8), it seems best not to understand this as death and resurrection. There are several reasons for this:

(1) In Revelation 13:3 and 17:8, the beast is explained as the composite kingdom. The reference to healing seems to indicate the resurgence of power in the Gentile kingdom that had been dead for so long.

(2) Satan is called the angel of "the bottomless pit" or "abyss" in 9:11. This means that 17:8 does not teach that the head of the empire arose out of the abyss, but rather that the empire itself was brought about "from the abyss," or by Satan.

(3) The Scriptures reveal that men are brought out of the grave by the voice of the Son of God (John 5:28-29). Satan does not have the power to give life. Since Christ alone has the power of resurrection, Satan could not bring anyone back to life.

(4) The wicked are not resurrected until the Great White Throne Judgment (Rev. 20:11-15). If a wicked one were resurrected at this point, it would set aside God's divinely ordained program of resurrection.

(5) Since all the references to this individual present him as a man, not as a supernatural being, it seems impossible to believe that he is a resurrected individual. We can conclude, then, that the beast will not be a resurrected person.

The doom of the beast

It is extremely interesting that the vast majority of passages that make reference to the activities of the beast also include a notice of his final doom. Therefore it must occupy a prominent place in the program of God.

In short, his doom is seen in Ezekiel 21:25-27; 28:7-10; Daniel 7:11, 27; 8:25; 9:27; 2 Thessalonians 2:8; Revelation 17:11; 19:20; and 20:10. While the movements leading to his overthrow will be seen later, we can observe at this point that God is going to ultimately and violently overthrow this satanic masterpiece of delusion and imitation.

The false prophet

It will be through the instrumentality of a second person empowered by Satan that this one-world government, one-world religion, and one-world economy will be introduced and men will willingly submit to it. This individual, called in Revelation 19:20 the false prophet, will be given power by Satan to perform miracles (13:12-15). He will apparently duplicate the miracles of Elijah (v. 13), perhaps to deceive the world into believing that he is the Elijah who is to fulfill the prophecy of Malachi 4:5. Further, he apparently will cause the lifeless image of the beast to come alive and to speak. Remember that Jesus offered the sign of Jonah, that is His resurrection, as proof that He is the Messiah who had come from God. The false prophet thus seems to be duplicating the sign of Jonah to persuade the world to believe that the beast is actually God.

Paul pointed out that God shall send them a powerful delusion so that they should believe the lie (2 Thes. 2:11). The lie is that this individual who will have instituted a one-world government, one-world religion, and one-world economy is actually the world's messiah, the world's god.

In close association, then, with the beast, the head of the federated empire, will be this "false prophet," also called "the second beast" in Revelation 13:11-17, where his fullest description is given. In that passage we find some important factors concerning this spiritual deceiver, including:

(1) He will evidently be Jewish, since he will arise out of the earth, or land, that is Palestine (v. 11).

(2) He will be influential in religious affairs (v. 12).

(3) He will be motivated by Satan, just like the first beast (v. 11).

(4) He will have delegated authority (v. 12).

(5) He will promote the worship of the first beast and compel the earth to worship the first beast as god (v. 12).

(6) His ministry will be authenticated by the signs and miracles he will do, evidently proving that he is "Elijah" that was to come (vv. 13-14).

(7) He will be successful in deceiving the unbelieving world (v. 14).

(8) The worship he will promote will be an idolatrous worship (vv. 14-15).

(9) He will have the power of death in order to compel men to worship the beast (v. 15).

(10) He will have authority in the economic realm to control all commerce (vv. 16-17).

(11) And he will have a mark that will establish his identity for those who live in that day (v. 18).

Finally, we can observe that the Book of the Revelation, in relating the second beast to the first, presents him as subservient to the first. He is called "the false prophet" (16:13; 19:20; 20:10), who ministers in connection with the first beast as his prophet or spokesman.

What we are faced with, then, is a satanic "trinity," an unholy trinity comprising the dragon, the beast, and the false prophet (16:13). The place occupied by God in His program is assumed by Satan; the place of Christ is assumed by the beast; and the ministry of the Holy Spirit is assumed by the false prophet. It is a counterfeit of the most hideous sort, but it is Satan's best effort to thwart the plan and kingdom program of God.

Thus through this system of deception and through this deceiver, Satan will realize his ages-long purpose to bring this world under his authority and to institute his kingdom here on the earth.

Nations in turmoil

Nations of the earth under Satan's authority are pictured in their rebellion against God and against His anointed Messiah in Psalm 2:1-3. To bring judgment on these rebellious nations, they will be drawn into the land of Israel for judgment. We find that the nations will be divided into four segments, which in turn come into the Middle East.

The first is referred to in Daniel 11:40 as the king of the south. This is to be understood as the Arab nations under the leadership of Egypt (vv. 42-43). They will immediately be joined by the king of the north (v. 40), a nation coming from the farthest north (Ezek. 38:15) which Bible students long have concluded would be Russia together with her allies (vv. 6-7).

After these two powers destroy the land of Israel (Zech. 13:8), they will be destroyed by God by a judgment from heaven in the same way the ancient cities of Sodom and Gomorrah were destroyed with fire and brimstone (Ezek. 38:22). In judging these two great political and economic powers, God will demonstrate that He is God and that the false king in the false kingdom is not a god to be worshiped and served (v. 23).

Satan's puppet, the beast of Revelation 13, will have risen to power from among the nations that have originated through the downfall and division of the old Roman Empire. After the destruction of the king of the north and the king of the south, this political ruler will move into Jerusalem and claim that city as the center of his one-world government, his one-world religion, and his one-world economy (Dan. 11:45). And he will hold sway in these realms over the world in a kingdom that will derive its authority from Satan. His uncontested reign, then, will span the last three and a half years of the Tribulation.

At the conclusion of that period, however, there will be a revolt against his authority and a coalition of nations referred to as "the kings from the East" (Rev. 16:12) will move from east of the Euphrates River into the Middle East to seek to overthrow that ruler. Before the battle can be joined, these two great powers will be "gathered together to make war against the rider on the horse and his army" (19:19).

Evidently the sign of the Son of Man, that will appear in the heavens (Matt. 24:30) and herald the second advent of Jesus Christ to the earth, will cause these two—who were preparing to fight for world supremacy—to ally their forces and try to prevent the Lord's return.

The victorious King

Notice in Revelation 19:11 that Christ in His descent is pictured as a Rider on a white horse. It was customary for a Roman general leading his troops into battle to provide a white horse, for to emerge from the battle riding on a white horse signified that the rider was victorious in the conflict. It would have been presumptuous for the general to ride that white horse *into* battle; but he provided it in anticipation of victory so that he might emerge on the white horse to symbolize his conquest.

When Jesus Christ returns as a righteous Judge, it will not be presumptuous for Him to come riding to this final judgment on that which symbolizes His victory. John wrote, "Out of His mouth comes a sharp sword with which to strike down the nations" (v. 15). A sword in Scripture is often used as a symbol for a spoken word. Jesus Christ, by the word of His mouth, will subdue all opposition to Himself. The beast will be taken, and with him the false prophet, and both will be cast alive in a lake of fire (v. 20). All who had joined themselves with the beast and the false prophet in opposition to Jesus Christ will be killed. And the false kingdom of Satan administered through Satan's masterpiece of deception will be brought into subjection to the authority of Jesus Christ, so that He truly is King of kings and Lord of lords (v. 16).

At his second advent, following the removal of all who were in the false kingdom in rebellion against Messiah, Christ will subject the ruler in that false kingdom to his authority: "He seized the dragon, that ancient serpent, who is the devil, or Satan, and bound him for a thousand years. He threw him into the abyss, and locked and sealed it over him, to keep him from deceiving the nations anymore until the thousand years were ended" (20:2-3). Thus not only the subjects of the false kingdom, but also the false king of that false kingdom will be brought under the authority of Jesus Christ.

An outpouring of grace

Christ the Judge, through the judgments that He will pour out during the seven years of the Tribulation period, will subject all things to Himself. But the years of the Tribulation will not only be a time of judgment; they will also be a time in which the marvelous grace of God is manifested to those who dwell on the earth.

Christ, in Matthew 24:14, said that in the period immediately preceding the establishment of Israel's covenanted kingdom, the Gospel of the kingdom will be preached in all the world. The "Gospel of the kingdom" is that message proclaimed by John the Baptist with its two parts: "Look, the Lamb of God who takes away the sin of the world!" (John 1:29) and, "Repent, for the kingdom of heaven is near" (Matt. 3:2). This was the Gospel Christ proclaimed as He offered Israel the covenanted kingdom and invited them to put faith in Him.

This same message will be proclaimed again during the years of the Tribulation period preceding Messiah's second advent to the earth. According to Revelation 7:1-8, God will set aside 144,000 of the physical descendants of Abraham whom He will call His servants (v. 3). Israel in the Old Testament was the servant of God and their ministry was to receive revelation from God and then to disseminate that revelation to the nations that were in darkness due to their ignorance of God. These 144,000, then, will be set apart as God's emissaries to the Gentiles to bring those in darkness a knowledge of the salvation that was provided through the death and resurrection of Jesus Christ. As a result of their ministry, an innu-

311

merable company will be brought to faith in Jesus Christ and experience the blessings of the salvation He has provided.

These who are saved out of the Tribulation period will "have washed their robes and made them white in the blood of the Lamb" (v. 14). They will be participants in the millennial kingdom that will be established at Christ's second advent (vv. 15-17). Thus we see that salvation during the Tribulation period will be by the grace of God received by faith based on the blood of Christ.

Not only will multitudes from among the Gentiles participate in the earthly millennial kingdom having been redeemed through faith by blood, but also a remnant from among Israel will participate in that earthly Davidic kingdom. In order to bring this remnant to faith in Christ, God will send two witnesses to minister to the people of Israel in Jerusalem (Rev. 11:3-12). They will be sent as prophets to minister in Jerusalem at the time Satan's deceiver is ruling over his false kingdom in that city. Their ministry will span the second half of the Tribulation period (v. 2), and they will be empowered by the Spirit of God in their ministry just as Joshua and Zerubbabel were empowered in the work of rebuilding the temple after release of the nation from bondage to Babylon (Zech. 4:1-7).

Since their ministry will center in Jerusalem (Rev. 11:8), we can conclude that their ministry will be to the scattered people of Israel who had sought refuge from the wrath of Satan among the Gentile nations (12:14-16). That they are God's prophets and that their message is God's message to the nation will be validated by their restoration to life after Satan's deceiver executes them in Jerusalem. And as a result of their ministry, a remnant from among Israel will be brought to salvation by faith.

That remnant will meet the requirements of Deuteronomy 30:1-6 and 2 Chronicles 7:14. They will repent. This is because of the grace of God extended to this people, for God has pledged, "I will pour out on the house of David and the inhabitants of Jerusalem a spirit of grace and supplication. They will look on Me, the One they have pierced, and they will mourn for Him as one mourns for an only child, and grieve bitterly for Him as one grieves for a firstborn son" (Zech. 12:10).

We find that the four things that were involved in true repentance according to 2 Chronicles 7:14 will be experienced by those who respond to the ministry of the two witnesses. The repentance required that the people humble themselves. In Zechariah's prophecy God will give them a gracious spirit. God required that they pray and Zechariah's prophecy said that they will offer supplications to God. God required that they seek His face, and Zechariah says they shall look (by faith) upon Him whom they have pierced. True repentance required that they should turn from their sin, and Zechariah predicts that they shall mourn for Him. Mourning was an acknowledgment of sin.

Thus the remnant in Israel will be brought to repentance through the sufferings they will endure under the judgments of God and through the persecutions of Satan during the Tribulation period. And through the preaching of the two witnesses they will come to faith in Jesus Christ. The redeemed multitude from the nations of the earth together with the redeemed remnant in Israel will constitute a kingdom over which Messiah will rule at His return.

Qualifying for the kingdom

The binding of Satan and his removal from the sphere in which Christ will reign for the thousand years of his earthly Davidic kingdom will remove every external source of temptation and enticement to rebellion against the authority of the King. David's greater Son will be able to restore the promised kingdom to Israel and institute a kingdom characterized by righteousness, peace, posterity, and plenty, as He exercises the authority God has given Him to reign.

Only those who have experienced the salvation that Jesus Christ provides through His death and resurrection and who have received the gift of eternal life will be accepted into Christ's earthly kingdom. Therefore after His return Christ will sit as a Judge (Matt. 25:31).

Jews

First of all He will regather all living Israel (Matt. 24:31) back to the land originally given by covenant to Abraham and to Abraham's descendants and they will be regathered for judgment (Ezek. 18:30; 20:33-38). As we saw in previous chapters, this judgment was described in the two parables in Matthew 25:1-30. In the Parable of the Ten Virgins, the virgins represent the nation Israel at the time of the Bridegroom's appearance at the marriage supper with His bride. It is revealed that those awaiting His coming fall into two groups: those with light and those with no light; those who are prepared and those who are unprepared. Those who are prepared are accepted into the marriage feast, that in this parable is used as a symbol for Messiah's millennial kingdom.

In the Parable of the Talents, it is taught that at the time of the absent one's return those who have been entrusted with the man's goods will be tested. Again the test reveals that those to whom a stewardship was entrusted fall into two groups: there were those who were faithful and those who were unfaithful. The faithful were welcomed into the joy of their Lord. That is, they will be received into the earthly Davidic kingdom, but the command is also given, "Throw that worthless servant outside, into the darkness, where there will be weeping and gnashing of teeth" (v. 30).

These two parables, then, reveal that Christ at His return will sit as a Judge on living Israel. At that time He will accept into His kingdom the saved who demonstrate their salvation by their faithfulness, but He will exclude the unsaved who demonstrate their state by their unfaithfulness.

Gentiles
Next Christ will sit as a Judge over living Gentiles (Joel 3:11-16). This judgment was depicted in Matthew 25:31-46 in the Parable of the Sheep and the Goats. After judging living Israel, Christ will gather together living Gentiles. This is not a judgment on nations as nations, but rather is a judgment on individual Gentiles. The Gentiles fall into two groups: those in the privileged position who are called sheep and are placed at the King's right hand; and those who are without privileges, called goats and placed at His left hand. The King says to those in the privileged position, "Come, you who are blessed by My Father; take your inheritance, the kingdom prepared for you since the creation of the world" (v. 34). These apparently have shown the true fruits of repentance by responding to the needs of a third group at this scene called "My brethren." The "brethren" may be understood as a reference to the nation of Israel as a whole that had undergone attacks of Satan during the Tribulation period, or it may refer to the 144,000 who are appointed as God's servants to proclaim the Gospel to the ends of the earth—the Gentiles— during the Tribulation period. Either group, because of their refusal to submit to the economic system of the beast, will be dependent on others for food, for shelter, for clothing, for protection. Those who demonstrate their faith in Christ by ministering to those who for

Christ's sake were deprived of their daily needs will be accepted into the King's earthly millennial kingdom.

On the other hand, those positioned on the left are excluded from that kingdom. The King said, "Depart from Me, you who are cursed, into the eternal fire prepared for the devil and his angels" (v. 41). These, even though they recognized the needs, refused to respond to those needs. They demonstrate that they have no faith in Christ and did not show the fruits of repentance. They therefore are excluded from the King's kingdom.

Thus in these parables we find that Christ will separate the saved from the unsaved, exclude the unsaved from the coming Davidic kingdom, and accept as subjects of His kingdom those who have received His salvation by faith and have demonstrated a true repentance by the fruits of faith in their lives.

Tribulation martyrs
Scripture also reveals there are others besides the saved Jews and the saved Gentiles who will participate in Christ's earthly kingdom. In Revelation 20:4-6 it is revealed that those in the Tribulation period who receive Christ as personal Saviour and seal their testimony with their lives will be resurrected and "will be priests of God and of Christ and will reign with Him for a thousand years" (v. 6). Thus the martyred Tribulation saints will have their part in that earthly kingdom. They will be joined by all the Old Testament saints who looked forward as Abraham did, "For he was looking forward to the city with foundations, whose architect and builder is God" (Heb. 11:10).

Old Testament saints
Old Testament saints who died in faith will be resurrected at the second advent of Jesus Christ to the earth (Dan. 12:2; Isa. 26:19-20) to have their part in the covenanted kingdom. In Hebrews 12:22-24 it is revealed that the city of the living God, the heavenly Jerusalem, will be inhabited by God the Father, by Jesus the Mediator of the New Covenant, by an innumerable company of angels, by the church of the firstborn (which we understand to be believers of this present age) and also by the spirits of just men made perfect (that is, all the Old Testament and Tribulation saints).

These resurrected, glorified ones will enter the heavenly Jerusalem by resurrection and become participants in the covenanted

Davidic kingdom along with the saved from among the Jews and Gentiles. That which was the hope given to Israel in the Old Testament will finally be realized as those who believed the promise will enter into and experience all the blessings of Messiah's kingdom as had been outlined through the prophets of the Old Testament.

The reign of David's Son

God's purpose for this earth is to subject all things to man (Gen. 1:26-27) and to bring all things into subjection to Himself through man. This ultimately will be realized as the Son of Man subjects all things to Himself and through Him to the authority of His Father.

Establishing the rule of David's Son as Sovereign over the earth demonstrates that Satan's kingdom is a false kingdom. Satan is a false king—God alone is God, and He alone has the right to rule. He has the authority and the power to bring all things into subjection to Himself.

Apart from the reign of Christ in a Davidic kingdom here on earth, God's promises and God's covenants would have failed. And apart from this rule, God's purpose for man would never be brought to conclusion. God's purpose for the earth would be unrealized and the problem generated by Satan's rebellion would never be resolved. Thus the physical, literal reign of Christ on the earth is *a theological and biblical necessity*—unless Satan is victorious over God.

Those from both Israel and the Gentiles who go out of the Tribulation period into Messiah's earthly kingdom will go in unredeemed bodies with an unredeemed nature within them. It will not be the citizens of the heavenly Jerusalem who will be charged with the responsibility of repopulating the earth. This will be done by the saved who enter the millennial kingdom in their natural bodies. And the multitudes born to them will be born with an unredeemed, fallen, sin nature within them. Even though they will be living under the benefits of the King's reign, they will need to be saved.

During the millennial reign of Christ, Israel as a nation will fulfill the function for which they were originally set apart by God. They will become a kingdom of priests (Ex. 19:6) who are intermediaries between those who need to be saved and the King who provides salvation. They will become, as they were originally appointed to be, God's lights to the world.

316

Those born in the Millennium who need salvation will approach the Saviour through Israel (Zech. 8:20-23). Salvation during that period will be provided through the benefits of the death of the Passover Lamb. That is why the Passover will be observed throughout the Millennial Age as a memorial of the death of Christ (Ezek. 45:21), and why blood sacrifices will be offered in the millennial temple as memorials of the death of Christ (43:19-27).

Jews living in the Millennium will live in perfect obedience to the law of the King. This will be possible because the redeemed will enter into the fulfillment of the promise of Joel 2:3-8 and Ezekiel 36:26-27, and the indwelling Spirit will empower them to obedience. In addition, there will be a universal knowledge of the demands the King made of those who would walk in obedience to His law (Jer. 31:34). What the King demands will not be written on external tablets as was the Law of Moses. Instead it will be inscribed on their hearts (v. 33). The outbreak of sin will be punished by immediate death (Isa. 11:4). Rebellion against the authority of the King will be immediately judged (Zech. 14:16-19). All those born during the millennial kingdom will have opportunity to receive the salvation that the King has provided, and because of fear of judgment and respect for the power of the King they will outwardly live in conformity to His law.

Since Satan will be removed during Messiah's millennial reign, there will be no one to entice them to an organized rebellion. Thus at the conclusion of the Lord's earthly reign, it will be necessary to test those who have lived during this period. For that reason Satan "must be set free for a short time" (Rev. 20:3).

When he is loosed he will organize a rebellion against the King and will draw after himself all those who have never received the salvation that was available. This great company of rebels will surround "the camp of God's people, the city He loves" (v. 9). Their goal will be to overthrow the King, to eliminate His kingdom, and to establish a new kingdom under a new king, Satan, in the sphere in which Christ has been reigning. But God will respond to this rebellion by causing fire to come down out of heaven and destroy this great multitude of rebels (v. 9).

Finally God will demonstrate His soverign authority over Satan by consigning him to the lake of fire, where he together with his emissaries—the beast and the false prophet—will be tormented day and night forever and ever (v. 10).

The eternal finale

All of the righteous dead of all the ages will have been resurrected before the institution of Christ's earthly Davidic kingdom, leaving only the wicked dead unresurrected after the Second Advent. At the conclusion of the millennial reign, Christ will demonstrate His authority not only by consigning Satan to the lake of fire, but also by judging and consigning to the lake of fire all of those who had been a part of Satan's false kingdom.

This will be done at the Great White Throne (Rev. 20:11-15), where their works will be reviewed to prove that they were sinners and consequently a part of Satan's kingdom. That is why the books will be opened. The Book of Life will be consulted to see if those who had been in Satan's kingdom were brought into the kingdom of God's beloved Son by faith in Him. Since their names will not be found written in the Book of Life, they will be cast into the lake of fire, where they will experience the second death. The first death was not the separation of the soul from the body, but rather the separation of the soul from God. All who are born into this world have tasted the first death, and physical death is the result of that first death. But both of these are reversible through faith in Jesus Christ. The soul that was separated from the body will be reunited to the body by resurrection. The soul that was separated from God may be reunited to God by faith in Jesus Christ.

However, those who have not experienced the new life in Christ will be eternally separated from God in second death. Even so, they will acknowledge that Jesus Christ is Lord (Phil. 2:11). Thus every member of the false kingdom who had been subjected to the authority of the false king will be brought into subjection to the authority of Jesus Christ. Jesus Christ will demonstrate the soverign authority that belongs to God which was assigned to Him in judgment. In addition, He will demonstrate the sovereign authority that belongs to God through His reign as King in the Davidic kingdom here on the earth. After this will come the time "when He hands over the kingdom to God the Father after He has destroyed all dominion, authority and power" (1 Cor. 15:24).

The kingdom established here on the earth, after it has run its appointed course, will issue into the eternal kingdom over which Jesus Christ will be appointed as eternal King (vv. 27-28). Then will be fulfilled ultimately that which the apostle anticipated when he said, "At the name of Jesus every knee should bow, in heaven and on earth and under the earth, and every tongue confess that Jesus Christ is Lord, to the glory of God the Father" (Phil. 2:10-11).

Those who enter this eternal kingdom will dwell in what Christ referred to as His Father's house (John 14:2). That dwelling place is called a city (Heb. 12:22; Rev. 21:2), a term that stresses the intimacy that those dwelling in the Father's house will enjoy. That dwelling place is a glorious place because it partakes of the glory of God (Rev. 21:11). It is a protected place, for it is depicted as being surrounded by walls (vv. 12, 14). It is a secure place, for it is built on a strong foundation (v. 14). It is a place that is accessible and grants freedom to those who dwell therein, for the city is described as having twelve gates. It is an adequate place for all of those who are included in that kingdom, for it is portrayed as being a city 1,500 miles long and wide and high. It is a place in which one will not only have access to the Lord God Almighty and the Lamb, but those included in that kingdom will dwell in His very presence (v. 22). Certain privileged individuals down through the course of human history have been given a revelation of the essential glory that belongs to our sovereign God, but all who are included in that kingdom will dwell in that very glory itself.

Little is said concerning the activity of the citizens of that eternal kingdom, but certain clues are given to us in Revelation 22:1-4. We will occupy ourselves with fellowship, not only with the Triune God but with the saints of all the ages. We can infer this from the reference to the fruit trees (v. 2). Throughout Scripture eating is used as a picture of fellowship, and without doubt unlimited fellowship will occupy us through the unending ages of eternity. And again we read, "His servants will serve Him" (v. 3). No clue is given as to the nature of the service that will be assigned to the members of this eternal kingdom. But just as in the present age each believer is gifted to contribute to the welfare of the whole body, so evidently ministries will be assigned to each individual which that one may discharge to the glory of God and for the benefit of all who are included in His kingdom.

Then further we read, "They will see His face" (v. 4). All through the Book of the Revelation, whenever saints gather before the throne on which the Almighty God sits, they give themselves to worship, to praise, to thanksgiving, and to adoration. The members of this kingdom will devote themselves above all to the worship of

319

the sovereign God in whose presence they dwell. Since we will be provided opportunities for fellowship, there can be no loneliness; and since opportunities will be given to the saints to serve, there can be no feeling of uselessness.

Individually and corporately, the people who have been satisfied with the riches of His grace will devote themselves individually and corporately to worship, to praise, to thanksgiving, to adoration for the unending ages of eternity. Amen.

Summary

The rebellion of Lucifer against the authority of God initiated a false kingdom characterized by its lawlessness and independence of God. In order to demonstrate His right to rule, God formed the earth and populated it with rational intelligent beings to whom He could reveal Himself, so that they would submit themselves to His authority because His right to rule and His worthiness to be worshiped would be recognized, thus answering Lucifer's challenge to God.

A perfect miniature theocracy existed in the garden, in which God was sovereign; His right to rule was invested in Adam, who was to subject all things to his authority and thus bring all creation into subjection to God.

Satan enticed man from obedience to God, and thus introduced his false kingdom into this sphere. God responded to man's disobedience in judgment, expelling Adam and Eve from the garden.

A new form of theocratic administration was established. All men were subjected to the law of conscience, through which God ruled. Again, Satan lured men from obedience to conscience and brought the race under his authority. God again judged the race, this time by a flood, thus demonstrating that He alone had the right to rule.

God then entrusted theocratic administration to human government, whose function it was to curb lawlessness and punish evildoers, thus providing an atmosphere in which righteous men might live in peace and in subjection to God. But the race rebelled against this form of administration. God demonstrated His right to rule again in judgment, this time scattering abroad over the earth those who had united in rebellion against Him.

God chose one man, from whom could spring a great race, and gave him a land for his possession and that of his descendants, in which God would establish a kingdom. This kingdom was determined by certain eternal, unconditional covenants which God gave to that people: the Abrahamic Covenant that guaranteed the perpetuity of Abraham's descendents, and their right to the land given to Abraham; the Palestinian Covenant that laid down the prerequisites for blessing from God on that covenant people; the Davidic Covenant that guaranteed that one of David's Sons would sit on David's throne and rule over David's kingdom; and the New Covenant that guaranteed God's provision for salvation, a new heart, and the empowerment by the Holy Spirit.

That nation forsook God and abandoned God's law, thus rejecting His right to rule. God responded in judgment, giving the northern kingdom over to Assyria and the southern kingdom over to Babylon. This discipline would continue during the centuries that that nation was ruled over by Gentiles, known as the "times of the Gentiles."

In the fullness of time the promised Messiah, David's Greater Son, came to call that nation to repentance with the offer of Himself as the true Messiah and the offer of the covenanted kingdom. That nation, however, refused to repent and put faith in Jesus Christ, the Messiah. Once again judgment came as the times of the Gentiles continued through the devastation of Titus in A.D. 70.

Because of the rejection of the covenanted form of the kingdom by the nation, a new form of theocratic administration was introduced as predicted by Christ in Matthew 13, which has continued through this present age. The church is within this new form of the kingdom. After the translation of all believers out of this earthly sphere into what Christ referred to as "My Father's house" (John 14:2), God will resume His program with the nation Israel. He will subject them to the disciplines of the period Christ called "the tribulation, the great one." As a consequence, multitudes from that nation will repent and turn in faith to Jesus Christ, the Messiah. They will be joined by innumerable multitudes of Gentiles who will be reached during that time with the Gospel of salvation by faith, through blood, because of the grace of God.

That period of discipline will end in the catastrophic judgments at the second advent of Jesus Christ back to this earth. By judgment all unbelievers will be removed and Satan will be bound, and Christ will ascend David's throne in Jerusalem, and will institute a kingdom characterized by peace and righteousness in which He rules as KING OF KINGS AND LORD OF LORDS. "At the name of Jesus every knee should bow, in heaven and on earth and under the earth, and every tongue confess that Jesus Christ is Lord, to the glory of God the Father" (Phil. 2:10-11). In subjecting everything to Himself, Jesus Christ is subjecting all things to God, thus demonstrating that Satan is an impostor, his kingdom is a false kingdom, and that God is sovereign and He alone has the right to rule, the right to be obeyed, and right to be worshiped. The original challenge by Satan that questioned God's authority finds its ultimate answer in the reign of Jesus Christ here on this earth in fulfillment of God's promises and covenants.

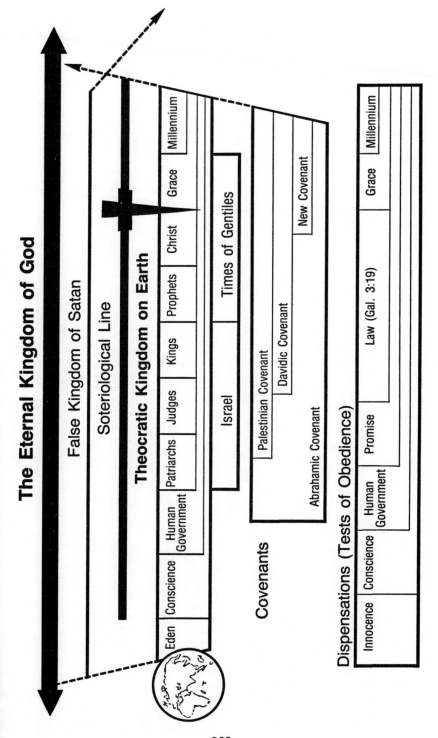

The Eternal Kingdom of God

False Kingdom of Satan

Soteriological Line

Theocratic Kingdom on Earth

| Eden | Conscience | Human Government | Patriarchs | Judges | Kings | Prophets | Christ | Grace | Millennium |

Israel

Times of Gentiles

Covenants

Abrahamic Covenant

Palestinian Covenant

Davidic Covenant

New Covenant

Dispensations (Tests of Obedience)

| Innocence | Conscience | Human Government | Promise | Law (Gal. 3:19) | Grace | Millennium |

Appendix:
The Kingdom Program in the Prophetic Books in Light of the Biblical Covenants

The Kingdom Program in the Prophetic Books in Light of the Biblical Covenants

I. PROPHECIES
   CONCERNING ISRAEL

   A. Israel's spiritual condition. The prophets described in detail the spiritual condition of the nation that brought about their dispersion, their future discipline in anticipation of the return of their Messiah.

   1. Spiritually blind
      Isaiah 6:10; 42:19; 59:9-10; 65:12

   2. Spiritually deaf
      Isaiah 6:10; 42:19; 48:8, 65:12

   3. Spiritually sluggish
      Isaiah 6:10

   4. Disobedient
      Isaiah 42:24

   5. Rebellious
      Isaiah 42:24; 48:4; 63:10

   6. Indifferent
      Isaiah 43:22

   7. Sinful
      Isaiah 43:24; 43:27; 48:8;
      59:2-15; 65:9, 12
      Jeremiah 5:25-26; 30:12-17
      Hosea 4:1-2

   8. Withheld sacrifices
      Isaiah 43:23-24
      Hosea 3:4

   9. Idolatrous
      Isaiah 44:9-20; 48:5

   10. Blasphemous
       Isaiah 65:7
       Ezekiel 36:17-22

   11. Deceitful
       Isaiah 59:13, 15
       Jeremiah 5:27

   12. Unjust
       Isaiah 59:14
       Jeremiah 5:28

   13. Repudiated God
       Isaiah 65:11
       Jeremiah 5:23, 31
       Ezekiel 6:9
       Hosea 4:1-2

   14. Forsaken by God
       Isaiah 48:17-19

   B. Israel's dispersion

   1. The warning of
      Israel's chastening

Isaiah 5:1-7; 5:15, 16, 25; 6:11,
12; 42:13-25
Ezekiel 7:8-9; 36:17-23
Amos 9:1-10
Micah 5:3
Zechariah 11:7-14

2. The method of
Israel's chastening
Isaiah 5:26-30
Amos 9:4
Jeremiah 5:15-19
Ezekiel 36:17-22

3. The chastening a
divine judgment for sin
Isaiah 17:4-6; 28:17-19; 42:13-25;
50:1; 65:12
Jeremiah 30:14-15
Ezekiel 36:17-22
Zephaniah 1:7-18
Malachi 4:1

4. The chastening
temporary in duration
Isaiah 50:1
Amos 9:8-9

C. Israel's preservation

1. By divine protection
Isaiah 52:12; 63:7-9
Jeremiah 5:18; 30:7-24; 46:7-9
Ezekiel 11:14-16
Daniel 12:1
Joel 3:16

2. Based on mercy
Isaiah 63:7

3. By divine provision
Joel 2:18-27

4. Entails deliverance from her
enemies
Joel 2:20
Micah 5:4-15
Zechariah 12:4-9

5. The preservation based on Israel's covenants
a. The Abrahamic
Micah 7:19-20
b. The Davidic
Jeremiah 33:20-26
c. The Palestinian

Ezekiel 16:60-63

D. The remnant

1. The fact of a
preserved remnant
Isaiah 4:2
Jeremiah 3:14
Ezekiel 6:8
Micah 4:6-7; 5:3

2. The remnant
preserved by divine power
Isaiah 1:9; 11:11-12
Jeremiah 23:3; 31:7
Ezekiel 6:8
Micah 2:12-13

3. The remnant will be small
Isaiah 65:8-9
Jeremiah 50:20
Joel 2:32

4. The remnant is a
believing remnant
Isaiah 10:20-27;
24:13-15
Jeremiah 50:20
Ezekiel 6:8-10; 39:22, 25-29
Joel 2:32
Zephaniah 3:13
Zechariah 13:9

5. The remnant of
Assyria a type of the remnant of
the Tribulation
Isaiah 37:31; 32

6. The remnant a
witness for Jehovah
Isaiah 24:14-15; 66:19
Ezekiel 14:22-23
Micah 5:7
Malachi 3:16-17

7. The remnant will be restored to
the land
Isaiah 11:11-12; 65:9-10
Jeremiah 23:3
Micah 2:12; 4:6-7
Zephaniah 2:6-7

8. The covenants will be fulfilled
in the remnant
a. The Abrahamic
Isaiah 65:8-9; 10:21-22
b. The Davidic
Micah 4:7

Jeremiah 23:3-6
  c. The Palestinian
    Isaiah 11:11-12; 65:9-10
    Jeremiah 23:3
    Micah 2:12; 4:6-7
    Zephaniah 2:6-7
  d. The New
    Jeremiah 50:20
    Joel 2:32
    Zephaniah 3:13

E. Israel's restoration to the land

  1. **The promise of restoration**
    Isaiah 1:25-29; 6:13; 10:20-27;
    11:10-16; 27:6, 12, 13; 43:1-21;
    46:3-4; 48:20-21; 49:6, 7-21;
    51:1-16; 54:7-10; 56:8; 57:13;
    60:4-5; 63:12-15; 65:8-10; 66:7-9;
    66:19-21
    Jeremiah 3:18; 12:14-16; 23:1-8;
    24:4-7, 29:11-14; 30:1-24; 31:7;
    32:36-44; 33:7-26; 50:4-7, 19
    Ezekiel 11:17-21; 20:33-44;
    28:25; 34:11-31; 36:7-10, 24;
    37:1-14; 39:25-29
    Hosea 1:10-11; 2:14-24;
    3:4-5; 6:2; 11:8-9; 12:9
    Joel 3:1; 3:20
    Amos 9:14-15
    Micah 4:6-8
    Zephaniah 2:6-7;
    3:10-20
    Zechariah 2:6-7; 8:8; 9:10-17;
    10:1-12

  2. **By divine power**
    Isaiah 11:10-16; 27:6, 12, 13;
    43:1-21; 46:3-4; 48:20; 49:8-21;
    51:3; 56:8; 65:8-10; 66:6-10
    Jeremiah 12:14; 16:14-15; 23:1-
    8; 24:4-7; 29:14; 30:3, 10; 31:4,
    11; 32:37-44; 50:19
    Ezekiel 11:17; 20:33-34; 28:25;
    34:11-31; 36:24; 39:25-29
    Hosea 2:14; 6:1-3
    Joel 3:1
    Amos 9:14-15
    Zephaniah 3:18-20
    Zechariah 8:8; 10:6, 10

  3. **By the Messiah**
    Isaiah 48:11; 49:6-7; 60:21; 61:2-3

Ezekiel 36:22-36; 39:21-25

  4. **Assisted by the Gentiles**
    Isaiah 66:12, 19, 20

  5. **The return from Egypt the picture of the final restoration**
    Isaiah 11:16; 48:20-21
    Jeremiah 16:14-15
    Ezekiel 20:36-37
    Hosea 12:9

  6. **The restoration a sign to the Gentiles**
    Jeremiah 16:19-20
    Zephaniah 3:19-20

  7. **The restoration will be permanent**
    Jeremiah 24:6-7;
    30:18-24; 31:36-40
    Ezekiel 39:29
    Joel 3:20
    Amos 9:14
    Micah 4:7

  8. **The restoration will fulfill the covenants**
    a. The Abrahamic
      Isaiah 10:21-22; 65:8-9
    b. The Davidic
      Jeremiah 23:5-8; 33:14-26
      Ezekiel 34:23-25
      Hosea 3:5
      Micah 4:7-8
      Zephaniah 3:15
    c. The Palestinian
      Micah 2:12; 4:6-7
      Isaiah 11:11-12; 65:9-10
      Jeremiah 23:3
    d. The New
      Jeremiah 31:31-34; 32:37-40
      Ezekiel 11:19-20

F. **The repentance of Israel prior to the Millennium**

  1. **The fact of Israel's repentance**
    Isaiah 2:5; 17:7; 26:11-18; 29:22-
    24; 63:7-19; 64:1-12
    Jeremiah 24:7; 29:11-14; 31:18-19
    Ezekiel 20:42-44
    Hosea 6:1-3; 14:3-9
    Micah 7:1-20
    Zechariah 12:10-14; 13:9

2. The repentance at Babylonian captivity a type of the repentance of the remnant
Isaiah 37:16-20

3. Jonah's repentance a type of the repentance of the remnant
Jonah 2:1-10

4. The invitation to repent
Isaiah 1:18; 55:1; 65:1
Jeremiah 3:22; 29:11-14
Hosea 14:1-2
Joel 1:13-14; 2:12-17
Amos 5:4
Zephaniah 2:1-3

G. The conversion of Israel

1. The fact of Israel's conversion
Isaiah 1:25-27; 2:5; 4:2-4; 17:7; 25:8-9; 26:9-18; 27:13; 29:22-24; 44:22-24; 45:17-25; 48:9-11; 50:8-11; 54:7-10; 55:1-8; 57:15-21; 63:16-19; 65:17-19; 66:7-13
Jeremiah 16:17-18; 24:7; 31:1-40; 33:8; 50:20, 34
Ezekiel 11:17-20
Joel 2:28-32; 3:21
Micah 7:18-19
Zephaniah 3:12-13
Zechariah 3:1-7

2. By divine agency
Isaiah 1:25; 2:5; 6:6-7; 28:16; 44:22-24; 45:21-22; 48:9-11; 54:4-11; 63:8, 16
Jeremiah 3:22-23; 16:21; 24:7; 31:11; 50:20, 34
Ezekiel 20:37; 36:25-29
Zechariah 3:4, 9; 13:9

3. By a cleansing and redemption
Isaiah 1:25; 2:4; 44:22-24; 45:17-25; 48:17; 55:7; 57:18-19; 63:16
Jeremiah 31:11, 34; 33:8; 50:20, 34
Ezekiel 36:25-26
Hosea 14:4
Joel 3:21
Micah 7:18-19
Zechariah 13:9
Malachi 3:2-3

4. By the exercise of mercy
Isaiah 54:7-8, 11; 55:7; 63:7, 9

Jeremiah 31:10
Ezekiel 39:25
Micah 7:18

5. By the exercise of love
Jeremiah 31:3
Hosea 14:4
Micah 7:19

6. Israel made holy and righteous
Isaiah 4:3; 45:24
Malachi 3:3

7. Israel justified
Isaiah 51:8
Hosea 14:9

8. Israel will glorify God
Isaiah 44:23; 45:25; 55:5

9. Israel will be converted by faith
Isaiah 51:10; 55:1-4, 7; 57:13; 66:2
Joel 2:32
Zephaniah 3:12

10. Israel will be given a new heart
Jeremiah 31:33; 32:39
Ezekiel 11:19; 36:26

11. Israel will be given a new spirit
Ezekiel 11:19; 36:26-27
Joel 2:28-29

12. Israel will be made obedient
Jeremiah 31:33-34
Ezekiel 11:20; 36:27

13. This conversion is based on the New Covenant
Jeremiah 31:31-34

H. The resurrection of Israel's dead

1. The fact of the resurrection
Isaiah 26:19-20
Daniel 12:2-3, 13
Hosea 13:14

2. The time of the resurrection
Isaiah 26:20, at the end of the time of indignation
Daniel 12:1-2, "at that time"
Daniel 12:13, at the end of the 1,335 days

I. The judgment and reward of Israel
Isaiah 40:10
Ezekiel 11:21; 20:33-44; 22:17-22

328

Daniel 12:3
Zechariah 3:7; 13:9
Malachi 3:16-18; 4:1

J. The future blessing of
Israel in the new heaven and new
earth
Isaiah 65:17-18; 66:22

II. PROPHECIES CONCERNING THE GENTILES

A. The times of the Gentiles
Ezekiel 30:3
Jeremiah 39:7-14 marks the beginning of the period

B. The course of Gentile powers
Daniel 2:31-45; 7:1-28. The entire
Book of Daniel describes the development of Gentile world powers.

C. The final form of Gentile world
power
Daniel 7:8; 8:23-24; 9:26-27; 11:36-45

D. The destruction of Gentile power by
the Messiah
Daniel 2:34-35, 44-45; 7:9-14
Isaiah 24:21

E. The judgment on Gentiles
Isaiah 2:12-21; 8:9; 14:4-11; 24:21-22;
26:9, 21; 27:1-9; 30:27-33; 32:16;
34:1-17; 49:25-26; 66:15-16
Jeremiah 30:11-16; 46:28; 50:31-46
Ezekiel 28:26; 39:17-24
Daniel 7:10-12
Joel 3:2-8
Micah 4:11-13
Zephaniah 3:8, 19
Haggai 2:20-22
Zechariah 2:8-9; 6:1-8; 12:9; 14:3, 12-15

F. The blessing on Gentiles in the
Millennium

1. Their participation in the
Millennium
Isaiah 2:4; 11:12; 16:1-5; 18:1-7;
19:16-25; 23:18; 42:1; 45:14;
49:6, 22; 59:6-8; 60:1-14; 61:8-9;
62:2; 66:18-19
Jeremiah 3:17; 16:19-21; 49:6;
49:39
Ezekiel 38:23

Amos 9:12
Micah 7:16-17
Zephaniah 2:11; 3:9
Zechariah 8:20-22; 9:10; 10:11-12; 14:16-19

2. The Gentiles will be Israel's
servants
Isaiah 14:1-2; 49:22-23; 60:14;
61:5
Zechariah 8:22-23

3. The Gentiles in the Millennium
will have been converted
Isaiah 16:5; 18:7; 19:19-21, 25;
23:18; 55:5-6; 56:6-8; 60:3-5;
61:8-9
Jeremiah 3:17; 16:19-21
Amos 9:12
Obadiah 17-21

4. The Gentiles in the Millennium
will be subject to the Messiah
Isaiah 42:1; 49:6; 60:3-5
Obadiah 21
Zechariah 8:22-23

III. THE DAY OF THE LORD

A. The Tribulation

1. The nature and character of the
period
a. A shaking of the earth
Isaiah 2:10-22; 13:13; 24:1-12, 16-20
Jeremiah 25:27-33
Joel 3:16
Haggai 2:6-7
b. Wrath, anger, indignation,
and fury
Isaiah 13:13; 26:20; 30:27,
30; 34:2; 63:3, 6
Jeremiah 25:15
Daniel 8:19; 11:36
Zephaniah 1:14-18, 3:8
c. Judgment
Isaiah 26:9
d. Destruction
Isaiah 24:3, 12; 24:19-20;
34:2
Jeremiah 25:18
Joel 1:12
Zephaniah 1:15, 18
Malachi 4:1

331

l. The Ancient of Days
Daniel 7:13
m. The Son of Man
Daniel 7:13
n. Messiah the Prince
Daniel 9:25-26
o. The Prince of princes
Daniel 8:25
p. The wallbreaker
Micah 2:13
Zechariah 14:9
q. The Lord
Micah 4:7;
Zechariah 14:9
r. The Son of Righteousness
Malachi 4:2
s. The Redeemer
Isaiah 59:20
t. The Most High
Daniel 7:22-24
u. Son of God
Isaiah 9:6
Ezekiel 21:2-12
Daniel 3:25
Hosea 1:11
v. The Servant
Isaiah 42:1-6; 49:1-7; 53:11
w. The Shepherd
Isaiah 40:10-11
Jeremiah 21:1, 3
Ezekiel 34:11-31; 37:24
Micah 4:5; 7:14
x. Jehovah
Isaiah 2:2-4; 7:14; 9:6; 12:6;
25:7-10; 33:20-22; 40:9-11
Jeremiah 3:17; 23:5-6
Ezekiel 43:5-7; 44:1-2
Joel 3:21
Micah 4:1-3, 7
Zechariah 14:9, 16, 17

2. **The Second Advent of the Messiah**
a. The fact of the advent
Isaiah 60:2; 61:2
Ezekiel 21:27
Daniel 7:22
Habakkuk 2:3
Haggai 2:7
Zechariah 2:8
Malachi 3:1
b. He is coming as redeemer

Isaiah 59:20-21; 62:11
Malachi 4:2
c. He is coming as judge
Isaiah 61:2; 62:11; 63:1
Daniel 2:44-45; 7:9-10
d. He is coming to reward the saints
Isaiah 62:12
e. He is coming as King
Isaiah 33:17-22; 40:9-11;
52:7
Daniel 2:45; 7:25-27
Micah 5:2-5
Zephaniah 3:15
f. He is coming to fulfill the covenants
Malachi 3:1
g. He is coming to the Mount of Olives
Zechariah 14:4
h. The signs of His coming
Joel 2:30-31
Malachi 4:5-6
i. The nearness of His coming
Isaiah 29:5-7; 46:13; 51:5;
56:1
Malachi 3:1

3. **Satan bound in the Millennium**
Isaiah 14:15

4. **Separation of sinners from the Millennium by judgment**
Isaiah 1:19-31; 65:11-16; 66:1-6,
15-18
Jeremiah 25:27-33; 30:23-24
Ezekiel 11:21; 20:33-44
Micah 5:9-15
Zechariah 13:9
Malachi 3:2-6; 3:18; 4:3

5. **The government of the Millennium**
a. Messiah will be the king
Isaiah 2:2-4; 9:3-7; 11:1-10;
16:5; 24:21-26; 31:4—32:2;
42:1-6; 42:13; 49:1-9; 51:4-
52:7-15; 54:5; 55:4-5; 60:12
Daniel 2:44; 7:15-28
Obadiah 17-21
Micah 4:1-8; 5:2-5, 15
Zephaniah 3:9-10; 3:18-19
Zechariah 9:10-15; 14:16-1
b. David will be the regent

Isaiah 9:7; 16:5
Jeremiah 30:9; 33:15-17, 21-26
Ezekiel 34:23-24; 37:24-25
Hosea 3:5
Amos 9:11

  c. Judges will be raised up
    Isaiah 1:26
    Zechariah 3:7

  d. Nobles and governors will reign under David
    Isaiah 32:1
    Jeremiah 30:21
    Ezekiel 44:3; 45:7-10, 17-25

  e. There will be a unified government
    Ezekiel 37:15-28
    Hosea 1:11

  f. Positions of responsibility will be assigned as rewards
    Isaiah 40:10
    Zechariah 3:7

  g. The Messiah will rule with a rod of iron
    Isaiah 11:4; 25:2-5; 29:17-21; 30:29-32; 42:13; 49:24-26; 66:14
    Daniel 2:44
    Micah 5:5-6, 10-15
    Zechariah 9:3-8

6. **Jerusalem in the Millennium**
  a. Jerusalem will be the center of the millennial earth
    Isaiah 2:2-4
    Jeremiah 31:6
    Micah 4:1
    Zechariah 2:11

  b. The safety of Jerusalem
    Isaiah 14:32; 25:4; 26:1-4; 33:20-24

  c. The glory of the millennial Jerusalem
    Isaiah 52:1-12; 60:14-21; 61:3-4; 62:1-10; 66:10-14
    Jeremiah 30:18; 33:16
    Joel 3:17
    Zechariah 2:1-13

  d. Jerusalem will be the center of the kingdom rule
    Jeremiah 3:17; 30:16-17; 31:6, 23

Ezekiel 43:5-6
Joel 3:17
Micah 4:7
Zechariah 8:2-3

  e. Jerusalem will be the center of worship
    Jeremiah 30:16-18; 31:6, 23
    Joel 3:17
    Zechariah 8:8, 20-23

  f. The dimensions of Jerusalem in the Millennium
    Jeremiah 31:38-40
    Ezekiel 48:30-35

  g. The accessibility of Jerusalem in the Millennium
    Isaiah 35:8-9

  h. The duration of Jerusalem in the Millennium
    Isaiah 9:7; 33:20-21; 60:15
    Joel 3:19-21
    Zechariah 8:4

7. **Palestine in the Millennium**
  a. The inheritance of Israel
    Ezekiel 36:8, 12; 47:22-23
    Zechariah 8:12

  b. The land will be enlarged
    Isaiah 26:15; 33:17
    Obadiah 17-21
    Micah 7:14

  c. The topography of the land will be altered
    Isaiah 33:10-11
    Ezekiel 47:1-12
    Joel 3:18
    Zechariah 4:8; 14:4, 8, 10

  d. Productivity will be restored
    Isaiah 29:17; 32:15; 35:1-7; 51:3; 55:13; 62:8-9
    Jeremiah 31:27-28
    Ezekiel 34:27; 36:29-35
    Joel 3:18
    Amos 9:13

  e. Rainfall will be plentiful
    Isaiah 30:23-25; 35:6-7; 41:17-18; 49:10
    Ezekiel 34:26
    Zechariah 10:1

  f. The land will be rebuilt after its decimation
    Isaiah 32:16-18; 49:19; 61:4-5

Ezekiel 36:33-38
Amos 9:14-15
g. The land will be redivided among the tribes of Israel
Ezekiel 48:1-29

8. Israel in the Millenium
a. Israel will be reunited as a nation
Jeremiah 3:18; 33:14
Ezekiel 20:40; 37:15-22; 39:25
Hosea 1:11
b. Israel will be related to Jehovah by marriage
Isaiah 54:1-17; 62:2-5
Hosea 2:14-23
c. Israel will be above the Gentiles
Isaiah 14:1-2; 49:22-23; 60:14-17; 61:6-7
Zechariah 8:22-23; 14:14
d. Israel will be made righteous
Isaiah 1:25; 2:4; 4:4; 44:22-24; 45:17-25; 48:17; 55:7; 57:18-19; 63:16
Jeremiah 31:11; 33:8; 50:20, 34
Ezekiel 36:25-26
Hosea 14:4
Joel 3:21
Micah 7:18-19
Zechariah 13:9
Malachi 3:2-3
e. Israel will be the subjects of the King's reign
Isaiah 9:6-7; 33:17, 22; 44:6
Jeremiah 23:5
Micah 2:13; 4:7
Daniel 4:3; 7:14, 22, 27
f. Israel will be God's witnesses during the Millennium
Isaiah 44:8, 21; 61:6; 66:21
Jeremiah 16:19-21
Micah 5:7
Zephaniah 3:20
Zechariah 4:1-7, 11-14; 8:23
g. Israel will be beautified to bring glory to Jehovah
Isaiah 62:3
Jeremiah 32:41

Hosea 14:5-6
Zephaniah 3:16-17
Zechariah 9:16-17

9. Worship in the Millennium
a. The fact presented
Isaiah 12:1-6; 25:1—26:19; 56:7; 61:10-11; 66:2
Jeremiah 33:11, 18, 21-22
Ezekiel 20:40-41; 40:1—46:24
Zechariah 6:12-15; 8:20-23; 14:16-21
b. The temple and its worship
Ezekiel 40:1—46:24
Haggai 2:7-9
Zechariah 6:12-15
(1) The gates and courts
Ezekiel 40:5-47
(2) The temple
Ezekiel 40:45—41:4
Haggai 2:9
(3) The chambers
Ezekiel 41:5-11
(4) The separate place
Ezekiel 41:12-14
(5) The interior
Ezekiel 41:15-26
(6) The chambers before the separate place
Ezekiel 42:1-12
(7) The purpose of the separate place
Ezekiel 42:13-14
(8) The measure of the separate place
Ezekiel 42:15-20
(9) The throne
Ezekiel 43:7-12
(10) The Altar
Ezekiel 43:13-17
(11) The offerings
Ezekiel 43:18-27
Jeremiah 33:18
(12) The Priests
Ezekiel 44:9-31
Isaiah 66:21
Jeremiah 33:21
(13) The worship
Ezekiel 45:13—46:18
(14) The place for the preparation of offerings

Ezekiel 46:19-24
(15) The river of the
sanctuary
Ezekiel 47:1-12
Isaiah 33:20-21
Joel 3:18
Zechariah 14:8
c. God the object of worship
Jeremiah 33:11
Zechariah 8:20-23; 14:16-17

10. **Judgment on sinners in the Millennium**
Isaiah 29:20-21; 65:20; 66:24
Jeremiah 31:29-30

11. **The Millennium will see the fulfillment of Israel's covenants**
Isaiah 19:25; 43:1, 4, 5; 49:14-16;
54:10; 61:8
Jeremiah 30:22; 31:1-4; 31:20;
32:38
Ezekiel 34:24, 30, 31; 36:28-29;
37:23-24; 39:28
Hosea 1:10—2:1
Zechariah 10:6; 13:9
Malachi 3:16-18
  a. The Abrahamic
  Isaiah 10:21-22; 19:25;
  43:1; 65:8-9;
  Jeremiah 30:22; 32:38
  Ezekiel 34:24; 30-31
  Zechariah 13:9
  Malachi 3:16-18
  Micah 7:19-20
  b. The Davidic
  Isaiah 11:1-2; 55:3-11
  Jeremiah 23:5-8; 33:20-26
  Ezekiel 34:23-25; 37:23-24
  Hosea 3:5
  Micah 4:7-8
  c. The Palestinian
  Isaiah 11:11-12; 65:9
  Ezekiel 16:60-63;
  36:28-29; 39:28
  Hosea 1:10—2:1
  Zechariah 10:6
  Micah 2:12; 4:6-7
  d. The New
  Jeremiah 31:31-34; 32:35-
  39; 50:5
  Ezekiel 11:18-20; 16:60-63;
  37:26

12. **Conditions in the Millennial Age**
  a. Peace
  Isaiah 2:4; 9:4-7; 11:6-9;
  32:17-18; 33:5-6; 54:13;
  55:12; 60:18; 65:25; 66:12
  Ezekiel 28:26; 34:25, 28
  Hosea 2:18
  Micah 4:2-3
  Zechariah 9:10
  b. Joy
  Isaiah 9:3-4; 12:3-6; 14:7-8;
  25:8-9; 30:29; 42:1, 10-12;
  52:9; 55:12; 60:15; 61:7, 10;
  65:18-19; 66:10-14
  Jeremiah 30:18-19; 31:13-14
  Zephaniah 3:14-17
  Zechariah 8:18-19; 10:6-7
  c. Glory
  Isaiah 4:2; 24:23; 35:2; 40:5,
  8; 60:1-9
  d. Holiness
  Isaiah 1:26-27; 4:3-4; 29:18-
  24; 31:6-7; 35:8-9; 52:1;
  60:21
  Jeremiah 31:23
  Ezekiel 36:24-31; 37:23-24;
  43:7-12; 45:1
  Joel 3:21
  Zephaniah 3:11, 13
  Zechariah 8:3; 13:1-2; 14:20-
  21
  e. Comfort
  Isaiah 12:1-2; 29:2-3; 30:26;
  40:1-2; 49:13; 51:3; 61:3-7;
  66:13-14
  Jeremiah 31:23-25
  Zephaniah 3:18-20
  Zechariah 9:11-12
  f. No sorrow
  Isaiah 25:8; 65:19
  Jeremiah 31:10-13
  g. Justice
  Isaiah 9:7; 11:5; 32:16; 42:1-
  4; 61:10; 65:21-23
  Jeremiah 23:5; 31:23; 31:29-
  30
  h. Knowledge
  Isaiah 11:1-2, 9; 41:19-20;
  54:13
  Habakkuk 2:14
  i. Instruction

335

Isaiah 2:2-3; 12:3; 25:7;
29:17-24; 30:20-21; 32:3-4;
49:10; 52:8
Jeremiah 3:14-15; 23-1-4
Micah 4:2
j. The curse removed
Isaiah 11:6-9; 35:9; 65:25
k. Plenty
Isaiah 4:1; 35:1-2, 7, 30:23-
25; 62:8-9; 65:21-23
Jeremiah 31:5, 12
Ezekiel 34:26; 36:29-30
Joel 2:21-27
Amos 9:13-14
Micah 4:1, 4
Zechariah 8:11-12; 9:16-17
l. No sickness
Isaiah 33:24
Jeremiah 30:17
Ezekiel 34:16
m. Healing of the blind and
crippled
Isaiah 29:17-19; 35:3-6;
61:1-2
Jeremiah 31:8
Micah 4:6-7
Zephaniah 3:19
n. Protection
Isaiah 41:8-14; 62:8-9
Jeremiah 32:27; 23:6
Ezekiel 34:27
Joel 3:16-17
Amos 9:15
Zechariah 8:14-15; 9:8;
14:10-11
o. Freedom from oppression
Isaiah 14:3-6; 42:6-7; 49:8-9
Zechariah 9:11-12
p. No immaturity
Isaiah 65:20

q. Reproduction by the living
peoples
Jeremiah 23:2; 30:20; 31:29;
36:8, 11
Ezekiel 47:22
Zechariah 10:8
r. Labor
Isaiah 62:8-9; 65:21-23
Jeremiah 31:5
Ezekiel 48:18-19
s. Universality of the kingdom
Micah 4:1-2
Zechariah 9:10
t. Unified language
Zephaniah 3:9
u. A fountain opened
Joel 3:18
Zechariah 14:8
Ezekiel 47:1-12
v. The manifest presence of
God
Ezekiel 37:27-28
Zechariah 2:2, 10-13
w. The Holy Spirit poured out
Isaiah 32:13-15; 41:1; 44:3;
59:10, 21; 61:1
Ezekiel 11:19-20; 36:26-27
37:14; 39:29
Joel 2:28-29
x. The eternity of the
Millennium
Isaiah 51:6, 8; 55:3, 13; 56:
60:19-20; 61:8
Jeremiah 32:40
Ezekiel 16:60; 37:26, 28;
43:7, 9
Daniel 9:24
Hosea 2:19
Joel 3:20
Amos 9:15

Scripture Index

Subject Index